MW01243678

August 06 2009

July 13, 2009

To patrons of the Canal Fulton Public Library —

May Mascot, Minister, Man of Steel — The Final Reunion transport you on a journey back to the days of your youth. May it also serve as a lasting reminder of everything that we hold most dear — especially family, good health and good friends.

In addition, may this book give you much to reflect on along with hours of sheer entertainment!

Mike Johnson
North Canton,
Ohio

Mascot, Minister, Man of Steel

The Final Reunion

Mike Johnson

authorHOUSE®

AuthorHouse™
1663 Liberty Drive
Bloomington, IN 47403
www.authorhouse.com
Phone: 1-800-839-8640

First published by AuthorHouse 9/1/2009

ISBN: 978-1-4389-8770-5 (e)
ISBN: 978-1-4389-8769-9 (sc)
ISBN: 978-1-4389-8768-2 (hc)

Printed in the United States of America
Bloomington, Indiana

This book is printed on acid-free paper.

Also by Mike Johnson:

Warrior Priest

Fate of the Warriors

God's Perfect Scar

To the Inspirations

Jim Blair – who kept smiling while battling a dread disease

John Crum – who overcame a devastating injury to teach lessons – in the classroom and about life

Francesca Femia Hahn – who proved unstoppable during a daunting journey from college mascot to career success

Jim Henkel – who persuaded me to attend my first reunion and later showed remarkable mettle amid dire circumstances

Sam Noah – who taught me much about bridging gaps – cultural and chronological

Patricia Shedenhelm Papenbrock – who took on cancer with courage and grace

Christine Straw – who taught me much about the value of reunions

Poh Hong Tan – who put aside doubts by family and friends and flew half way around the world to attend a reunion

June Went – who tucked away mementos of friendship and told me to never forget her

And to the others who inhabit this story that pays tribute to the resilience of the human spirit

CONTENTS

1963

Winston Churchill becomes honorary U.S. citizen

Tom Jones   Irma La Douce   Dr. Strangelove

The Group   The Spy Who Came In From The Cold

Rose Bowl: Southern Cal 42, Wisconsin 37

Jack Nicklaus wins Masters   Arnold Palmer is top money winner

Pope Paul VI is elected

Surfin USA   Danke Schoen

Those Lazy Hazy Crazy Days of Summer

Beatles first album released in U.S.

Fidel Castro visits Russia

Sonny Liston knocks out Floyd Patterson

The Unicorn   The Centaur

Michael DeBakey implants first artificial heart

Valentina Tereshkova becomes first woman astronaut

Martin Luther King's 'I have a dream' speech

JFK assassinated

Jack Ruby murders Lee Harvey Oswald

China and Russia sever relations

Great Britain, Russia and the U.S. sign a nuclear test ban treaty

PREFACE - LETTING MEMORIES BUBBLE UP

Let's begin in the here and now. It's 2009 and too many of the kids I grew up with are dead. Jerry was the first to die – at age 28 and quickly from a rare disease. You'll read more about him. Larry G, Lonna, Nancy, June, Joel, Jim B, Bing, Randy, Fred, Steve, Larry M and Jim H. They're gone too. They fell to accidental choking, kidney failure, cancer, heart attack, unexplained seizure, complications from stroke and diabetes, Lou Gehrig's Disease, pulmonary hypertension, leukemia and, well, it's a long and sad toll.

Another, Diane, survived a stroke – with lasting physical limitations but undiminished pluck. Still another, Pat, showed grace and grit while dueling colon cancer. Another, John, suffered a freak accident, leaving him a quadriplegic but not preventing him from becoming a highly esteemed teacher. Another, DeeDee, stayed devoted to her husband during a long Multiple Sclerosis decline ending in death. One of the class lights, Jane, contracted and struggled with agoraphobia, and another class light, Chris, endured a long siege of chronic fatigue syndrome.

Here in 2009 when we survivors have reached a certain stage, we can expect our ranks to keep thinning at an accelerating rate. I dread that. I hate grieving. I'm not one who can weep his or her way through grief and move on. I just don't cry. Only once can I remember crying in grief, and that was when I was a little boy and first learned what death meant. So how does my body react when someone close to me dies? I feel like I've been sucker punched – like a powerful vacuum cleaner has sucked out my vital organs, leaving my torso an empty shell.

But, this isn't a story about death and suffering so much as it is a tale of spunk, grit, resilience and GUP – grace under pressure. In other words it's a story that pays tribute to the resilience of the human spirit. So let's back up for a few moments and start with 1983. From there we'll occasionally dip back in time but mostly move forward. Ready? Here we go.

You could call this a serendipitous or even accidental book. Or if you regard a new book as a newborn, then a long overdue book. Its gestation began with a simple question posed by my wife Lynne – in 1983. But before I relate her question near the end of this preface, here are two other questions: Have you ever gone to a class reunion? Ever thought seriously about doing so?

If you've been to one or more, you know how much you can learn – or remember. Class reunions can be powerful. They can even change the way you think about people, about experiences and their value. That's what happened when I decided to go to one – our high school class's 20-year reunion in 1983. (Circumstances – overseas Army duty, adopting an international child and being in a wedding party – had prevented me from attending earlier reunions.) And what I experienced there spawned this story – a story that, as you'll see, is or could be a lot like yours. I regard my classmates as special, just as you do yours and rightly so. They've had the same range of experiences – good and bad, funny and poignant. Some impart lessons, unintended for the most part, but ones that might affect the way you think about life and living.

When I decided to tell this story, the most unexpected aspect was remembering with amazing clarity events and discussions that I had long forgotten or let slide into my memory's deepest recesses. In fact, if someone outside the context of class reunions had asked me about certain people, events and conversations, there is considerable doubt that I would have remembered. But once I began telling this story – and I started barely more than a week after our 25-year reunion in 1988 – a lot of those deeply buried memories came bubbling to the surface. The same thing happened after our 1993 reunion, our 1995 class birthday party and our 2003 and 2008 reunions. I'll bet the same thing would happen to you if you let it.

As the years have rolled – sprinted – by, my reunions haven't been limited to individual high school classes. As you will see, they also have included numerous one-on-one mini-reunions, high school multi-class reunions, and reunions of undergraduate and graduate college classes. Nor have reunions been limited to schoolmates. Increasingly, former faculty and staff have become central to reunions. Still another kind of reunion reconnected me with a friend made decades ago in a far-off land.

For those of us who have managed to keep our minds pried open to possibilities, all those reunions have whispered strong messages and taught lasting lessons. All have graced us with their special moments – funny, poignant, uplifting.

I owe a sizable debt of gratitude to my wife Lynne. Now about that question she asked more than 25 years ago. After returning from the 1983 reunion and telling her about people and events and conversations, she asked, "Why don't you write some of it down while it's still fresh?" That was like uncorking a bottle of champagne.

All of the events in this book are true. All the dialogue is verbatim or nearly so; none has been merely made up.

Names? Most are actual but some have been changed out of respect for personal feelings.

CHAPTER 1

ACUTE AMBIVALENCE

Class reunions aren't for everyone. I'll admit that right off. Some people couldn't be dragged to one. They still are carrying way too much heavy baggage from their teen years. Memories of being tormented, teased, excluded, on the outside looking in. Others attend one reunion and decide that's enough. They see or sense the same cliques, feel the same hurts and just plain fail to connect. Some people vacillate, overcome their qualms and go – and get hooked. I'm one of those and I'm glad.

Our class held its first reunion in 1968, five years after graduation from Shelby High School. I was still in the Army in Korea, and I don't remember if I even received an invitation. But if I had been able to go, it's doubtful I would have attended. Why? I think so much was happening in my life and it had only been five years since graduation that I just wasn't very eager to see my old friends. I was in love with a girl I was separated from and I was dying to see her. Besides, I had made many close friends in college and, at the time, felt closer to them than to my high school friends. That would change but it would take time.

In 1973 attending the 10-year reunion would have been problematic. I was very busy and preoccupied. I had started a new job with a new company about a week before the reunion. I was getting ready to start law school in September, and my wife – the girl I had been dying to get back to from Korea – and I were in the homestretch of adopting an international child. Taking the time to drive to Shelby for the reunion just wasn't a high priority.

In 1978 I was somewhat interested in going to the 15-year reunion, but I couldn't sort out my feelings. There were some classmates I wanted to see, but I was nervous about what I would say to them. And I was even more nervous about what I would say to classmates I didn't know very well during our SHS days. Fifteen years seemed like a huge gap and what on earth could we possibly have in common after all those years? Sound familiar to you? And I was still very busy and preoccupied. We now had

1

three kids, one bio and two adopted. I had finished law school and was studying for the bar. My dad was in a nursing home after suffering a stroke. And that same reunion weekend, I was to be in a wedding party in our hometown. I finally decided not to try squeezing in getting to the reunion. But then Jim Henkel weighed in and things began to change.

Jim had been a good high school friend. He was a terrific athlete and had lettered in football, baseball and basketball and was named senior co-athlete of the year. Years later he was twice elected mayor of Shelby. But most of all, Jim was nice. I was also soon to learn that he could be very persuasive. I don't remember when I had last seen Jim. It hadn't been 15 years but it had been quite a while. I do know that after high school our lives had taken different paths. I left Shelby for Ohio University. Jim stayed in Shelby and went to nearby Ashland University, married Susie Bashore (who was a year older and on whom I had had a boyish crush back in third or fourth grade and which Susie, as evidenced by her occasionally teasing me, has never forgotten) and went to work at the Shelby Building & Loan on West Main Street.

The 15-year reunion was held in July of 1978. Well, Jim had heard I was in town and phoned me on Saturday evening. It was after the reunion had started. The phone in my mom's apartment rang and the call was for me.

"Mike, this is Jim Henkel."

"Hi, Jim. How are you?"

"Fine, fine. I want you to come to the reunion." As you can see, Jim wasn't beating around the bush.

"Oh, I don't know, Jim."

"Come on. You'll have a great time. Lots of the kids are here."

"I don't know. I don't think so."

Jim went for the jugular. "Look, I'm going to come over and get you."

"Wait a minute…"

"No, I'm coming over."

"Okay, okay, you win." We both chuckled. "Just a minute, though." I put the phone down and explained to Lynne who was on the line and what was happening. I asked whether she minded if I went to the reunion for a while. She said of course not. "Jim? Okay."

"That's great. I'll be right over."

"What should I wear?"

"It's real casual. Just slacks and a sport shirt."

Well, I went and it's strange but I don't remember very much about it. We got there late and I do remember I didn't stay long. I only have a clear memory of talking with one person, Jim Williams, and I don't remember anything we discussed. I know I talked with some other people, but I just don't remember with whom or what was said. I felt a little out of place, self-conscious. That was strange, too, because I was not known for shyness in high school.

I knew most of my classmates and quite a few of them pretty well. I was real friendly with some of my teachers, and I think most of the teachers liked me – despite my having harassed some of them with teasing and pranks. I emceed a couple of school assemblies. I was a starter on the football and baseball teams and, although I didn't date anyone steadily, I tended to date girls who were pretty popular. Which is not to say that I didn't suffer the usual teenage anxieties. I dreaded pimples and I sometimes sweated bullets before asking girls out, because there was always the chance of REJECTION.

Some classmates saw me as nice, some as arrogant and some – a few classmates wrote variations of this theme in my senior yearbook – as "arrogant but nice." Well, anyway, I didn't stick around the reunion long, but I was still there when the photographer took the class photo. I think I left soon after that. I think that my lack of clear memories of that reunion says something about the ambivalence that I was experiencing.

1983

So along came 1983 and, early in the year, I received an invitation to our 20-year reunion. I thought it over and decided that this time I really wanted to go. Probably the biggest reason was this: I had made friends in college, but I was still in touch with only three of them. I had no idea where most of the rest were. Right after graduating from OU, we had scattered to the four winds. The Army took a lot of us, some went to grad school, some took jobs in distant places, a couple joined the Peace Corps, and so on. We lost touch. In Korea, I got real close with a handful of guys, especially Mike Hood from Far Rockaway, Long Island; Emmett Zimmerman from Madison, Wisconsin; Mike Schwartz from Queens in New York City; and Don Schauer from somewhere in the midwest. But we didn't leave Korea at the same time and when our time came to return stateside, we weren't focusing on maintaining our friendships. Instead, we were dying to get home to girlfriends and families and grad school, and so on.

So what I'm saying is that all of the friendships I had made in college and the Army didn't turn out to have the same deep roots and strong bonds as the ones I had made at SHS. And, at long last, I had begun to realize that.

I asked Lynne if she was interested in going to my reunion and she said, "No, not at all. I've met Bill Anspach and Jim Henkel but I don't know anybody else. You go and have a great time."

"You sure?"

"Yes," she smiled, "go."

So I went, but not before doing some thinking. My Type-A side kicked in. *If I'm going, I want to make the most of it.* So I decided two things. One, I would arrive early, about 5:45 p.m., or 15 minutes before it officially began, and I would stand near the door for the first half hour or so and try to greet everyone. Two, as the evening moved along, I would target people and try to engage them one-on-one. I didn't have anyone in particular in mind because I didn't know who would be there. I would just spot someone and approach and start talking. As you'll read later, that's what I did, with some surprising outcomes.

1988

By now, my early ambivalence had surrendered entirely to anticipation. I was flat out eager to go to our 25-year reunion. Although I was living about a two-hour drive from Shelby, I even helped with planning the gathering. Great fun. But this involvement turned out to be merely a warm-up for what would happen five years later.

That year was pivotal in another respect. Thanks to Ohio University publishing its first all-alumni directory, I found myself reconnecting with some friends from my college years. Later in this book I recount some of those very special reunions.

1992

During the months following our 25-year reunion in 1988, some classmates expressed the same sentiment: for 1993, plan a longer reunion so

4

we can spend more time together. Among those urging a longer gathering were June Went in Nashville, Tennessee and David Spangler in Tempe, Arizona. They had several suggestions.

In early July of 1992 on a Saturday morning, I received a call from Ralph Thauvette. After exchanging pleasantries, Ralph said, "Mike, I guess it's time to begin thinking about next year's reunion, and I'd really like you to help out. You've got a lot of good ideas, you know? I know we're all busy, and it would be a little difficult for you to get to meetings, so if you can only make it to some, that would be fine."

Without hesitation, I replied, "Ralph, I'd love to help. I'm glad you asked me."

"That's great. I really appreciate it."

"When is the first meeting?" I asked.

"Frankly, I was thinking if you said yes, we'd pick a date that's good for you."

I chuckled. "And then all the others?"

"Right."

A month earlier, in June of 1992, our family had moved from an eastern Cleveland suburb about an hour south to North Canton. That put me about 85 miles from Shelby and a few miles farther to Crestline where Ralph was living.

On Saturday, August 8, 1992, when the planning committee had its first meeting at Ralph's house, there was quick agreement to structure a reunion that went far beyond the traditional Saturday night affair. Within a couple hours, the committee had settled on this expanded agenda:

- Friday, July 30, 1993, 7 – 9 p.m. Knights of Columbus Hall set-up and decorating session. In the reunion invitation, we would bill this as an opportunity to get an early start on the weekend. Pizza party after the meeting.
- Saturday, 9 a.m. Golf outing. A "scramble" so that even those lacking rudimentary golf skills could have a fun time. This would be open to spouses, companions, kids.
- Saturday, 4:30 p.m. A tour of Old SHS which, upon the opening of the new high school in the fall of 1965, had become the junior high.

5

- Saturday, 5:30 p.m. The traditional Saturday night gathering.
- Sunday, noon to whenever. A picnic, also open to kids.

Over the next 10 months, we had five more meetings, another at Ralph's house and others in Shelby at the homes of Bill Anspach, Anne Lafferty Stock and Elaine Lybarger. I made it to four of the six. These meetings served two purposes: they got us organized and they built anticipation.

At the last meeting, about a month before the reunion, Ralph said he would again serve as master of ceremonies but asked me to take charge of the Saturday night program's traditional humorous interlude. This meant I had to dream up some dubious achievements we traditionally cite, select the appropriately dubious prizes and emcee that part of the program. That chore turned out to be great fun. We wound up "honoring" numerous achievements, among them:

- Oldest and youngest male and female classmates in attendance. (Upon their arrival at the reunion hall, we asked classmates for birthdates.)
- Classmates in attendance who shared birthdates. (Two pairs did.)
- Classmate who can talk the best game of baseball ever played or watched.
- Classmates who admit to taking LSD. (Two did.)
- Classmates attending their first reunion. (Two.)
- Classmates living in the state:
    - o Which had given birth to the most fads.
    - o Which was the setting for Gone With The Wind.
    - o Where Elvis died.
    - o And so on.
- Classmate who had visited the most continents.
- Classmate who has spent the most years in classrooms – studying and teaching.
- Luckiest classmate in attendance. (Criterion: except for attending school or serving in the military, had lived entire life within the city limits of our hometown.)
- Most youthful appearing classmate and thus best equipped to represent us as we move into the next decade of our lives.
- Etc.

1993

The next summer, this humorous interlude began with a Name That Tune contest, with tables of classmates competing. The tunes were two dozen 25- to 35-second excerpts of songs popular in the 1960s, played without interruption from a specially prepared tape. Lots of howls and shrieks. Great fun.

Twenty of us participated in the golf outing. Also, about 20 of us plus spouses toured Old SHS. That was a hoot. Mark Stock, then principal of Old SHS, served enthusiastically as tour guide. Some things, such as office locations, had changed but much remained the same in the sprawling three-story, L-shaped, red brick building. The original section had been completed in 1924. Additions came in 1939, 1951 and, after we graduated, in 1965.

It was amazing how we were able to recall so clearly which teachers had taught which courses in which classrooms. Some classmates thought they could even identify their former lockers. Or come darned close. Amazingly, Mark informed us, the lockers we used were still in use. The doors had been painted – changed from gray to red – but never replaced (which still is the case now in 2009). As students, we didn't really think of SHS as having particular character or class. Today we see it clearly in the high ceilings and windows, the rich wood trim you would be hard-pressed to find in newer schools, and outside in the old-fashioned lamp poles topped by antique glass globes.

The tour caused a torrent of memories to come bubbling up...Dueling orally with a despised teacher...Smoking in the girls rest room...The "blue room" where teachers who smoked went to light up...Hallway flirtations... Pranks. During that Saturday afternoon tour, the old hallways were echoing with the hearty, memory-charged laughter of alums who once again were feeling very young. The tour, simple as it was, clearly was a reunion highlight, one that still is cherished.

Later, during and after the '93 reunion, comments from classmates told us we had done good. Fifty-four classmates attended the 1993 reunion. Nineteen of them participated in the Friday night set-up and decorating session. As it ended around 9 p.m., about a dozen of us and some spouses and kids adjourned to the local Pizza Hut where we partied till about 11:30

p.m. Lots of kidding, reminiscing, laughing and, of course, some serious reflecting. A good start.

Before the Saturday night gala had ended, our class had decided not to wait five years to gather again. Bill Anspach had a suggestion: in two years, in 1995, put together a class 50th birthday party. There was much backing for the idea. Three months after the 1993 reunion, in October, eight of us gathered to begin brainstorming just such a party. Elaine Lybarger and Margie Parsons Hoover Earick agreed to head the planning team. Both volunteered – sort of. You'll learn more about that party – a two-day affair – in subsequent chapters.

Since 1995? Those old bonds formed in our youth have just kept on getting stronger. We made sure to create opportunities for that. Of course, we had our 35-year reunion in 1998. Then we had another class party in 2000 to celebrate our 55th birthdays. In 2002 our class participated in an 11-class reunion that brought together the SHS classes of 1957-67. And in 2003 we had our 40-year reunion to which we invited the classes of 1962 and 1964. You'll learn more about those gatherings and the '63ers who attended them in the chapters to come.

In addition you'll meet some memorable classmates – with whom you'll share some singular moments – from my college alma maters. Moreover, you'll get to sit in on a reunion with a Korean I met while soldiering and with whom I reconnected after nearly 40 years.

CHAPTER 2

"I WAS IN A FOG."

Christine Straw and I never had much to do with each other in high school. It's not that we "hated" each other in some sort of teenage way or even disliked each other. Well, at least I didn't dislike her. I didn't know what if any feelings she had for me. There was just no chemistry between us. None at all. I have only one personal memory of Chris from SHS – just one – and I'll tell you about that in a bit.

Chris was smart, really smart. I graduated fourth in our class of 157, and I'd bet anything she was one of the three ahead of me. For reasons unknown, SHS didn't have a valedictorian in 1963 as it had in previous years and would do so in ensuing years. But if it had, Chris might well have been the one. Heck, in college at Baldwin-Wallace she was named outstanding freshman woman. She was the daughter of Dr. Norman Straw, a respected general practitioner and, if anybody had asked me to predict what Chris would become, I would have said a doctor.

In our 1963 *Scarlet S* yearbook the caption under Chris's picture reads "A worthy player of the game of life." Pretty bland. I wouldn't be surprised if Chris wrote that herself. No color, no presence, no snap. To reprise a word from that era, no charisma. Looking back, it's almost as though Chris didn't want to be noticed. To me, she always seemed distant, and she projected an air of certainty or resolve. Plus maybe arrogance.

I wouldn't have dreamed of dating Chris. Why? Because I was barely aware of her. Chris was not a public girl. She wasn't a majorette, cheerleader or even a member of the Pep Club. She just wasn't there. She might have been in some of my classes, but I don't remember. We moved in different orbits. Does that ring a familiar bell? Think back to your own high school days. Now pause for a few moments and reflect. Can't you think of a few classmates who circled outside your orbit? And perhaps for reasons you might not recall with any appreciable clarity. That's just the way things were.

If you look under Chris's *Scarlet S* caption, here's what you would see: Biology Club 10, 11, 12; Officer 11; Class Play 11; G.A.A. (Girls Athletic Association) 9; Choir 11, 12; Sextette 11, 12; Annual Staff 12; Tri-Hi-Y 10; Girls State 11; Speech & Dramatics Club 12; Thespian Club 12; Senior Stand (a noon hour concession stand staffed by seniors).

As you can see, Chris was active but, with one exception, our activities took us in separate directions. Under my *Scarlet S* picture and caption, you would see: Reserve Football 9, 10; Varsity Football 11, 12; Reserve Baseball 9, 10; Varsity Baseball 11, 12; Whippet Tales (the school paper) 11; Buckeye Boys State 11; Class Executive Committee 11; Annual Staff 12.

As I said, I do have one clear personal memory of Chris. It has to do with our annual or yearbook. We were both on the *Scarlet S* staff, Chris as co-editor with Anne Lafferty Stock, and I as co-sports editor with Malcolm McKinney.

As co-sports editor, my job didn't include writing the senior class photo captions. It was, however, part of Chris's job. I did write one caption, though. It was for Anne Lafferty Stock. At a *Scarlet S* editorial meeting, I happened to hear a couple staffers saying they were having difficulty coming up with a suitable caption for Anne. One immediately came to my mind and I suggested it and they liked it right away: "Little Miss Laughing Eyes." If you could see Anne's picture, you'd see right away why it was so appropriate. By the way, more than 45 years later, Anne's eyes still shine brightly and laugh, but I'll tell you more about her later.

Now, you know, it's funny, but there I was on the yearbook staff, and I never was curious about my own caption. Didn't give it a thought. I never saw it until the yearbook came out, and then I'm sure I blushed. It sure as hell embarrassed me. There, under my senior picture, was the caption: "It's hard to be humble when you're so great."

Aarghh...Whew! Talk about a body blow. That was harder, much harder to handle than the caption under my picture when I graduated from eighth grade at St. Mary's. That one reads: "The only boy in the class who can throw a curve without a ball." I laughed that one off pretty easily, was even kind of proud of it.

Well, I didn't even try to laugh off "It's hard to be humble..." It just plain hurt. So I did some asking around among members of the yearbook staff. No one seemed to know for sure who wrote it, or maybe they just weren't saying, but a couple thought it might have been Chris. I never confronted her. I'm not sure why anymore. School was nearly over and perhaps I thought *What the hell, it's not worth the trouble.* But you can see I never forgot it. And I admit I continued to half-suspect Chris.

If it was Chris, she actually did me a favor. Lots of my fellow seniors kidded me about the caption, and I think I handled it pretty well. Just sort of shrugged it off. But I'll bet not any of my classmates knew that that caption sparked an epiphany, a major turning point. From that moment, I vowed to stop putting people down, even in a kidding way, which I did a lot but which a lot of people mistook for real meanness because I've always had a talent for keeping a poker face while teasing. And I did bunches of that in high school. The night after I first saw that caption, I decided to learn to poke more fun at myself and less at others and to be very gentle in the poking. No more biting comments or hurtful wisecracks. So, in a way, I owe a debt of gratitude to whomever wrote that caption, although it still was plenty embarrassing at the time.

So in 1983 there I was at our 20-year reunion, and I saw Chris and, on impulse, I decided she would be one of my targets. Of course, I had absolutely no idea where this arrow would go. If it missed the bullseye, I was prepared for that. I could always make a reasonably graceful withdrawal.

"Hi, Chris."

"Hi, Mike."

I offered my hand and she shook it.

"You look very nice," I said and I meant it. Chris had learned to present herself very well, and she looked pretty, radiant even. She had on a multi-hued dress with a swirling design. Except for two thin straps, her shoulders were bare. Very fetching. Her hair was long and the red was tinged with gray.

"Thank you," she said, "so do you."

"Thanks. How are you?"

"Fine. How are you?"

Scintillating conversation, huh? But that's the way it started and, I'll tell you, that's the way many reunion conversations begin. You just don't let it throw you. Sometimes it takes a while for the conversational engine to warm up.

At that moment, I'm not sure why, I decided to take a plunge. Instead of letting the conversation build gradually or just sputter out, I decided to barge ahead. I wasn't sure how Chris would respond.

"Chris, when we were in high school, if there was anyone in our class who struck me as knowing exactly who she was and where she was going and how she was going to get there, it was you. You seemed to be really in command of yourself."

Chris smiled and shook her head, her long red-gray hair swishing slowly across her cheeks. "It was all a façade. I was in a fog."

I thought she was joshing me and said so.

"No," Chris said, smiling wryly, "I wasn't in command of anything. I was so unsure of everything. I didn't know who I was or where I was going or how I was going to get there or anywhere. I was a long way from finding myself."

"That's hard to believe."

"But true."

As maybe you are beginning to see, this conversation turned out to be one of the reasons I've come to value reunions. In some cases, you start to learn something, at long last, about your classmates. If you don't already have a bond, you begin to form one.

Chris continued. "If you remember, I didn't date much."

"Well, to be honest," I replied, smiling, "I don't think I noticed."

"Well, I didn't and the reason is that I was afraid to date."

"Why?"

"Because I didn't know how to act around boys. I just didn't know. So I made sure that not many boys asked me out. I built a wall around me. I didn't let too many boys get too close."

When she told me this, my emotions felt like they were in a mixing bowl. I felt sadness. I felt sympathy. And I felt gratitude that she was opening up and telling me. Why me? I don't know for sure. Maybe because she sensed I would listen without judging. Whatever, I'm glad she did. At that moment, I was alone in that American Legion hall with Chris. Yes, it was crowded and, yes, it was noisy. But I don't ever remember concentrating more fully on what someone was saying.

Right then and there I wished the hell I had tried to get to know Chris in high school. Maybe she wouldn't have let me but I wish I had tried. We could have been friends right along.

You know, teenagers aren't totally insensitive, but only with measures of living and suffering do we begin to develop consistent understanding and compassion. Or at least some of us. That isn't likely to change. But it's still too bad that many of us as teenagers were so hung up on ourselves, on our pretensions and prejudices.

Chris and I talked and talked and I know that we could both begin to feel a bond taking hold. It was a very warm and satisfying feeling. Unlike her dad, Chris hadn't become a physician. But she had become a psychologist, working for the Milwaukee public schools.

"It's only recently," she said, "that the fog has begun to lift."

"Boyfriend?" I asked gently.

"Yes," she beamed. "It's a serious relationship. It's one of the first I've been comfortable with."

After 30 minutes or so and with mutual reluctance, we ended our conversation. We each had other people we wanted to talk with. Although I regretted we didn't have longer, I felt that we had begun to form a friendship. This one encounter, as much as anything I experienced that night, told me that I had made the right choice in coming to the reunion.

1988

As our 25-year reunion was approaching in 1988, I phoned a classmate in Shelby and asked her if she knew whether Chris was coming and she said yes. So I sent off a postcard to tell Chris how pleased I was that she was coming and that I'd look forward to resuming our conversation.

On July 16, 1988, about 5 p.m. or an hour before the reunion was to start, I was alone at my mom's apartment. I was getting ready to shower when the phone rang. I picked up the receiver. "Hello."

"Mike?"

"Yeah, who's this?"

"It's Chris."

"Chris?"

"Chris Straw."

"Chris! Talk about a surprise. The reunion's only about an hour away."

"I know," she said. "I just felt like giving you a call."

"I'm glad you did. Where are you?"

"At my parents."

"I heard you got in town early," I said.

"How did you know?"

"Shelby's a small town, remember? My mom saw you walking on Main Street." Chris laughed. "What have you been up to?" I asked.

"My sister and I have been going through things in my parents' attic. It's been a lot of fun. You wouldn't believe some of the things we found."

"I'll bet."

"Well," Chris said, "I just wanted to call for a minute and say I'll see you tonight."

"I'm really glad you did. I'm looking forward to seeing you. Right now I'm going to hit the shower and dress. See you in about an hour."

"Okay."

"See you."

How about that? Boy, I could hardly believe it. This was a girl I was barely aware of in high school. Son of a gun. Chris's call made me feel very good. It was the kind of gesture a friend would make.

When I saw Chris enter the hall that evening, I knew I had been right about our becoming friends five years earlier. Simultaneously, we exchanged heartfelt hugs. There was no hesitation and the hugs weren't of the "A-frame" variety where two people embrace tentatively from the waist up, their feet still far apart. These were toe-to-toe-coil-your-arms-tightly type hugs.

We didn't talk as much as we did back in 1983, but the learning process continued. For example, I mentioned to her that nine of us had left SHS in 1963 for Ohio University in Athens. Chris had gone to Baldwin-Wallace.

"I spent two and half years in Athens," Chris said.

"When?" I was hugely surprised.

"Right after you left. I got my master's in psychology there."

"You spent a lot of time in Porter Hall," I said.

She smiled. "I spent a lot of time in Porter Hall." That's where psychology classes were held and I had taken a few.

"There's still a lot we don't know about each other," I said. "But we're learning."

At the end of our 25-year reunion, by the way, Chris was just a dissertation away from a Ph. D. "A piece of cake," I told her.

"Hardly," she smiled.

"But you'll get it."

"I'll get it."

For Chris and me that reunion had a "postscript" that was delightfully memorable. It had to do with a post-reunion party at the home of a classmate who lived on a country road. About 20 of us made our way there. Some of us were clustered in the kitchen, and others were sprawled around the family room, including Chris and me who were lying on the floor and propped against large cushions in front of the fireplace. We simply weren't eager for the night to end. Too many fond memories were bubbling up, too many thoughts on life and living were emerging, too many laughs were erupting.

Finally about three in the morning, Chris said she had to get going as she had a train to catch later in the morning. Chris had used Amtrak to travel from Milwaukee to nearby Crestline where her Shelby family picked her up. I told her I'd drive her back to town as 3 a.m. was a tad later than this non-night owl was accustomed to being up and about.

It took another half hour to say goodbye to everyone. The hugs and kisses were hard and long. Jim Blair, whom you'll meet later in this story, went outside with us since he had to move his car so that I could back mine out of the driveway.

"You leaving now too, Jim?" I asked.

"No," he laughed. "I came outside here in the middle of a good story, and I want to go back and hear the rest of it." Later I heard that Jim and the rest of the gang finally began vacating at 4 a.m.

I backed out of the driveway. "Where to?" I asked Chris.

"High School Avenue," she said.

"High School Avenue? Your parents still live there?"

"Same old place," said Chris. Her dad kept his office in the family home.

"Is your dad still practicing?"

"Sure is."

For the ten minutes or so that it took us to drive to Chris's parents' place, we were in a reflective mood. We talked about how great it was to see everyone and to keep learning things about each other. It also struck me that I was riding with a classmate who was highly intelligent, attractive, successful, independent and adventurous. Was she among women ahead of their time?

I also think melancholy was beginning to set in. And the lateness and darkness must have added to our somber mood. Three a.m. in a little semi-rural town like Shelby is really black, not like a metro area where hundreds of thousands of blazing shopping center nightlights mean it never gets truly dark.

We were coming up on High School Avenue now.

"Tell me where to stop, Chris."

"Right after that crosswalk."

I slowed and braked in front of the Straw's gray-shingled house, and I felt a lump growing in my throat. "Here you are."

I turned and Chris leaned in and we hugged.

"Good night," she said simply as she got out.

Before July of 1983 I didn't know much about Chris Straw at all. But after those two reunions, when I would think of her, it was with much respect and a large measure of affection.

1993

Chris Straw was in a fog no more. In the five years since our 25-year reunion in 1988 she had successfully presented her dissertation and "finally" earned her Ph. D. in psychology. Dr. Straw. Just like her dad. That triumph occurred in 1990, a year that also included a harrowing incident. Chris was mugged and her arm was broken. "I had $2.50 in my purse," she recounted wryly. She also had learned to master the bass and helped form a bluegrass band called Pickin' Up Speed. Shortly before the 1993 reunion, her band recorded and released an album called *Don't Say Goodbye.* She brought a cassette of it with her. Not bad at all.

Those same five years also brought Chris a measure of distress. She had been stricken with chronic fatigue syndrome and an array of debilitating allergies. During the worst of it, her hair, already graying, turned snow white. At the '93 reunion, it was gray again.

On Saturday of reunion weekend I phoned Chris's parents' house to ask whether she would like to join me, June Went and Elaine Lybarger for breakfast at The Coffee Shop, one of the few establishments on Main Street still bearing the same name as it did in the 1960s. Her dad answered the phone and told me that Chris was still sleeping. She had driven from Milwaukee, arriving in Shelby at 1:00 that morning. But Saturday afternoon, Chris joined us for the tour of Old SHS.

At the picnic on Sunday I asked her, "What's next?"

"My house. During my illness, it got away from me. I'm painting, getting new carpet in the living room, that sort of thing."

Chris's house was a 1922 brick duplex she had owned for the last 17 years. As the picnic was winding down and Chris was preparing to leave, we hugged with our accustomed gusto. Arms still wrapped around each other, I said, "Whether it's two years or five, I'll look forward to seeing you again."

"Two years or five," she replied, smiling, "I'll be here."

1995

It turned out to be just two years. As I said earlier, back in '93 we had decided to have a class 50th birthday party. We had settled on July 31 and August 1, 1995, for a two-day party. On Saturday night we would have a catered picnic at Rabold Park, on the western fringe of Shelby and surrounded by fields of towering corn stalks. The next morning, Sunday, we would board a chartered bus for a trip north to Cleveland and a luncheon tour on the Goodtime III, a party boat that runs along Cleveland's Lake Erie waterfront and then south on the snaking Cuyahoga River.

On Saturday afternoon I was already at Rabold Park when I saw Chris get out of a car in the parking lot a couple hundred feet away. As she began walking across the grass, I went moving to meet her. We hugged and then, on impulse, I kissed her on the lips. Her widened eyes told me she was startled but her smile told me it was okay.

Chris had a great time at the party. We spent time with each other at the barbecue, but spent our best time at Anne Lafferty Stock's house. About 9 p.m., darkness was closing in on Rabold Park and buzzing mosquitoes were beginning their relentless attacks. It seemed a good time to wrap up the barbecue. But Chris, Anne and I felt like continuing our chat, so we adjourned to Anne's place.

Chris had big news. She had sold her brick duplex that she had owned for 19 years and bought a small house with an innovative Frank Lloyd Wright-type design. Was Chris excited? Well, she had brought pictures and she got them out of her purse. Her eyes were glittering as she showed the pictures to Anne and me. You could tell that now, for the first time, she felt like she really had a home in Milwaukee.

Her old home in Shelby? Her dad, Norman, was having health problems and had retired from his medical practice. But he and Chris' mom still were living in that old house on High School Avenue, just down the street from Old SHS.

1998

Chris came but I couldn't. It killed me not to be there. I was attending the Executive Program at Stanford University's Graduate School of Business. The program was intense, requiring weekend work and Sunday night study groups, and was obscenely expensive. My employer was footing the bill, and I knew I wouldn't be able to tear myself away for a cross-continent flight to Shelby for the 35-year reunion. But I did manage a mini-reunion in the Bay Area, and I'll tell you about that later.

2002

Right. 2002, not 2003. Here's why. In early 2001 Janet Page Whitehill, a member of the SHS Class of 1962, began advancing a concept: have a multi-class reunion. Her idea took root and spread. Several months later, a decision was made: in August of 2002 there would be a reunion that would bring together 11 SHS classes – 1957-1967 plus teachers from that era. It would be a three-day gathering and include nine events in a variety of venues.

The ninth and final event was a Sunday afternoon picnic at Siegfried Park. It followed an ecumenical memorial service that paid respects to deceased schoolmates and was conducted by three of our schoolmates from those 11 classes. Two had become clergy and the third – in a surprise to all of us – had become deeply religious. The day was gloriously sunny. Chris was there.

Everyone at the picnic seemed to have a camera, and they were being put to heavy use. At one point, seven or eight of us were yakking it up around one of the picnic tables in the shade of a pavilion. With a poker face, I said to Chris, "There's something we need to do that we've never done before."

By now, she knew me very well. "And what would that be?"

"Have our picture taken together."

Her face lit up. "You're absolutely right." The Milwaukee psychologist and the Ohio businessman eased ourselves up and away from the table. I handed my camera to Jim Henkel – which seemed appropriate given that he had persuaded me to attend my first reunion. Chris and I moved out from the shade of the pavilion into the bright sun. We wrapped our arms around each other, and Jim aimed the camera.

"Ready?" he asked.

"Ready," we replied.

Jim pressed the shutter button.

In the picture, you can tell one thing right away: Chris and I were glad to be in it together.

By this time Chris had joined a group – three women backed by two men – called The Moxie Chicks. Chris and the other two women did vocals, Chris played the bass, and the two men were guitarists. In 2002 the group was among 15 individuals and groups included on an album titled *One Ball of Clay*. In 2006 The Moxie Chicks released their own album – *Cross Me, Fool!* – with 14 songs of which Chris wrote several. I have both CDs and the talented Moxie Chicks provide fun listening. You can see and learn more about them at www.mootownproductions.com.

2008

I met Jon. That's right. Chris's long-time beau accompanied her to our 45-year reunion. It was easy to see why Chris had connected with him. Jon is smart, friendly and easy to talk with. He also is a man after my own heart, with a love of history, particularly military history. Jon, a dentist, served in the Marines.

19

Looking ahead, Chris's outlook seems as buoyant as her zest for music. "The Moxie Chicks are going strong, loving singing, songwriting and each other for over eight years now! We are starting to discuss a second CD; our first CD still gets airplay sometimes! We have such fun singing and playing at coffee houses, farmers' markets and churches."

Of course, Chris and I again made time to talk, in particular on Saturday morning over coffee with Jon, Ralph and Bob Boyce at the local Wendy's. And we were pictured together in several group photos.

Know something, though? I still don't know if she is the one who wrote that *Scarlet S* caption for my yearbook picture.

CHAPTER 3

THUMBING WEST AND FLYING EAST

David Spangler I knew, or so I thought. David and I were born just two days apart in Shelby Memorial Hospital. When we were young, David had the best backyard in town. It was five lots deep, full of trees, and great for playing cowboys and Indians and cops and robbers. How do I know the yard was five lots deep? Because later that fabulous yard was divided into lots and sold. And where decades ago boyhood fantasies were played out, today sit four ranch-style houses and a small medical office building owned by my nephew Gary, a dentist.

David and I went to St. Mary's for eight years together before going on to SHS. In 1954 on a school day afternoon, David lost his mom, Tillie. She was walking behind the family car in the driveway at their house when the car rolled back over her. The parish priest came to our classroom to get David. A couple days later, the whole school went to the funeral. I don't remember anything about the service, but I remember crying all the way through it.

David was the first boy in our St. Mary's class to reach puberty. Orally and visibly. For a while, his voice was cracking often and we would laugh and David always seemed to take it with good humor. In class, when he was standing and reciting and his voice would start cracking, he would smile shyly, eyes downcast, and blush, try to clear his throat and continue talking. David was also the first to shave, and we're not talking about a dusting of peach fuzz. At age 13, David had a five o'clock shadow. Ironically, some years later, he was among the first of us to begin balding.

David was one of the shorter guys in the class and one of the fastest. His stumpy legs pumped like a pair of half-mad pistons. He could run like hell. He went out for football in the ninth grade, and in an early practice he was decked by one of the bigger and stronger guys on the team. That was enough. David decided he didn't like being hit and channeled his speed into track which he ran all four years while at SHS and where he specialized in the half-mile.

David was on student council in our junior year and was president of the council in the twelfth grade, so you can see that David had earned his share of popularity and respect, even though he perceived himself as something of a rebel or outcast.

Actually, in high school David never impressed me as someone who was marching to a decidedly different drummer or who was in any visible way a rebel. He had a variety of interests, but they were all quite conventional, even admirable. He took piano lessons for several years and once aspired to be a concert pianist. He also enjoyed working with radios, playing chess, swimming, roller skating and working as a disc jockey during lunch hour dances in the gym. But I had been wrong about David and the drummer's beat he heard.

Immediately after high school graduation, David showed me just how wrong I had been when he decided to unlimber his thumb and began hitchhiking west. Way west. His goal was to travel around the world in two years. Now NOBODY in Shelby dreamed dreams like that, much less set out to live them. Not at 18.

David's thumb got him as far west as Kansas where he picked up the ultimate ride. It happened like this. In Shelby, David's closest buddy was his neighbor, Marty Yarman, who was a classmate of ours at St. Mary's but had chosen to go to high school at St. Peter's in nearby Mansfield. In the spring of 1963 Marty's family had decided to take a summer trip to California. Now this seems improbable, but David and Marty swear it's true. Before David had begun his odyssey, Marty's parents had told David that if he wanted a ride to California, then he should be on a particular stretch of Kansas highway at a particular time on a particular day. If David was there, BINGO, he could spare his thumb and feet some miles. If he wasn't there, Marty's family would assume that David had elected to continue hitchhiking. Well, as the Yarmans were driving across Kansas on the designated day at the designated time, ahead they could see David standing along side of the road.

The Yarmans went on driving to Los Angeles where they dropped David off. At LA's port of San Pedro, David signed on with a Liberian-flagged West German freighter that was homeward bound. But David quickly grew disenchanted with sailing, at least that variety. "My job," says David, jokingly describing his work, "was to keep the third mate's cabin clean." At the freighter's first port of call south of San Pedro in Mexico, David disembarked. As he told me years later at a reunion, his wanderlust had waned: "I was just too lonely to keep traveling alone."

So he began thumbing east but never got closer to Ohio than Arizona. "I got as far as Phoenix and liked it. It grew on me." He enrolled at Arizona State and got his degree there and became a teacher and then a counselor. He still lives in Tempe across the street from the ASU campus.

Even though David never made it back to Shelby to live, it's clear that he had developed strong ties to our hometown and our SHS classmates and that our reunions are important to him. Now I say that, despite David's assertion today that he used to feel like something of an outcast. I mean, he really believes that he was one of our class rebels. The most I'll concede is that David's drummer was tapping out a slightly different cadence. But David was never completely out of step, witness his two years on student council and his year as council president. Besides, David is one of the relatively few class members who attended all of the first five class reunions. And he had the perfect excuse for not attending our 25-year reunion.

His determination to make it was nothing short of remarkable. Here's why. David remained single for 19 years after leaving SHS. Then in 1982 he married Kathy, a nurse. Before the 1988 reunion, he wrote to a friend in Shelby. He said that Kathy was expected to give birth to their first child on July 5 – just 11 days before the reunion. "If the baby is born more than a week before the reunion," Dave wrote, "I will come. Less than a week and I won't be able to make it."

Well, the baby, Andre Joseph Spangler, didn't make his appearance until July 12, a scant four days before the reunion. With his bride and baby just out of a Phoenix hospital and resting at home, David nonetheless boarded a plane and went jetting to Ohio. At the reunion, the proud father joked that he had become a parent at a time when several of his classmates had become grandparents. Seemed like David still had some of that youthful spirit of adventure that led him to begin thumbing west in 1963.

He also still was feeling the pull of his roots. Four weeks after that 1988 reunion, I heard from David. Once more, David's drummer was tapping out a slightly different cadence. David would be flying back to

Ohio again, this time with his bride and baby so that he could have Andre Joseph baptized in Shelby. "Why have the baby baptized in Shelby?" David said, asking the question before I could. "I am a traditionalist and I want my child to be baptized in the same church that I was baptized in. Perhaps it is a form of 'roots' that will be passed on."

I'll tell you something else. After David got to Shelby for the baptism, done on August 14, he and Kathy and baby Andre paid a surprise visit to my mom, who was stunned and thrilled.

Different drummer and a good man.

1993

David drove this time instead of flying but he made it from Arizona for our 30-year reunion. With him were wife Kathy and son Andre, now just five years old.

2003

David and Kathy came to our 40-year reunion. As we were shaking hands and hugging, David asked, "Is your wife here?"

"Yes," I said. I turned and pointed across the expanse of the K of C Hall. "That's her sitting at the table with the elderly woman." Lynne was sitting with Karen Reimsnyder, a retired SHS teacher who had suffered a stroke and was one of 15 former SHS teachers who had accepted our invitation.

"We want to meet her," said David.

"Let's do it."

I led David and Kathy over to Lynne. She saw us coming, got up and approached. "Lynne," I said, "this is David Spangler and his wife Kathy." I didn't have to say anything else. Lynne already knew all about David.

CHAPTER 4

TRUEST GRIT – "WHO WAS THE FOURTH?"

Adversity. Physical, emotional or financial. It visits and becomes a companion for most of us at one time or another. But when during life do we begin to understand and appreciate its impact on others?

More fundamentally for many if not most individuals, there is a prerequisite, and let me frame it in the form of a question. To wit, when during life do we begin to learn about ourselves? Our strengths and weaknesses? Physical, intellectual, emotional and moral ones? Some individuals, we know, begin to acquire, store and use such knowledge early on. For others, however, such knowledge remains elusive until later – the very end – or never.

Take a few moments and reflect on your adolescent years. For many if not most the teen years stand as the least likely for acquiring, absorbing and putting to productive use knowledge of self. Why should that be? Is there any stage of life during which a person – boy or girl – is more awkwardly self-conscious? More prone to embarrassment? More worried about fitting in with peers? More concerned about being accepted without reservations? More immune to healthy introspection?

Boys and girls seem equally affected. Raging hormones, blotchy skin, sprouting hair, enlarging breasts, monthly bleeding, swelling penises and more. For millennia they have undermined self-esteem, fueled self-loathing and proven effective preventatives to serious self-examination. Perhaps the clearest – and most tragic – evidence is the suicide rate among teens.

All of which leads to this observation. While during our teen years most of us endured periods of uncertainty or anxiety, sometimes profound and lasting, we tended not to consider the extent to which our friends were able to cope. How resilient were they? How able were they to absorb and handle hardship? Could they shrug it off? In later years, then, we could be surprised when friends from our youth demonstrated emotional toughness or gritty resilience.

John Crum has shown more grit than a dozen John Wayne characters. Compared to John, Sylvester Stallone's Rambo was a pantywaist. In fact, as far as I'm concerned, the last 35 or so years of John's life have been downright inspirational.

Certainly, nobody was more determined than John Crum to make our 25-year reunion in 1988 and, after he told me that he planned to come, there was no one I wanted to see more.

I've known John since we were nine or 10 years old and playing Little League baseball. In fact, we played baseball together right on through high school and American Legion. But I didn't really get to know him well until we got to high school where we became good friends.

In the fall of 1967, just months after graduating from college, we found ourselves on a bus together, going to Fort Hayes in Columbus to take our Army physicals. There was a lot of joking about what the doctors might find wrong that would keep us out of the military. Truth is, we were as healthy and strong as a brace of Belgian draft horses and knew we would pass. We joked too that, a la Cassius Clay, we might flunk the Army intelligence test.

That was the last day I saw John for six years. The Army took him to Taiwan and me to Korea. Upon returning, I went to Schenectady, New York and John to Centerburg, Ohio, where we began our careers.

On September 1, 1973, John was at a party where people were horsing around. They were doing handstands, headstands, and so on. John tried a flip but something went amiss and he landed face down in a beanbag chair. At that moment John's life changed forever. His neck broke and he became a virtual quadriplegic. He has no use of his legs. At first he had no feeling below his neck. Gradually John regained control of his shoulders and right arm down to his wrist. At the time of the accident, his wife Linda was pregnant, and the trauma of John's accident sent her into labor. Their only child, John Casey, was born the next day.

As you can imagine, John had some really tough moments. His first look at his new son was wrenching. "I was so discouraged," John said. "We had been married for six years and had looked forward to our first baby for so long, and I couldn't even hold him or anything. It was probably the worst time of my life."

On September 15, about two weeks after the accident, I visited John in Riverside Hospital in Columbus. When I walked into his room, he was suspended face down from his bed. It was a sight that rocked my stomach, and I had to struggle to maintain composure. Hospital staff were rotating John regularly. He saw me, smiled weakly and said, "You're the last person I expected to see."

I'm not surprised he said that. He didn't know that I had moved from Schenectady to suburban Cleveland and, if he had thought about it, he probably would have guessed I hadn't heard about his accident. After that hospital visit, we exchanged letters every once in awhile during the years to come.

Soon after the accident, John began to show the grit he had long demonstrated. He had been a feisty ballplayer and crusty person for as long as I could remember. His language was blunt and salty, sometimes in the extreme. He had hurt some feelings, though not mine. Two years after the accident, he went back to teaching at Centerburg High School – in a wheelchair. He was nervous. How would students regard him? Treat him? Soon after returning, John spotted on a classroom desk a note written by a student: *Crum's a bastard.* "Then I knew I was back."

John himself wasn't finished learning. Subsequently he earned a master's degree via correspondence from California State University at Dominguez Hills. Ever modest, John said only, "Getting my master's was quite an accomplishment."

In mid-1987 I happened to write a letter to John, congratulating him on a teaching award that I learned he had received. He replied in December and closed by writing, "Hope to see you at our 25th reunion this coming July."

As our reunion approached, there was no one I was looking forward to seeing more than John.

On July 16 John was one of the first to arrive at the Knights of Columbus Hall in Shelby. I saw Linda pushing him in his wheelchair, guiding him through the doorway and to the registration table. John saw me. He smiled an incredibly kind smile and said simply, "Hi, Mike."

God, I wanted to crush him in my arms. Of course, I didn't want to knock anybody down getting to him, so I moved forward carefully. "John,"

I whispered, smiling. I bent down and gently hugged him. My emotions were running high and I swallowed hard.

I didn't know what John would say next, but what he said was a big surprise and caused me to grin broadly, because I then knew John had arrived in high spirits and was ready for fun. As I straightened up, he looked at me and asked, "Do you remember Hixon, Berger and Gaul?"

I just never, never expected a greeting like that. "Sure," I replied, "they were great players."

"They were terrific," John agreed. "But who was the fourth?"

His question so surprised me that it threw me for a second. "Uh, uh, Bob Walters."

"No, no," John said. "That's not it. You're close, though."

"Roger Walters!"

"That's it!" cried John. He was absolutely beaming. "I knew if anyone could remember that name it would be Mike Johnson. Do you know that you just ended fourteen years of frustration?"

"What do you mean?"

"After the accident, when I was trying to figure out how I could live with a broken neck, and I was trying to keep my sanity, I played memory games. I remembered Bill Hixon – he was a hell of a third baseman." Bill later went to the U.S. Military Academy at West Point.

"He sure was," I said. "He may not have fielded every ball cleanly, but nothing got through him. Remember how he used to have the coach hit one hard grounder after another at him just to see if he could stop everything?"

"Yes, yes, I remember," said John. "And there was Ken Berger and Chuck Gaul. But I couldn't remember the fourth." Ken went to Miami University and then joined the Air Force and served in Korea at Kimpo Air Base. Decades later Ken provided research assistance for my third book, *God's Perfect Scar*, part of which is set at Kimpo. Chuck joined his dad's business.

Hixon, Berger, Gaul and Walters were from nearby Ontario and played on Shelby's American Legion baseball team. All four were superior players.

"Neither one of us will ever forget now," I said, laughing.

"Walters was a hell of a pitcher," said John.

"You have a hell of a memory, John."

"I remember something else, too." The devil's own gleam was in John's eyes.

"What's that?"

"A certain Little League tournament game. Against Bucyrus. When we were twelve."

"Oh, my God, I didn't think *anybody* else remembered that game."

"Do you remember how it ended?" John asked.

"John, have mercy...I struck out to end the game."

"You were called out."

"You don't know how painful that was," I said, smiling now at the old memory. "I'd hit the ball earlier in the game and I was confident. We were down by one run and the tying and winning runs were on base. The count went to three and two and when the next pitch came in it was so far outside that I dropped my bat and took a step toward first. When I heard the ump call 'strike three' I froze. I can still see that pitch and it's still outside."

"I agree," said John. "Do you know how I remember that?"

"How?"

"I was the tying run, standing on third."

"I'll tell you something you don't remember because I don't think I ever told anyone. After the game, I cried all night. I felt like I'd let the whole team and the whole town down. The next night, my dad wanted to take me to watch the next tournament game and I didn't want to go because I was so ashamed. It took some doing for my dad to persuade me that the whole town wasn't down on me."

"Aww, Mike..."

"It's true. I thought the whole town hated me." In that era, when baseball games were televised only infrequently, attendance at Little League games was routinely large, easily running into the hundreds for tournament games.

John Crum is a hell of a man. His wife Linda is a hell of a woman, too. As John had observed, they had been married six years before his accident, and she has been with him every step of the way since. Still is.

That evening, classmates clustered around John from beginning to end. It was clear that his presence was a highlight – *the* highlight – for many.

1992

Long-term adversity notwithstanding, John's wit remained sharp. At his son Casey's high school graduation ceremony, John was a guest speaker. Afterward he observed dryly, "Mom was very surprised that her son had progressed beyond the monosyllabic stage."

A few years later, after moving to Florida, he and Linda got acclimated quickly. "All paralyzed people should live in a warm climate," John observed. "It really changes your outlook." Was the new location perfect? "Florida has many shortcomings," he added, "but overall I'd give it an 85 – good beat and easy to dance to."

1993

John Crum made it to another reunion. Despite another five years of wheelchair confinement, John's face still looked remarkably unburdened. And once again, his spirits were high.

Months earlier, after Ralph Thauvette had again given me responsibility for planning the reunion's humorous interlude, an idea began to percolate. I wanted to create an achievement for which there could be only one possible honoree. Yes, I was about to exercise some leadership license, in effect stacking the deck and with a particular purpose in mind.

Later, at the reunion, about midway through the interlude, I said, "The next award will go to our classmate who can talk the best damn game of baseball ever played *or* watched. Now, you may have your own idea about who should win this, but to me it's a hands-down no-contest choice. And besides, as I said at the start, this responsibility carries with it a measure of license. So, with that in mind..."

I then stepped toward John and Linda and handed her a bag. "Linda," I said, trying to suppress laughter, "please, take the prize out."

She reached in the bag and, amidst spontaneous applause, held aloft a carved wooden hand, forefinger extended, painted in SHS colors red and gray, and declaring *SHS #1*. You could feel the warmth of the applause as it was breaking out and building.

CHAPTER 5

AN ODE TO US

A few nights before the 1988 Class of '63 25-year reunion, I was sitting in our backyard in Lyndhurst which had lots of trees and backed on to a woods. It was incredibly peaceful on summer evenings, the house shading the western sun, soft breezes off Lake Erie rustling the leaves, squirrels scurrying and hoping for one of my occasional handouts of nuts.

My wife, Lynne, was sitting beside me, reading, and I was relaxing and thinking about the upcoming reunion. A bit of inspiration struck. I stood and opened the sliding rear patio door, went inside the house, retrieved a pen and pad of paper, and moved back outside. Vivid memories of classmates such as John Crum had sparked an idea. I began writing:

25 YEARS
AN ODE TO US

Our bodies were temples but the temples are crumbling.

Without our glasses, we can't see our shoelaces.

After shampooing we have to clean the hair out so the water can drain.

When eating we think more about calories
and cholesterol than about taste.

When we run no one will mistake us for Olympians.

We're far less intelligent – just ask our kids.

When we wrap it all up, here's what we get: our vision is weaker,
our hair is thinner, we're dumber, slower and clumsier.

But despite all that we're better people. Oh, we're flawed all right,
but now we're more likely to see the flaws and try to correct them.

Twenty-five years ago a wart induced dread and a pimple caused
panic. During the last 25 years most if not all of us have learned
what the *real* problems are.   We've had to cope with problems
concerning health, marriages, children, home and jobs. And more.

Because of these problems we've become wiser, more thoughtful,
more understanding and more compassionate. We've
left our teenage pretensions by the side of the road.

We've come a long way – and overcome more than a few obstacles to get
here. We should be proud of each other. We really were the *class* of '63.

July 16, 1988

I made 100 copies and took them to Shelby and showed the ode to
Lucy Myers.
  "What do you think?" I asked. "Will the kids like it?"
  "Cool. I love it and so will they."
  We then inserted them into the booklet that each classmate would
receive upon arriving at the reunion.

CHAPTER 6

DISGUSTINGLY YOUTHFUL

Jim Blair's senior picture and the caption under it say a heck of a lot about Jim Blair. In the picture, there is nothing tentative or forced about Jim's smile. It is wide and it is genuine. The caption reads, "But, Mom! Stealing second base isn't illegal!"

That was Jim, he of the perpetually sunny disposition, always smiling and always talking with exclamation points. His laugh was more like a giggle and infectious. He was also a perfect example of one category of classmate you see at any reunion: Jim was one of those people who hadn't aged. His whole appearance was disgustingly youthful. I guess that's what great genes and a great attitude will do for you. In 1988 you could have taken his picture, and he still would have looked like the Jim Blair in the 1963 *Scarlet S*. Hell, he was even cutting his hair again the same way. And it was all still there and still brown. And no lines. His face had no lines. He still had his high school effervescence.

Now, if you are thinking Jim's life had been a thick bed of lush rose petals, think again. Jim had the heart of a lion. Always had. And he needed it. His dad drank way too much and was abusive. His sister Lynda, five years younger, was born with deformed legs. Jim was caring and protective. As a boy, he would put Lynda on his shoulders and carry her to the Little League field so she could watch practices and games. Jim's brother Tim, younger by three years, was hit by a car and killed while walking along a road when he was still at SHS. Through it all, Jim kept smiling and kept others smiling, too.

Jim had not attended our 20-year reunion but was present for our 15-year gathering. Though as I said earlier, I don't remember much about that one, and I don't recall seeing or talking with Jim. But he is in the class picture taken that night. The last memory I had of Jim before 1988 goes back to the mid-1960s when I was at Ohio University and Jim was in the Air Force. One Thanksgiving when we both were in Shelby for family gatherings, someone – I don't remember who – organized a touch football game among ex-highs at Skiles Athletic Field, the SHS football stadium. I went with Bill Anspach, a classmate, my closest friend, and next door neighbor for 15 years. Jim Blair was there, too.

It was a wonderful Thanksgiving morning for touch football. There was no snow on the ground, but the air was see-your-breath cold and dry and clear. We took the field and it seemed strange. It was the first time I had ever played a game (okay, so this was only touch) at Skiles Field when there weren't screaming fans and blaring bands in the stands. For varsity games, thousands jammed Skiles. But even for jayvee games there were gatherings large enough to make themselves heard. On that Thanksgiving morning there wasn't a soul except us guys on the field. It was wonderful.

Now, we did make some noise. We were hollering at each other, all of us in great spirits. We were having a blast. And we were playing some pretty good football. After all, we weren't that far removed from our high school glory days. Jim Blair was a left end in high school and a very good one. Jim stood about six feet tall, was fast and had good hands. He could block, too. In high school practices, I used to hate going one-on-one against him. He was one guy who used to hit in practice as hard as in games. Most of us, as I recall, were better game players than practice players. Jim went all out all the time. Well, anyway, in this touch football game, we naturally all were doing lots of running. After we'd been playing awhile, Jim ran a deep sideline route and caught a long pass which he ran into the end zone for a touchdown. Whereupon he went staggering to the back corner of the end zone, dropped to his knees, retched and tossed his cookies. All of them.

Now, we all thought this was hilarious and laughed uproariously. I think Jim would have laughed, too, if he hadn't been so nauseous. He pushed himself back to his feet, tried to clear his throat and gasped, "I guess I'm not in such great shape." He kept on playing.

On Friday, July 15, 1988, at about 6:30 p.m., I was driving into Shelby for the reunion the next night. On the way to my mom's apartment, I saw Bill Anspach standing outside his home. I honked and pulled over. We shook hands through the car window and greeted each other. Bill and I always are glad to see each other but, as to him and me, the reunion was not such a big deal. We have stayed in touch, seeing each other once or twice a year. Earlier in 1988 he and his son had driven to visit me in our home in Lyndhurst, a leafy suburb east of Cleveland.

"What are you doing tonight?" I asked.

"Not much," said Bill. "Why?"

"I thought we might go out for a beer."

"Okay. Hey, Blair just drove by a few minutes ago. How about if I try to track him down and the three of us go out?"

"Sounds good," I said. "It'll take me a while to get settled in over at my mom's. I gotta change out of this suit and talk with her a while."

"I haven't eaten yet, so I'll need a while, too."

"I'll call in about an hour."

About 8 p.m., I swung by Bill's house to pick him up, and we headed for the American Legion Post bar to meet Jim. By this time, I wasn't feeling well. I hadn't taken time to eat anything at my mom's which meant that I hadn't had anything to eat since breakfast, and my stomach was getting queasy. Jim was tired, having driven up alone the day before from Columbus, Georgia where he was a government meteorologist. Beer on an empty stomach didn't do much for me, but we started on some wonderful reminiscences. Jim's effervescence made it fun.

"Do you remember when we played Mansfield Senior?" Jim asked.

"You mean when we were seniors?" I asked.

"Yeah."

"We won."

"You hit a grand slam homer."

"Jim, you just made my weekend, no matter what else happens. I didn't think *anybody* else remembered that."

"How could I forget? Do you remember the situation?"

"The score was tied 2-2," I said, "there were two out and I had two strikes on me. Their pitcher had thrown a fastball and a changeup, and I guessed he'd throw another fastball. He did and I got all of it."

"All right, Mike!" exclaimed Jim. "Now, do you remember that we played Mansfield a second time that season?"

"No, are you sure?"

"Positive," Jim laughed, "but I'm not surprised that you don't remember. It was the Monday after prom weekend and they killed us by something like 26-1."

"We probably all were half-dead," I said.

Jim giggled his infectious giggle. "I told Coach (Chuck) Williams it was the biggest scheduling mistake he ever made."

"It's no wonder I don't remember."

Jim plunged on. "Do you remember the Upper Sandusky game that year?"

"Yeah, I lost the game."

"Whaddaya mean, you? I lost the game." Jim said this good naturedly but with rock-hard certainty.

"No," I said, "it was me. I made an error that cost us the game."

"No. Wait a minute. I'm the one who blew it," Jim insisted, smiling. "Well, my error wasn't exactly an error, but it cost us the game. Don't you remember? I was playing left field, and the sun was setting in my eyes. A guy hit a blooper, and I never saw it. Well, actually, I saw it when it left the bat, but I lost it right away. Hell, Denny Kidwell had to run out from shortstop to pick up the ball. Don't you remember?"

"Yes, now I do." And I did. "I also remember we had to beat Upper to tie Galion for the Northern Ohio League championship. It was the first year the NOL had an organized baseball season and awarded a championship. I was playing first and it was late in the game and the batter hit a grounder to me. A routine play. I picked up the ball, stepped on first to get the batter, and then I saw the runner on third trying to score. I threw home and the ball bounced a good ten feet in front of our catcher. He didn't have a chance. I'd made that throw a zillion times, and I blew it."

"I remember that," Jim said, smiling.

"Thanks," I said dryly.

Jim Blair helped make that reunion special, not only for me but for many. Throughout the night he went floating about the Knights of Columbus Hall, sharing memories and igniting laughter. Inside, Jim was troubled, though. At a post-reunion gathering at a classmate's home, Jim confided to the small group there that he felt his long-time marriage might be in jeopardy. There was pain in his voice, not what we were accustomed to hearing from Jim. He asked for advice. Basically, what he heard were murmurs of encouragement to try to stick it out. At three in the morning, I sensed that none of us was up for playing marriage counselor. Nonetheless, Jim thanked folks sincerely "just for listening" and for their encouragement.

Before we broke up at about 3:30 or 4:00, Jim was again seemingly upbeat. It's clear that Jim was the kind of classmate that livens up a reunion, and any reunion can use at least a couple Jim Blairs.

1993

Jim once more made the drive to Shelby from southern Georgia. His marriage had solidified, he said. He was jovial as ever – and still disgustingly youthful.

2003

Things had changed. After our 40-year reunion in July, a classmate emailed me. "Could you believe Jim Blair?" he wrote. "He looked awful. I think I've seen what death looks like when you're still alive."

A few weeks before that reunion, Ralph Thauvette phoned me. As usual, Ralph was coordinating reunion plans in Shelby.

"Mike Johnson," I said into the receiver at my office.

"Mike, it's Ralph."

"Hi, buddy, how are you?"

"I have something really awful to tell you," Ralph said. "It's really upsetting me. I had to tell someone." I was about to be the someone whatever the news was. Ralph's grave tone, never mind his words, was unmistakable.

"Go ahead, Ralph."

"I just got a letter from Jim Blair. He thinks he might have Parkinson's Disease. This is really choking me up." And that's precisely the way Ralph sounded, choked up.

"Oh, Lord…" That was all I could think to say.

"You should see his handwriting," said Ralph. "It looks like scribbling. Barely legible."

"Is Jim planning to come to the reunion?" I asked.

"Yes," said Ralph. "Angie is coming with him." Angela was Jim's wife but hadn't previously accompanied him to our reunions.

"What does Jim's letter say?"

"Well, basically, he is alerting us that he has Parkinson's so we won't be shocked. Man, I feel really terrible about this. What do you think we should do?"

"Spread the word," I said, "so people won't be shocked when they see him. Other than that, I don't think there's anything we can do."

"No, I guess not," said Ralph. His sadness at this development was overwhelming him. Jim, perpetually friendly, seemingly forever youthful, had been stricken, and Ralph's pain was acute. "He's signed up for golf," said Ralph. "I don't see how he can play. His handwriting looks so weak and shaky."

"We'll make sure Bill Anspach (who was organizing the golf outing) is fully plugged in."

"Right," said Ralph. "Well, I'm sorry I called with such bad news. But I had to tell someone."

"No problem. I'm glad you called." And I was.

Jim did come to the reunion. In fact, he and Angela were the first to arrive at the K of C Hall on Friday afternoon. It was about four o'clock. Ralph and I were the only ones inside, setting up the sound system. We heard the hall doors swing open and close noisily and looked up. There was Jim with Angela.

"Hey, Jim!" Ralph and I both said. We began walking toward him. He continued walking – slowly – toward us. When the three of us came together, we shook hands and hugged. Then Ralph and I greeted Angela the same way. No, we'd never met her, but at reunions we aren't exactly slow to bestow hugs on anyone within arm's reach. We could see Angela was warmed by our greeting.

We also could see that Jim was visibly weakened. After a couple minutes, we realized he would have difficulty standing for long. So I hustled across the hall floor to a storage room and brought back four folding chairs. Ralph and I put aside thoughts of the sound system, and we all sat. The conversation got rolling.

"When did you first notice symptoms, Jim?" I asked.

"In January, right after I retired I started feeling funny." After completing his Air Force duty, Jim had continued working as a civilian government meteorologist in Georgia. Now, there were a few lines in his face, but his hair still was brown and thick, and his perpetually sunny disposition was firmly in place. "They think it might be Parkinson's," said Jim. "But I'm not sure. Look," he said, extending his arms and hands. "I don't have the shakes. My strength is down, but I don't have any shakes."

"And did you fly or drive up from Columbus?" I asked.

"Drove," said Jim. "Angie did most of the driving."

"Jim did his share," Angela quickly interjected. Angela was tall, blond, pretty and soft-spoken with an accent that told me where she and Jim had met. In fact, as I was to learn later, she was a native of the Columbus, Georgia area.

"I've got another test next week to try to figure out what this is," Jim said.

Pretty soon, other classmates began arriving to help set up and decorate. As they clustered around Jim, Ralph and I returned to setting up and testing the sound system.

That evening, Jim pitched in, helping to position red tablecloths and affix twisted red and gray ribbons to tabletops. The next morning, he went golfing. He fell once but kept on playing. He was in fine spirits at the Saturday night gala and at the picnic the following afternoon.

The next week, back in Georgia, Jim did undergo more testing, and he did get another diagnosis. It wasn't only Parkinson's. It was worse – ALS – amyotrophic lateral sclerosis, or Lou Gehrig's Disease.

On September 4, Jim sent me this email: *Mike, I thought I'd write you to let you know what the Mayo Clinic said about me. I do have ALS, but I also have symptoms of Parkinson's. The doctor said there is very little they can do for me. I do take a medicine every 12 hours, and all it does is slow the disease down and give me a little more time. I got another appointment at Emory* (University Hospital) *in Atlanta the 18th of this month. I'll let you know what they say to me. Mayo said this is very rare.*

My family is going to the gulf this weekend. We rented a house with a pool right on the beach, and it sleeps 12 people. I really enjoy my whole family being there...You take care, Mike. I really enjoyed coming to Shelby. I'm proud to know you're my friend. Jim

His condition began to worsen quickly. In October of 2003 Margie Parsons Hoover Earick, one of our '63 classmates who lives in Bucyrus, Ohio, and her sister Nancy Parsons Schmidt, class of '67, who was living near Columbus, Ohio, drove to Columbus, Georgia to visit Jim. The Parsons kids and the Blair kids had been neighbors in their youth and had become very close. Upon returning to Bucyrus, Margie emailed me. She reported that Jim was fully aware of his fate. Margie said that Jim observed that it would "take a miracle" for him to cheat death.

We'll continue Jim's story later in this book within the context of a memorable road trip.

CHAPTER 7

REACHING OUT – "SQUEEZE HARDER"

My mini-reunion with Patricia Papenbrock was unexpected and perhaps even unique. I mean, the front of a busy store in a bustling shopping center is a hell of a place to reunite with someone you haven't seen in 25 years but that's what happened.

On top of that, we hadn't been together for more than a few minutes when Pat reached into her purse and pulled out a pack of cigarettes and told me she smoked. Now, when you consider who she is and what she did, you'll understand why I was taken aback. But that can wait a while. First I'll recount our two-person reunion that took place on July 24, 1988, or a week and a day after our class's 25-year reunion.

At one time or another, a goodly number of SHS boys likely had a crush on Pat. Yes, you can include me in that number. I even worked up the courage to ask her out a few times and, in something of a continuing miracle, she said yes each time. Why, I'm not sure. Generally, like many high school girls, she dated some older guys. When I went out with her, first in our junior year, I was thrilled but not totally comfortable. That first date was for a Snowball, a big December dance. One of my older brothers, Gene, a car salesman at the time, offered me a new Pontiac for the date and I accepted. Nothing like showing up in a shiny chariot. Pat was impressed but her dad was more so. Not so much with me but with the car, a "marimba red" Pontiac. After shaking hands and calling for Pat who still was upstairs, he stepped past me and walked out to the curb where he gave the new Pontiac a thorough inspection.

Pat's poise and maturity were daunting. She was a woman among boys, or so I viewed her. Maybe she agreed to date me because I was less immature than other boys in our class, but even all these years later I'm not at all sure about that.

Pat Papenbrock (nee Shedenhelm) was a high school boy's idea of perfection. She moved with athletic grace and was a cheerleader for one year, a majorette for four, and homecoming queen. She was on the staffs

41

of the school newspaper and the *Scarlet S*, and she was a member of the Thespian Club. To me she wasn't the most beautiful girl, but she was pretty and she was nice, very nice.

In our senior year, the spring of '63, we went to the Senior Party and later, on May 18, to the Senior Prom together. The prom was one of those all-night affairs. Dance, movie, bowling and breakfast at classmate's house. I think Pat may have outscored me in bowling. I didn't bowl often and I was strong but wild. I could never figure out whether I should bowl left-handed – the way I threw a baseball – or right-handed – the way I shot a bow or rifle and the way I write. (I was born a lefty but my confusion's roots lie with a Franciscan nun who was determined to see lefties write righty.) I remember Pat and I laughed a lot, probably at my string of gutter balls.

Afterward in the early morning hours, as we cruised through the farm country outside Shelby, we talked a lot about our post-graduation futures. I was going to be heading south to Ohio University's renowned journalism school and she north to Mt. Sinai Hospital's acclaimed nursing school. Pat's decision to study nursing didn't surprise me. For me, a single incident demonstrated her aptitude. It happened when we were juniors. We were sitting in an otherwise empty classroom during lunch hour. Just chatting. Three warts had formed on the back of my right hand between thumb and forefinger. One was small but the others were large and ugly. I mentioned to Pat that I had a doctor appointment to have them removed. Without hesitation she took my hand in her left hand. With her right hand she first examined the growths and then she gently rubbed them. I have no recollection of what she said, but her words were soothing – the words of a caring nurse-to-be. As the eastern sky began to brighten, we went to classmate Martha Keil's house for a sunrise breakfast. Sometime around nine o'clock on Sunday morning, I drove her home. We kissed politely on the front porch.

The last time I remember seeing Pat was on graduation night. She did go off to Mt. Sinai in Cleveland, and we quickly lost touch.

Pat came to the five-year reunion in 1968 when I was soldiering in Korea, but she hadn't been to once since. However, on July 12, 1988, four days before our 25-year reunion, she wrote a letter to the class that was made part of the reunion booklet. She wrote that she would be "unable to attend because of two kids working (different places, different time schedules) and out-of-town guests arriving Sunday AM, the 17th." Hmmmm…As you have seen earlier with David Spangler, those aren't the kind of obstacles that will stop a person who is really determined to attend a reunion. Her closing sentence fascinated me: "I hope there are plans for a 'next' reunion; I plan to be there." Pat sounded like a classmate suffering from acute ambivalence, a common affliction among grads torn between coming and staying home. I had once been similarly afflicted.

Right after the reunion, I dashed off short letters to several classmates. Some of the notes were thank you's to members of the reunion planning team. Some were brief updates of things I had learned at the reunion and went to classmates who had not attended but who had written letters to the class. Thus, one of my updates went to Pat. Just a few days later – it was a Friday – I returned home late from a business trip. I'd nearly missed a connection in Chicago – I had to run from one end of O'Hare Airport to the other to catch my flight – and was worn out. Before crashing I decided to look through the mail and, much to my surprise, it included this note from Pat:

Dear Mike,

How wonderful to hear from you twice! I am grateful for your interest and updates.

You neglected to say much about you other than about your father in Crestwood nursing home. I'm sorry about your father – that's never easy. I'd like to know how life is for you – the choices you've made, your mother, & all other.

We live very close to one another. I would be delighted to meet you for a cup of coffee or if you prefer, we could talk by phone. My number is 000.0000.

Again, thanks Mike for the letters. It feels good to be in touch.
Pat

(Side notes. Pat refers to hearing from me twice. She was one of a dozen classmates to whom I had sent brief notes about three weeks before the reunion, urging them to attend. She mentions my dad in a nursing home; in my post-reunion letter to Pat, I mentioned that classmate Anne Lafferty

Stock delivered library books to residents of Crestwood "where my dad has been confined for a dozen years." Dad would pass away on Christmas morning that year.)

I discussed Pat's note with Lynne, and we agreed quickly that it was more than a polite response. Pat seemed to be reaching out. And since only a few days had passed since I sent my note to her, she must have written her note immediately upon receiving mine. In other words, she must have responded when her emotions were on the loose, and I wanted to reach her before she caged them and got to the point where she might have second thoughts about wanting to talk with me. I didn't want to make it easy for her to dodge such a conversation. So I decided to call her soon. In fact, had I not been so tired that night, I would have phoned right away. But I decided to wait until Saturday morning. At 9:30, I picked up the phone, figuring that a mother of three teenagers probably was not still in bed.

"Hello" was the way she answered the phone. Since it was an adult female voice, I assumed it was Pat.

"If you can recognize this voice," I said with a hint of mischievousness, "I'll put a gold star right on your forehead."

"Say something more."

"How much more do you want me to say?"

"I'm afraid I'm drawing a blank. I'm sorry."

"Think back to the events of the past few days," I said.

A brief pause, then, "Mike!"

"Very good. You get the gold star." I chuckled.

"Mike! How are you?"

"That's a hell of a way to begin this conversation."

She laughed. "Oh, I know."

"Well," I said, "that's the way a lot of reunion conversations start. Then they get rolling and get better."

"I'm so glad you called."

"Yes," I said, "but the telephone isn't the way to have this little reunion. We need to see each other."

"I agree. Let me look at my calendar. Oh, my, I don't see...You work on week days, and..."

As I said, I wanted this meeting to happen soon, before chilly feet or second thoughts got in the way. "I caught you off guard," I said.

"You did."

"Compose yourself."

"Okay."

"Do you want to do this today?"

"It won't work today."

"I can be flexible."

She paused and what I heard gladdened me. "Would tomorrow be okay?" she asked.

"Sure. Now we have to decide where and when."

"About one-thirty?"

"Fine."

"We have to decide on where," she said. "I'm trying to think of this little restaurant in Eastgate Shopping Center. It's next to Bernie Schulman's. Oh, for the life of me, I can't remember the name."

"Why not Bernie Schulman's?"

"Okay...How will we recognize each other?"

"Good question. It shouldn't be too hard. Look at our senior yearbook. I wear glasses now. I have less hair and it's not as brown. Gravity has taken a certain toll. But other than that...How about you?"

"Well, I, uh..."

"Well, tell me, are you about the same?"

"Yeah, about the same, I guess, but you can be the judge of that, Mike."

"I'll be gentle, Pat." We both laughed. "I have a proposal. Instead of going to a restaurant, let's go to a park. I think it would be – "

She interrupted me. "That's a marvelous idea, Mike."

"I'll throw a couple lawn chairs in the trunk."

Pat started to ask me a couple questions about me, then checked herself. "Let's save it." Then she added, "I do have to ask one quick question. How's your mother?"

"About as good as can be expected under the circumstances. She's been under a lot of stress for the last dozen years." Of course, I was alluding to my dad's confinement in a nursing home.

"Your mom and I used to work together," Pat reminded me.

"I remember. At Keil's Department Store."

"Please tell her I said hello."

"I'll tell her about this meeting. She'll be thrilled."

"Oh, good. Tomorrow then. One-thirty at Bernie Schulman's."

"See you there."

"Bye, bye."

"Hey," I said, "bring pictures. Of your family."

"Okay."

"Bye."

So there you have it. A girl – a woman – whom I had not seen in a quarter century has just agreed to meet me in front of a general merchandise emporium in a shopping center. Words like bizarre and ironic seem appropriate here. In 28 hours, two people who were close once but who had taken up residence on different spaceships were going to alter course and converge on the same landing site. Destination: Bernie Schulman's.

So how did I feel about this? Pretty good. I was glad I had not ignored her reaching out. Later that Saturday, I decided a couple things. One, I would try to make her feel as comfortable as possible about this and, two, I would try to make the meeting fun and memorable. I had a brainstorm as to accomplishing that, the fun and memorable part, I mean.

Sunday, July 24, 1988, dawned blue and bright. The morning inched along, and then I got in my car about 1:15 p.m. Pat had to travel a bit farther and I envisioned her already on the road to our Bernie Schulman's rendezvous. I figured we both were excited. I know I was. I arrived precisely at 1:30, parked and walked across to Bernie Schulman's entrance. I had not wanted to be late because I was concerned that, if Pat arrived before I did, she might conclude I'd changed my mind, or she might have a last minute change of heart if she didn't see me and wheel right around and out of the parking lot. Too little faith in Pat? Maybe, but she had shied away from attending reunions.

After I'd stood in front of Bernie Schulman's for about five minutes, I thought I heard someone call my name. I looked around and saw a woman in white levis and a white top and sunglasses walking toward me. She had Pat's athletic stride. The woman smiled and waved, and I began moving toward her. When we were perhaps 20 feet apart, I smiled and said, "Pat." A brief pause, then I said, "Take off your sunglasses."

She did and we closed quickly, arms outstretched. We embraced and squeezed. "Squeeze harder," I said and she did.

"Oh, Mike..."

It was a long hug and then we kissed. She pulled away slightly and looked at my eyes. "About the same?"

"About the same." Indeed, her figure was as trim, perhaps a tad leaner, than 25 years before. Her face was a wee bit fuller, and it also appeared softer and wiser. Still very pretty.

We strolled to my car. We got in and I began driving to Strawberry Lane, an area in the North Chagrin Reservation, a large park about 10 minutes to the north.

"Talk," Pat said in what amounted to a mock command.

I laughed. "Where do you want me to start?"

"Tell me about the reunion. How many were there? Who?"

"Let's start in a different way," I said. "Tell me how your family reacted to this meeting."

"Oh, Mike, what an interesting way to begin. My husband was puzzled and a little uneasy."

"Why?"

"Well, in the past," she said, "I hadn't done anything to stay in touch with my classmates. And none of them had stayed in touch with me. I didn't think our class had been very close in school. It was sort of a chapter that had been closed. So he wondered why I wanted to do this."

"Your kids?"

"Andrea and Rob, my oldest ones, didn't have much to say. My youngest, Christi, was all for it. She was excited for me." We laughed. Looking ahead, imagining Pat returning home, I could picture Christi grilling her for all the details.

"My wife," I told Pat, "thought it was neat. She knows how much value I've come to place on these reunions, and she was for it. Like yours, my two older kids had zilch to say. My youngest, Ben, was full of questions. One after another. I finally asked him if he wanted to come along. Now, of course, I didn't really want that. If Ben had said yes, I'd-"

"You'd have said, 'Stuff it, Kid.'"

I laughed. "It never got that far. I told him the meeting was not going to take place in a restaurant and that killed his interest. Ben is an eating machine and loves to go anyplace where eating is involved. He loves restaurants, the fancier the better."

We laughed. I pulled into Strawberry Lane and circled around a small lake. I parked and we walked to the rear of the car and I opened the trunk.

"You look young and strong," I said. "You carry the chairs."

"That depends," Pat joked. "What are *you* carrying?"

"These." I lifted out a tripod and large black camera bag and a container of water and cups. "Let's go."

We went walking across a meadow to some trees where we placed the chairs side by side facing the lake.

"Sit," I said.

She reached into her purse and pulled out a pack of cigarettes. "I smoke."

"I like to light up an occasional cigar."

"I smoke regularly."

"Pat, knowing what you do – "

"Mike, please don't give me the anti-smoking lecture." She was smiling but serious. "I've heard it too many times."

"Okay." And that was the last I said about it. Our time together today, however long, would be too short to waste debating smoking. I couldn't help thinking, though, *Here's Pat, a hospice nurse. In her hospice and bereavement work, she must have comforted many people who were dying from cigarette-caused diseases or consoled their survivors.*

We took turns summarizing our personal histories of the past 25 years. To me, the most notable element of Pat's history was her hospice work. "I'm very impressed," I told her. "Whenever I visit my dad at Crestwood, I have to work up my courage. Years ago, my brothers and I used to kid my dad that we expected to learn that he had died climbing a ladder or shoveling snow."

"And I'll bet that's the way he wanted it," Pat said.

"Yes, well, it's not easy for me to go in there."

"This may surprise you," Pat said, "but it's not easy for me either. I had to learn to control my emotions, and I'm pretty good at it. I don't show my emotions very much."

"You know," I told her, "it occurred to me on the way to meet you that there's a whole lot more I don't know about you than I ever did while we were in school."

"I had the same thought."

"Well, this is a start. I think you'll find any bonds we had will be strengthened by this. Let's switch to the reunion."

"Okay."

"But rather than just tell you about it, let me show you." From my camera bag, I pulled a set of 20 pictures I had taken at the 25-year reunion. I handed them to Pat.

"I don't recognize her," Pat said as she intently studied the woman in the first picture. I told her who it was. She looked at the second picture. "I don't recognize this one either. Oh my, I wonder if I'll recognize any of them. This is what I was afraid of."

Now, I thought, she's revealing one of the reasons she hasn't been attending reunions. Anxiety. But she did recognize the classmates in the next two pictures. Then I looked up, and this woman who had learned to control her emotions was weeping. Tears were welling under both eyes and had begun trickling down her face.

"Would you like a hanky?" I asked. "I have a clean one in my pocket."

"Yes, please, I'm not carrying tissues."

I'll admit this: I was glad to see those tears. As clearly as any words she might have spoken, those tears told me she cared.

We went through the rest of the pictures, and her comments became more animated. Occasionally she dabbed at her eyes. I then told her about Chris Straw, John Crum and Jim Blair and the others I've been telling you about. I made a point of telling her about David Spangler's iron determination to attend the reunion.

"I feel kind of sad," she said.

"I understand. You're not alone with those feelings. After the reunion ended, a feeling of melancholy set in and it didn't begin to diminish until a couple days later. I didn't have any trouble understanding why. You know that some of the kids you won't see for at least another five years. Some you won't ever see again. And some have very serious problems to deal with. It's no mystery why you feel sad."

Without any questioning or probing by me, Pat then disclosed the biggest reason why she hadn't come to the reunion. "My husband and I talked about my coming to the reunion. I said I was thinking of going. He said, 'You are? Well, if you really want to go, I can go.' I said, 'No, you don't have to go. I can go myself and stay with one of my sisters.' He said, 'No, if you want to go, I don't want you to go by yourself.' Then I said, 'That's all right, I won't go.'"

I shook my head. I was certain that that conversation had taken place between millions of couples around the country and had been one of the chief roadblocks to attending reunions. Fear.

"Pat," I said very gently, "lots of your classmates were there without spouses."

"Oh, I thought so." You could hear the ache of regret in her voice.

"Hell, Pat, my wife wasn't there. She has zero – or less – interest in going to my reunions. And I'll tell you something else. I think the people who have the most fun are the ones who go without spouses. Classmates with spouses think they have to entertain them. Or somehow keep them included. Or spouses sit on the periphery in desultory little groups or shadow their spouses but never really become part of the conversations." Nor, I should add, have I attended any of my wife's class reunions.

She was silent for a long moment, and so I decided to share more of my feelings. "My closest friend in college was Andy Blank. (My second book, *Fate of the Warriors*, is co-dedicated to Andy.) You think of your closest friend, and Andy and I were that close. He got cancer and was dead nine months after we graduated. The guys who were going to be in his wedding party wound up as his pallbearers. I was in Korea when I heard about Andy's death from his dad. I told myself that sometime, I didn't know when, I would visit Andy's grave for a last reunion. Years went by and I never did it. I was too busy to take time from the present and the future to look back, even briefly. But five years ago, when I attended our 20-year reunion, I decided it was equally healthy to occasionally look back and remember where you came from and what got you there. So last summer one day I happened to think about Andy and decided the time had come. His parents had moved and I didn't know where. So I took a stab and called some graves registration offices. Two phone calls and I had the name of the cemetery. Then soon after that, on a Saturday in July, I told my wife, 'Lynne, the time has come. Tomorrow I'm visiting Andy's grave.' I got up early and got on the road. It was a beautiful morning, and I had no trouble finding Andy's grave. I stood there and remembered. Yes, I felt sad. The time was long past when I could do anything for Andy, but I'll tell you, it felt good to be standing there. I was very glad I had taken the time to step back and look back. The thing is, it took me 19 years to do it, and it shouldn't have."

"I'm so glad we got together," Pat said.

"Me, too."

She handed me my hanky and smiled. "I hope you don't mind some mascara."

As I was putting the hanky back in my pocket, I saw Pat glance at her watch. "Are we in a hurry?" I asked.

"No. I just told Bill I'd be home by four."

"He *was* a little worried."

"Yes."

"So, four is the witching hour," I said. She smiled. "Well, we'll make sure you're at least close. Will you mind if you're a bit late?"

"No."

"Good. Now it's time to take a picture, but not just any picture." I stood and positioned my tripod. I checked the lighting and told Pat to stand.

"You look uncomfortable," I said.

"I am."

The nearest people were maybe 30 feet away. "Look, do you really care what these other people might be thinking?"

"No."

"Then, relax." And she did, breaking into an easy smile.

"Are you going to be in this picture with me?" she asked.

"You got it." I switched the camera to the time delay setting. "But it won't be just you and me. It'll be you, me and something else. We're going to make this picture part of the reunion collection. That means we need to do something special." She was visibly puzzled but also enjoying this. I moved back to my camera bag and pulled out an old cellophane wrapper. As I removed the contents, Pat started to laugh. It was one of my old varsity football letters, a large gray block S embroidered with a scarlet football. I handed it to her.

"Hold it against your chest," I said. "And don't move."

"You're bossy."

"Only when I'm directing a picture."

We laughed.

"Now, when I press the end of the timing cord, you'll see this red light begin to blink. It will blink slowly at first, then rapidly. When it blinks rapidly, smile, because it will be ready to take the picture. Ready?"

"Ready." Pat was beaming.

I pressed the end of the cord, then moved to Pat's side. We wrapped an arm around each other as she held the big gray S against her chest. The red light blinked slowly, then quickly, we smiled, and the shutter clicked.

"Two more," I said. "That'll mean one for you, one for me, and one for the reunion committee."

And then we were done. We started to gather our things.

"Pat, I'm hoping this isn't the last time we see each other. I'm hoping we'll meet again, but not in front of Bernie Schulman's. A class reunion would be nice."

She smiled, her face showing both kindness and sadness. "You've given me a lot to think about."

"I hope so."

We walked back to my car and drove back to Eastgate Shopping Center. We walked to her car and then we hugged again. It was another long one.

As she eased into her car, she said, "Mike, thank you for taking the time to see me."

"Pat!" I exclaimed, as I threw my arms skyward in mock exasperation. "That's what I would expect a business acquaintance to say."

"I mean it," she said. "Thank you."

"You're welcome. Pat, I'm glad we had our mini-reunion."

I returned to my car. As we pulled away, we both waved. Pat was smiling.

1993

About two weeks before the 1993 30-year reunion, knowing our planning team had not received a registration form from Pat, I wrote her this letter:

Dear Pat,

Well, it's July 1993 and our 30-year reunion is nearly upon us. I'm writing this because my instincts tell me you are not planning to join us. I hope I'm wrong.

A bunch of your classmates would love to be with you. Am I exaggerating? No.

Now, you may be telling yourself again that you and your classmates 'weren't that close' or that you 'have no desire to get close to them.' Those are just two of the reasons you could cite for not going. Of course, as you know very well, deciding not to do something is rather easier and less courageous than deciding to do something.

Saying what I'm saying, I realize, is presumptuous. Being so is merely one example of my inglorious set of flaws.

If you don't go? Life will go on with no visible loss. If you do go? Life will go on – enriched. Is it 'safe' to occasionally look backward as we move forward through life? My belief? It's safe and healthy and strengthens us for the journey ahead.

Should you muster the courage to go, I know you would be touched by your reception. And should you go, I offer this counsel: consider participating in one of the activities leading up to the Saturday night gathering. It'll build your comfort level.

Should you find yourself on the fence and like to discuss this with someone, you could give me a ring.

On behalf of Ralph, Chris and others, I hope you climb behind the wheel and find your way to Shelby later this month.

Your flawed but reliable friend.
Mike

On reunion weekend, on Saturday afternoon at 4:30, about 20 classmates had gathered for the tour of Old SHS. Upon entering the school, we began reminiscing immediately and laughter was bouncing through the hallways. After about 15 minutes I happened to turn around and there was Pat. I'm sure my surprise was visible. She had arrived late and, following the echoes, had caught up with us. She immediately was enveloped in a series of hugs, mine first.

Later, as the group was again moving through the halls, I said to her, "You got the letter,"

"Yes," she replied softly, "and it made me angry. I almost decided not to come."

"You were planning to come?"

"Yes."

I supposed that the presumptuousness of the letter had irritated her. But I quickly decided that any more meaningful conversation could wait.

She obviously enjoyed the tour. In the old Band Room, Pat, a former majorette, was reminiscing and took some teasing: "I'm surprised they let you in here," I said, "since you wore that short little uniform and twirled that piece of metal. I thought you had to play music."

"Hey," she protested laughingly, "how about the clarinet?"

"Barely qualifies…"

At the K of C Hall after the tour, she was greeted warmly by many and seemed to be having a grand time. We chatted briefly a couple times. About 6:30, all the class members moved outside for the reunion photo.

Later in the evening, a group, including Pat, was clustered around Jeanette Egleston, one of three former teachers who had accepted our invitation to the reunion. Jeanette had been one of our favorites and, as we were to learn that evening, was only 13 years older than we. A former SHS majorette and a member of the class of 1950, she was still petite and effervescent. Jeanette had good naturedly endured considerable teasing by the guys in her classroom. I had been one of the chief tormentors. Indeed, before the reunion, I had heard that Jeanette had accepted our invitation, at least in part "to get even with Mike Johnson." Well, at this juncture, I was recalling some of the things we had done to Jeanette and she was relating what she had done to retaliate. Then I heard Pat, who had not been in the same classroom, say "It's clear; you guys were all in love with her."

My response, "Probably."

All laughed.

Later still in the evening, I asked Pat whether she was joining us for the next day's picnic. "No," she said, "I'm driving home tonight."

Still later as midnight was nearing, she was among a circle of six or so girls, sitting between Chris Straw and Cindy Wray. I squatted down between Pat and Chris and whispered in Pat's ear, "Before you leave, I'd like a brief, private word with you."

"Fine, when I walk to my car."

Later, in the parking lot, we stood face to face under a canopy of stars. The air was cooling pleasantly. A few other classmates also were outside but, possibly sensing our desire for a few moments of privacy, gave us a wide berth.

"I have a question," I said. "How did you feel about your reception?"

"You were right," she said. "It was wonderful." Then Pat said, "I have a question for you."

"Okay."

"Why are these reunions so important to you?"

I paused for a long moment before speaking. "I might have some difficulty articulating this, but I think there are several reasons. As I've told you, I used to be ambivalent about them. Then about 10 years ago, some relationships, not just these, started to take on more meaning. I wanted to nurture them. As to our reunions, I've come to enjoy them more and more. Each one seems to be a building block for the next one. These people are special to me. Also, as I think you know, I tend to bring a measure of intensity to anything." Pat chuckled at this. "Passion. Whether it's reunions, business, coaching or whatever. How's that for an answer?"

"Not bad." Then we hugged tightly. With her face against my chest, I heard a happy sigh. Then we let go.

"I hope this won't be our last meeting," I said. "I hope there will be another reunion." We hugged again, just as hard, and I heard a happy "Mmmm."

Still hugging, Pat looked at me and said, "Say hello to your mom for me. She's special."

"All right."

Then we parted and she continued walking toward her car. "Drive safely."

2007

February 17 brought a jolt. It was an email from Pat. It was rather chatty and she said almost in passing, *I suppose you know about my surgery and rehab.*

Surgery and rehab? I was thinking she'd had an accident of some kind. Playing tennis. Skiing. A fall at home. I replied that I'd heard not a word about her surgery.

There followed another email from Pat. *On December 12, Bill and I were told that I had colon cancer after a rather urgent colonoscopy* *had been done on the 5th. I had a colon resection done on January 9. I was 11 days in the hospital, due to complicating factors. The prognosis is very good but because of just ONE (out of 24 harvested) lymph node involvement, that one bought me a round of chemo which I start this week. I am recovering nicely from the surgery, but having chemo is another foreign territory to travel. I will be taking the therapy for six months.*

I lost my first friend to cancer when he was just 16 and I was 15. My closest college buddy fell to cancer at age 23. Since then many more friends have fallen to that dread disease. Still, whenever I learn that another friend has been stricken, it's a jolt.

A few days later came another email from Pat. *The chemotherapy I'm taking is in pill form, therefore I'm doing it from home. It was my option, versus going to the hospital twice a week for 2 weeks with 2 weeks off and having a mediport inserted. Both that method and what I am doing are standard treatment for colon cancer. The oncologist did not have a recommendation for me one over the other, so the decision became a no-brainer for me and Bill. This pill form of treatment has been around since 2005. The cycle is a lot of pills for two weeks, then one week off before starting again. Both regimes are for 6 months. I started Sunday AM. Wish me luck.*

As you can see, Pat was handling this crisis with a calm and grace consistent with her being – both professional and personal.

Luck is good to have on your side, but I thought something more couldn't hurt, so a couple weeks later, I told Pat about a college buddy, John Edwards, who is a Methodist minister and who keeps an active prayer list. Pat replied that she wouldn't mind being added, wittily observing that "you can't get any closer than that." John gladly added her and then occasionally asked me how Pat was doing. You'll learn more about him later within the context of his own tests of character.

July 13 brought this email from Pat: *I am doing well, will start the last cycle of chemo on Monday, lasting two weeks. The 'off week' (2 on 1 off) seems to be the most difficult. It seems my body likes the chemicals while I am on it, then takes it out 'on me' when I am off. So I'm ambivalent about ending it – can't wait and yet feel somewhat depressed that I can no longer be an active participant in fighting it. Very optimistic; now the waiting begins. I told Bill the other night I have forgotten how it feels to be me, the me before this began. Perhaps that me is in the past. Will try to be understanding and try to like the new me if that is to be.*

In October she did it. She came to Alumni Homecoming.

On October 12 at about 5:00 on Friday afternoon, I was in a hallway at Old SHS, chatting with fellow alums who were staffing the registration table. I heard footsteps and turned to see who was approaching. First I saw Pat's oldest sister and her husband. Pat was following.

I shook hands warmly with her sister and brother-in-law, and then Pat and I hugged vigorously. We exchanged pleasantries for a couple minutes and then I said, "Don't take this as a chauvinistic comment" – she started laughing – "but given what you've been going through, you look a lot better than I expected."

"Thanks. I really feel good."

It showed. Her eyes were radiating good health and happiness.

A little later inside the school cafeteria where alums were gathering, Pat clearly was reveling in the company of fellow grads. She was laughing during the Whippet Quiz – trivia questions based on Whippet sports with winners receiving Whippet logo'd merchandise and apparel with the grand prize a football helmet – and applauding the performances by the Whippet band and choir.

The next morning, Pat and her brother-in-law visited the "new" SHS, checking out the science classrooms and labs. Then on Saturday night before and after the Hall of Distinction dinner and induction ceremony, we exchanged more hugs. She also met Lynne for the first time. When I stepped to the podium to give an update on a cancer-stricken classmate, Jim Henkel, I saw Pat dabbing at tears.

A few days later, I received this email from her: *I know it must have been difficult for you to give us an update on Jim on Saturday evening. You did it well. Thank you. I remember, just on the outskirts of my memory, playing with June Went, Jim, John Crum, Bill Shaffer over on June's street. I think there may have been others but we were playing "war" with June and I as nurses and running to "care for" the wounded. I hope and pray that Jim does not die from this deadly cancer "bullet" that has targeted him.*

Re the alumni weekend. Along with seeing classmates, I was thrilled to go to SHS and hear about the new science wing to be and then out to Pioneer (Career & Technology Center) *to see and hear about that complex. Thanks for the encouragement to include that. My brother-in-law accompanied me.*

More about the reunion: have you ever seen the TV series, Cold Case? It's about unsolved murders from the past, "showing" the characters as they "were" 30, 40 years ago then to the present day. That's where my thoughts were. I felt like it was an episode, me "seeing and remembering" from 1963, then fast forwarding to 2007! It was nice to see Janet. Who could ever forget her doe-like eyes and full lips? She is lovely as always.

It was nice to see both you and Lynne. Wish I'd had more time to talk with her as well as others. Perhaps another time.

Sounds good to me.

CHAPTER 8

MOMENT OF PRAYER FOR THE "QUEEN OF THE ROCKING K"

Our 20- and 25-year reunions were very upbeat. A ton of fun. But make no mistake about one thing: reunions can put some lumps in your throat, and eyes have been known to mist and teardrops to drip. That's especially true as the years begin to pile up behind you.

Bob Blankenhorn was chairman of our 1988 reunion planning committee. Bob's a real friendly bear of a guy. Big chest, bigger waist. In our 1963 *Scarlet S*, Bob is sporting a crewcut and smiling broadly. In 1988 his hair was fashionably long, brown tinged with gray, and he was wearing a full beard and mustache and his girth was wider. His baritone voice seemed a perfect match for his frame, and it was as resonant as ever.

At our reunions, we have a few traditions. I've already told you about the humorous interludes. Another is taking a class picture. About 7 p.m., Bob called for attention and asked everyone to step outside and assemble for the class picture. It was fun getting organized, about 70 of us crowding together on three rows of rickety, portable wooden bleachers. As the photographer composed and focused, I was urging everyone to get closer. "We want to fill this frame. We don't want a picture of the grass and sky. Act like we actually like each other. The closer we get, the closer the photographer can get and the better the picture."

This, of course, produced some good-natured jesting and jostling, but everyone did get really close. "Just be sure," I cautioned, "that your face isn't blocked by someone else's head."

After the photo session, we all were kidding around as we slowly moved back inside the K of C Hall. Bob waited a few minutes until we were all inside and then again asked for our attention. It was time for another of our reunion traditions.

"As we are gathered here for this reunion," Bob said somberly, "some of our classmates can't be with us. What I would like is for everyone to bow his head for a moment of prayer." Bob then spoke a warm, from-the-

59

heart conversational prayer in which he asked for blessings for our troubled classmates.

One of them was Nancy Kuhn. During our days at Shelby High School, Nancy was a friendly, cheerful girl who lived on a family farm. Her *Scarlet S* yearbook caption read "Queen of the Rocking K." But busy farm girl though she was, she made time to be much more. Nancy was treasurer of the Speech Club and a member of the Shelby Whippet marching band, the Girls Athletic Association, the Pep Club and the Thespian Club. She acted in two comedies – *Inner Willy* and *The Death and Life of Larry Benson*. She was easy to like and respect. As we gathered for our 25-year reunion, Nancy lay in a Columbus hospital in critical condition without kidneys. A transplant had failed.

After the reunion, I wrote to Nancy, and three of the '63 girls were planning to visit her. I hope they did.

Like I said, reunions can put a lump in your throat. Unfortunately, there are more lumps to come.

1993

On December 20, 1989, I received a letter from Nancy. In it she summarized the doings of her husband Jerry and her kids Brian and Betsy. With a tone of hope, she wrote, "I am finally regaining some of my strength. It has been a long process. I'm able to do my dialysis at home so that helps."

More than three years later, in April of 1993, Ralph Thauvette saw Nancy, and she seemed to be doing well. She was very optimistic and was planning to attend our 30-year reunion, a mere three months away. But then, just a week later, Nancy passed away. Ralph, one of the most caring men walking the planet, had flowers sent to her family in the name of the Class of '63, and he attended Nancy's funeral. At the reunion in July we observed her passing with heartfelt comments from Ralph, eyes reddening, and a long moment of silence for the Queen of the Rocking K.

CHAPTER 9

"I REALLY DO LOVE YOU."

Jane Bell Henning was one of the class zanies, but also one of the class lights. She was luminous, glowing with energy and enthusiasm. She was pretty, with long brown hair, slender, and she seemed to float when she walked. She was 5'5" and weighed no more than 90 pounds. Years later she would say, "I looked like Twiggy. Thin was in." Her smile came easily and often.

Jane also could be guileless, which she was on one hot summer evening. I was walking home from one of our off-season football conditioning sessions. As I was to learn a few years later, Army basic training had nothing on these summer workouts. I had run Lord-knows-how-many quarter-mile laps, wind sprints and the stadium steps and finished up by playing touch football. I was whipped and thirsty. Jane was working the soda fountain in Heck's Rexall Drug Store at the corner of West Main and North Gamble. Despite Shelby's being home to fewer than 10,000 folks, there were three drug stores – all on Main Street – with soda fountains. I stopped in for a coke, and we engaged in relaxed conversation.

Actually, Jane was doing most of the talking, which was the usual state of affairs. After a few minutes, starting to feel refreshed, on an impulse, I said, "Jane, would you like to go out, maybe take in a movie?"

Her answer was a question and anything but what I expected. "Are you going to be playing first string?"

I was taken aback but answered straightforwardly, "Yes."

"Okay."

We wound up dating several times off and on and I took her to a homecoming dance. We also dated some during the summer after our freshman year of college, hers at Muskingum College in Cambridge, Ohio from where she was transferring to Ohio State for her sophomore year. But I occasionally wondered whether she would have gone out with me that first time had I been less than certain about playing first string.

Jane's energy level…Think of that cartoon character, The Tasmanian Devil. She was a dynamo and had some terrific house parties. Her parents Al and Maxine, now both deceased, would roll up the rug, move the furniture out of the way, the music would start, and the dancing would begin. Dancing with Jane was fun. "Our" specialty at those parties was twisting to Chubby Checker. Lord, could we twist up a storm. Now, I fear my knees and hips would stage a mass rebellion after two minutes of twisting. Another of our favorites was fast dancing to *Shout, Shout* by Ernie Maresca. I can still hear the pulsing beat and cute lyrics and see the light in Jane's luminous eyes.

Shout, shout knock yourself out
Come on, yell, yell, loud and swell
You gotta scream, scream you know what I mean
Put another dime in the record machine

Hey we're havin' a party and now it's just begun
We're all over here and a havin' fun
Joe's all alone and he wants to be kissed
Mary's in the corner and she's doin' the twist.

Hey, play another song like Runaround Sue
Oh, let's do a dance that we all can do
We're turning that jukebox up mighty loud
And liven up this crazy crowd.

Every party that I attend
Believe me now, it's the livin' end
Movin' and a groovin' with some friends of mine
Saturday night now and we're havin' a time.

Hey, doin' the fly with our hands in the sky
Yeah, foot stompin, Baby, just you and I
School was out about a quarter to three
And we're havin' fun now it's plain to see.

So let's shout, shout knock yourself out
Come on yell, yell, loud and swell
You gotta scream, scream, you know what I mean
Put another dime in the record machine

I can still feel the sweat beginning to pour as Jane and I went whipping through *Shout, Shout.* In school, we used to talk about what a "great song" it was and, for us, it was.

Jane's middle name was Bell and it fit her to a 't'. Jane Bell was not silent. Rarely did she stop talking. Listening to Jane was like listening to an endless series of jaunty exclamation points.

Lest you be thinking that Jane Bell's bell rang inside an empty head, let me put any such notion firmly to rest. She was plenty smart, got mostly A's, quick and witty. Once, in explaining the Cuban missile crisis in an essay, she wrote that "Cuba is a bad, nasty, puny, little spot." Another time, a sociology teacher happened to ask Jane where she had seen an amoeba. Her quick reply: "In biology – with a telescope."

Jane provided me with one of my lasting high school memories. It had to do with our senior *Scarlet S.* In the spring of '63, a classmate hosted a massive yearbook signing party at her home. I think about half the class jammed into the modest house. We each brought our new *Scarlet S* and started passing it around, signing in each other's book.

Now the idea, of course, was for each person to sign over his or her picture in each book. After the party, when I got home, I started looking through my book. When I saw *my* picture, here is what was written over it:

Mike –
In my books you
Are tops
In just about
Everything (add that
To your
Superiority)
I really do love you
J.B.

So I turned the page to Jane Bell's picture and here is what I read:

Don't know
What I'm
Thinking of –
I signed
On your
Picture
J.B.

Jane was at our 20-year reunion and, to me anyway, she seemed like the same old Jane. Perhaps just a bit subdued.

Well, Jane was *not* at our 25-year reunion. In an ultimate and cruel irony, Jane was suffering from agoraphobia. A fear of open places. I'd known one other person, a woman co-worker, with agoraphobia and learned that, in some cases, it can be successfully treated. But at least temporarily, a class light had been dimmed.

1993

In the weeks before our 1993 reunion, Jane wrote an upbeat, chatty letter to the class. Regrettably, she didn't come from her new home in Pennsylvania for our gathering. Still, her letter was an encouraging sign that, perhaps, our class light was growing brighter.

1995

Jane sent in a reservation for our class 50th birthday party. But a week or so before the party, she called to say that a business-related conflict would keep her away.

At the party, we talked about Jane and her duel with agoraphobia. I wondered whether we'd ever again cross paths.

2002

Jane came to the 11-class reunion. She looked good. Her face was fuller but still plenty pretty and trim. Her husband Dick, her senior by 10 years, was along. After the dinner and program on Saturday night, I sat for a while with a group of six or so including Jane. Lots of eager chatting was taking place. But Jane had little to say, virtually nothing. Very strange. She looked kind of disengaged. When that little group was breaking up, we all hugged. When Jane and I hugged, nothing was said. Not a word. We just smiled. It just didn't seem at all like the Jane of old.

2003

2003 brought a surprise. A nice one. Here's the context. In the months leading up to the school's first-ever All-Alumni Weekend in 2004, I decided to produce a video. During a 12-month period, from November 2002 through November 2003, I took and collected some 225 photos – new as well as vintage – that were to "tell the story" of both Shelby the town and SHS. For a rousing, funny finish to the video, set to the song *All-Star* by Smashmouth, I wanted newly taken photos of former athletes in "action," former cheerleaders doing cartwheels and splits, former majorettes twirling batons, and so on. I sent emails to such alums, asking for their cooperation. And I asked all to wear the school colors, red and gray. Boy, what good sports! Alums into their 60s had themselves photographed doing all of the above and more. You should see the photos that came pouring in. Priceless shots.

Anyway, to a bunch of other alums, I sent an email, asking that they be photographed wearing something red or gray, with an arm raised skyward and their forefinger extended in the "We're #1" sign. I included Jane on the email list but considered getting a photo from her to be a long shot. Sort of like expecting the Berlin Wall to come crumbling down during our lifetime. A few weeks later, after slicing open that day's mail, you could have bowled me over with a bluejay's feather. I was holding a large photo of Jane – wearing red and gray and posed just the way I'd asked. I knew it would look terrific on a big screen. And it looked like our class's bright light might be shining again.

2007

January 16 brought an even bigger surprise – literally. The postman delivered a sizable box – about 12"x12"x18" – to our door. What the heck, I wondered, is this? Despite the box's size, it wasn't particularly heavy. I walked to our kitchen and set it on the table. Then I looked at the return address and saw the name, Jane Bell. I'm sure my eyes widened. What in the world would Jane be sending me?

I reached for a paring knife and sliced open the box. The first thing I saw was this handwritten note:

1/12/07
Dear Miguel,
Jerry Warshower was my Aunt Ruth's second husband. When he learned I was from Ohio, he gave me this blanket. I think you will truly appreciate it. Love ya',
Jane Bell

I began laughing. I pulled the blanket from the box, stepped into the living room and spread it out. And kept on laughing. The blanket was green with white trim and white lettering – Ohio University's colors are green and white – and a large white block 'O' in the middle. From top to bottom, the wording on the blanket reads:

Jerry Warshower

Football 1929-30
Halfback
Basketball 1930-31
Guard

O

Baseball 1929-30-31
Catcher
All Buckeye Conference
Basketball 1931
Baseball 1930-31

This gift, I decided immediately, merited a phone call. So I emailed Jane, acknowledging the gift and thanking her and asking for her phone number. Her next day's reply included both her home and work numbers and a brief message: *I'll look forward to talking with you.*

I reached her at her work number and we chatted for some 20 minutes, our words punctuated frequently with laughter. She spoke openly of her agoraphobia and the meds that have helped combat it. The 'O' blanket? Jane said she came into possession of it some 20 years ago. Jerry Warshower subsequently had passed away, and there were no family members who could shed more light on the blanket's origins.

"I don't care what you do with it," Jane said. "You could put it away or maybe offer it to OU."

I thought that a good idea but immediately a nearer-term idea popped into my mind. When I attended meetings of the SHS Alumni Association, many members wore red and gray logo'd apparel of either SHS or Ohio State. I often would wear the green and white of OU and take lots of joshing for my "bleeding green." So at the next meeting I came early and then greeted other arrivals draped in Jane's 'O' blanket. You should have heard the yuks.

During our phone chat, I loved hearing the energy in Jane's voice. Small wonder that she was one of our class's bright lights – damned smart, witty, pretty and full of piss and vinegar.

Postscripts:

Back during our SHS days, did Jane really love me? Mmmm...maybe as long as I was playing first string. ☺

Several months after Jane sent me the OU blanket we reunited again and as you will see later in this story, I learned much more about her duel with agoraphobia.

CHAPTER 10

THE BACON SAVER'S FINAL REUNION

Joel Stentz saved my bacon in freshman geology in 1963-64 at Ohio University. But let's back this up to the summer before our freshman year at SHS. It was August 1959. I first met Joel when I found myself standing behind him in line while waiting to take our football physicals. I found him insufferable. He was overweight and he was bragging to no end about everything, including his football ability. I quickly concluded that he was an arrogant clod.

It was an early lesson in why it's unwise to let first impressions create lasting conclusions. I couldn't have been more wrong about Joel. He probably was just very nervous that morning, standing virtually naked with a bunch of other guys in a gym. That can be very unnerving for many a pubescent youngster.

Joel turned out to be a great friend. He was congenial, considerate, kind to a fault. Joel never played first string in football. He was plenty big and strong but he wasn't quick enough or fast enough. But he stuck it out and stayed with the team all four years.

My only other football memory of Joel is from our senior season and is in stark contrast to that first exposure to him four years before. SHS had remarkable and sustained success in football for a good 40 straight years. In fact, from 1948 through 1987, the school had to endure just two losing seasons, in 1958 and 1970. During that span, the school won more than 75 percent of its games.

Our senior team, the 1962 squad, was loaded. In 10 games we scored 302 points – and could have scored another 100 had Coach Bill Wilkins not been opposed to running up scores to embarrassing levels. In one game we scored 32 points in one quarter and had four other touchdowns called back because of penalties. In another we led 30-0 at halftime. In that game Coach Wilkins played the second and third strings most of the second half. But he grew so disgusted – not because they weren't scoring but because they were playing sloppily – that he put us first stringers back in with about eight minutes to play, and we scored another 22 points.

In those same 10 games we gave up only 26 points and had six shutouts. We never gave up more than eight points in a game. Unfortunately, in the one game – against Bellevue, also undefeated – in which we allowed eight points, our generally potent offense sputtered whenever we closed on Bellevue's goal line and we scored but six points.

In the fourth quarter, I was kneed in the pelvis. The bone was bruised and it felt like someone had plunged in a four-inch knife blade. It was called a "pointer." I was slow to get up off the grass and looked like a DUI suspect as I staggered back to our huddle.

"Are you okay?" asked Bill Anspach, my best friend and next door neighbor.

"Yeah."

"You sure?"

"Yeah."

Even the referee expressed concern. "Maybe you should go off, son."

"No. I'm okay."

"You sure?"

"Yeah."

I wasn't and I felt like I wanted to puke, but we were driving again, and I felt the team needed me. Besides, about 7,000 people were screaming, and my adrenalin was still pumping.

Would you believe it? On the next play, I got kneed in the same spot. This time I got no farther than my hands and knees and someone had to help me up. I shuffled to the sideline where I dropped to my hands and knees. Somebody helped me up and to the bench. It was Joel Stentz.

Doctor Grant Dowds looked me over, smiled around the pipe clenched between his teeth and decreed that I would live. Any further diagnosis could and would wait until a visit to the hospital for x-rays the following morning.

Joel stayed with me the balance of the quarter. When the final gun sounded, I was crying. Not from the pointer so much but from losing the Northern Ohio League championship by two maddening points. Joel served as my crutch and helped me off the field and into the locker room, which was a damned depressing place that night. You've been in noisier funeral parlors. Joel helped me pull off my pads, strip down and into the showers. The pain was worsening and my hip was stiffening. Walking was getting harder by the minute.

A group of women – I don't remember which group – had decided they would host us and our opponents for chow after that game in the school cafeteria.

I finished dressing in front of my locker. Joel waited patiently. I think we might have been the last two guys to leave.

"You feel like going over to the cafeteria?" Joel asked.

"I don't think so."

"I'll drive you home."

"No," I said, "let's go over to the cafeteria for a while."

"Yeah, okay."

Man, the pain was excruciating now. I leaned heavily on Joel for the short walk to the cafeteria. I had tears rimming my eyes again, and this time it was pain from the injury plus the losing. I shook a few hands of Bellevue players and had to swallow hard each time. They were good guys and were showing their respect of us by refraining from celebrating. But, damn it, when you are a competitor, losing a big game and then having to break bread with your victors is wrenching. I sat down carefully and forced down a couple bites of potato salad. I almost gagged.

"Let's get the fuck out of here," I muttered to Joel.

He helped me up and we moved gingerly out to his car. At my house, he helped me to the front door. My dad met us there. There was no way I could climb the stairs to my room, so Joel and Dad helped me to the first floor bedroom. They eased me down on the bed.

"Okay?" Joel asked.

"Yeah." I know I was grimacing.

"I'll check on you tomorrow."

"Thanks."

My dad thanked Joel and he left then. But I had visitors later that night, classmates concerned about me. One of them was Jane Bell Henning.

Joel and I both enrolled at OU, and his thoughtfulness and generosity quickly showed. Of the nine members of our SHS class who went to OU, only Joel arrived in Athens with a car. Almost right away, Joel spread the word that anytime a few of us were ready for a weekend visit to Shelby we should let him know and he would load us up and make the run. His "fare" – a dollar apiece to help pay for gas. Let me tell you, not only were we grateful, so were our parents.

From day one at OU, Joel was a geology major. That was his academic true love. As things turned out, in my freshman year, I had to take a natural science course, and I chose geology. A questionable choice. It taught me the definition of dread. It was *boring.* For me, anyway. By sheer chance Joel and I wound up in the same geology class. That was serendipity in-the-making.

I flunked my first geology test. Got a 47 which was an F on the most generous of curves. The cause was simple enough to identify: failure to study. To that point serious study had been taking a back seat to player-coaching an intramural football team and partying. I'd had my first date before attending my first class. I knew I was in trouble and I knew I had to get serious fast. I leaned on Joel again.

Some academic knuckling down got me on track in the classroom, but I still had some heavy catching up to do in geology lab. One day we had a lab test for which we had to identify a bunch of rocks. Ugh. Joel again was by my side, very literally. Slowly, we began moving around the back of the lab. Shoulder to shoulder. Joel would study the rock, then whisper the identification which each of us would write down on the test paper.

After a few of these whisperings, the base voice of the graduate assistant running the lab section came booming from the front of the room. "Stentz! Johnson! Are you guys talking?"

We replied together, "No, not us."

I passed. It was the only time I ever recall cheating in school.

Another vivid memory of Joel goes back to the late 1970s. He was in Shelby for a Saturday funeral, and I was there for a wedding. On Friday night, unbeknownst to each other, we wandered down to Skiles Field to watch an SHS football game. Early in the second half, I was standing behind a restraining fence along the sideline. I heard someone call my name.

"Mike?"

I looked around but couldn't locate the source of the voice.

"Mike Johnson?"

A man, smiling, approached but I didn't recognize him.

"You don't remember me, do you?"

"Should I?"

The man laughed. "Hell, yes. It's me, Joel. Joel Stentz."

"Joel!"

We clasped hands. I was having a hard time believing my eyes. Joel realized that and he was enjoying it immensely. He had dropped mucho pounds and had grown a full beard and mustache. After I got over the shock of his vastly altered appearance, we began yakking and talked away the rest of the game, barely aware of what was going on out on the field. After the final gun, we walked from Skiles Field to Weber's Bar where we chased our reminiscences with a few beers. Joel brought me up to date on himself. He had gotten a master's degree in geology and had settled in California. After some years in geology, he had tired of it and bought a restaurant. He seemed very pleased with himself and his station.

I was looking forward to seeing Joel at our 20-year reunion in 1983 but he didn't show. Before our 25-year reunion, I decided to write him to encourage him to make the trip to Shelby. I phoned a friend in Shelby to learn if I could get the addresses of Joel and 10 or so other classmates I intended to write.

"I assume Joel is still living in California," I said.

There was a long, silent moment. "No, he's not."

"Where is he?"

"Joel Stentz is in Shelby."

"What?" It was virtually impossible for me to imagine what circumstances would have uprooted Joel from California and brought him back to Shelby. "For crying out loud, how long has he been back in Shelby? *Why* is he back in Shelby?"

There was another pause, then my friend said, "Mike, it's a sad story."

"What?" I was puzzled and beginning to feel vaguely worried.

"Joel has suffered a stroke and is unemployed. He's on welfare, I think."

"Shit." That was the only word that came to mind.

"I've seen him," she said, "and he doesn't look good at all. I got the definite feeling he doesn't want to be seen. He's put on a lot of weight."

"Oh, man, that's terrible. Is he married?"

"He's living with a woman but I don't know if they're married."

"Look, give me his address. Do you have it?"

"Yes."

"I'm going to write him anyway and tell him that there are a bunch of classmates who want to see him, problems or not."

I did write to Joel but I didn't hear back from him. Besides the one friend, nobody else at the reunion had seen Joel recently. He supposedly was still having trouble walking and speaking clearly.

A couple months after the reunion, Bill Anspach and I decided to see Joel. Since the reunion, we'd heard from a couple more classmates that Joel was in pitiful physical shape. They told us his weight had ballooned, that the right side of his body was nearly useless, that his speech was slurred, and that he didn't want to see people.

Bill and I agreed that, alone, we weren't sure whether either of us was brave enough to go see Joel. We figured we could do it together,. We agreed on a date when I could make the drive to Shelby and Bill could meet me.

On that morning, we first stopped at the Shelby police station on Main Street to visit with Fred Eichinger, police captain and another classmate. We told Fred of our intent to see Joel. Fred was escorting us from the police station, and we were girding ourselves to see Joel when Fred said, "There's Joel now. That's him walking up the street with his wife." Fred was pointing to two people several blocks away.

"Thanks, Fred. See you." Bill and I hustled over to my car, got in, drove up the street past Joel and his wife, around a corner, parked, got out and began approaching Joel. I could see just a hint of recognition in his eyes.

"Joel," I said, "it's Mike Johnson and Bill Anspach."

"Well, I'll be..." He was stunned.

Without hesitating, I hugged him and so did Bill. We each took and shook his right hand which was somewhat clawed from the stroke.

"Joel, it's great to see you," I said.

"It's good to see you, too. This is my wife, Bev."

"Hi, Bev," we said, shaking hands with her.

"Hi, Mike. Hi, Bill."

"How long have you been married?" I asked.

"Four years," Bev answered. "It will be five years in December."

"That's nice," I said. "Joel, did you get my note before the reunion?"

"Yes." A pause. "You know I had a stroke," Joel said.

"Yes, Joel, I know."

"I don't look so well."

"You look fine." He was dressed shabbily, as was Bev, and his hair needed cutting and shampooing, but he was not nearly as heavy as we'd been led to believe. When he walked, his pace was slow but his limp was barely noticeable. "How long has it been since your stroke?"

"Two years." That would have been 1986.

"It's obvious you've come back a long way," I said.

"I still can't speak too clearly."

"Bullshit." The word just came out naturally. "I've understood every word you've said."

"Thanks."

"I mean it." And I did.

"Thanks."

"Joel, I bring greetings from one of your classmates."

"Who?"

"Pat Papenbrock. Pat said to say you played a mean clarinet."

"Clarinet? I played the saxophone."

"My mistake," I said, and we all smiled.

I then asked Joel if he remembered the night he helped me home after I was hurt in the Bellevue game and the time we cheated in the geology lab. He smiled widely and remembered clearly.

It was now late morning, and it was sunny and hot. "Joel, we don't want to keep you standing here too long, so we'll let you go. It's been great seeing you." Again I took his clawed hand and shook it. "Can we give you a ride?"

"No, thanks," said Joel. "We like to walk."

Then Bill took Joel's hand and said, "It's been great seeing you, buddy."

"It's been nice seeing you guys, too," Joel said.

"Take care. Bye, Joel. Bye, Bev."

Then Bill and I turned and began walking toward my car. Out of earshot, Bill said, "The best thing you said to him was 'bullshit.'"

"He can use some pats on the back and some self-esteem."

"Yes," said Bill, "but maybe what he needs more than that is a regular kick in the behind to help him along."

"Do you think he'll get it from Bev?"

"No."

"Neither do I." We had been told by several people, including Fred Eichinger, that Bev had some serious problems of her own.

"I'd like to help Joel," Bill said. "Maybe there's a way."

1993

Son of a gun. Joel did join us for our 30-year reunion.

At the Friday night set-up and decorating session, I learned that Joel had sent in his registration form, with payment. I was very pleased.

A classmate, a woman, told me that evening that Joel and Bev had moved from their rundown house on Walnut Street to a nice house on Louise Drive. She speculated that Joel's or Bev's family had financed the purchase. She just wasn't sure.

On Saturday evening I happened to see Joel and Bev come into the K of C Hall vestibule and approach the registration table. He was dressed spiffily, including colorful suspenders. I moved quickly to greet him. I took his somewhat misshapen right hand in mine and then hugged him. "Joel, it's good to see you. I'm glad you came." Then I greeted Bev.

There was a softness in Joel's eyes, and his smile was warm. "I'm glad to be here, Mike. Thanks."

Moments later, I excused myself, hurried back into the hall and quickly informed others, including Bill Anspach, that Joel had arrived. It didn't take any urging to get them to go greet Joel right away. He was in good company the rest of the evening. I hope Joel was glad he came.

1998

In addition to having suffered the stroke, Joel had developed diabetes. Perhaps the diabetes had come first. In any event, his condition kept worsening. He endured several amputations that first cost him toes and then a foot. On September 16, 1998, that "insufferable" 14-year-old and first-rank bacon saver passed away. He was 53.

CHAPTER 11

FIRST TO DIE

Jerry Russell was the first of our classmates to die. When I heard about his passing, I felt as though Muhammad Ali had punched me in the gut.

I learned about his death from a newspaper clipping mailed to me. The headline: *Former Shelbian Dies Today In Plano, Texas.*

Jerry was born in Toledo, Ohio on April 2, 1945, and his family moved to Shelby when he was a preschooler. He was a fun guy and highly respected by his classmates. He was a "crossover." He could be – and was – comfortable with anyone and they with him. The whole class was Jerry's clique. Part of his popularity was his easy laugh and his crinkly eyelids. Jerry just had a gift for putting people at ease. His *Scarlet S* caption reflected his easygoing manner: "If at first you don't succeed – Ehh!" We all heard Jerry say "Ehh" lots of times.

Jerry liked fun. "What I remember most about Jerry is Halloween, " recalled Anne Lafferty Stock whom you will learn more about later. "We used to race through the neighborhood, soaping windows, seeing how many we could do without getting caught."

Jerry was on the tennis team and was elected our senior class vice president. Still, classmate Jeff Dawson is convinced Jerry suffered from an inferiority complex. Jerry's parents divorced when he was a preteen. "Remember, back then divorces were fairly rare and Jerry felt very left out," recalled Jeff. "He did not bond with his father until shortly before he died. So, in the critical years of having a male image, he did not. He tried to overcompensate and could not stand attacks on himself or to be made fun of. He preferred to make fun of other people. I remember in geometry how he gave Doyle such a hard time because he was his main rival as the best student in the class."

As Jerry entered his teens, his mom remarried and, according to Jeff, his stepdad worked hard at creating a positive relationship with Jerry.

Jerry went to Purdue and struggled – academically and emotionally. Jeff remembers that a breakup with a girlfriend so upset Jerry that he "punched the wall so hard he hurt his hand and was in the psych ward for a short time." He flunked out and then enrolled at Ohio State. There, Jeff recalled, "Jerry worked hard to be a good student, and I think this was driven by wanting to be better than others because he was not feeling that good about himself." He graduated, albeit with less than stellar grades.

While working a summer job at a large printing company plant in Willard, just 14 miles from Shelby, Jerry met a lovely young woman, Sharon. She was from a large family – 14 – who lived in Norwalk, about 30 miles north of Shelby. Sharon also graduated from Ohio State – with high grades as an economics major.

Jerry and Sharon had a son, Jason.

When Jerry fell ill, at first, his doctors didn't deem his condition all that serious. Then he began to decline. Before long he was confined in an iron lung. He lost so much weight that his skin looked as though it had been stretched over his skeleton as tautly as shrinkwrap. His illness turned out to be Guillain-Barre Syndrome – a rare disease the cause of which is unknown. In about 60 percent of cases, an infection affecting either the lungs or digestive track precedes it. A victim's immune system begins attacking nerves that transmit signals between body and brain. The result is severe weakness that quickly worsens. The entire body can become paralyzed. Guillain-Barre occurs most often in the elderly and young adults. About 30 percent need the help of a machine – iron lung in the early 1970s – to breathe. Most people recover. Jerry didn't. Six weeks after falling ill, Jerry was gone – just 10 years after graduating from SHS.

The young family was living in Texas when Jerry died. What happened to her, unexpectedly widowed at such a young age? Eventually, she remarried, gave birth to twins at age 40 and another child at 42. Later, she divorced.

As I think back, at every reunion since his passing, classmates have talked about Jerry. We hope he is resting peacefully.

CHAPTER 12

THE LOVELIEST WIDOW

Why I never fell for DeeDee Milligan is beyond me. We were friends but not especially close ones. We kidded around but I have no memory of ever flipping for her. It wasn't as though I never noticed her. That was impossible. Maybe DeeDee was involved so deeply with someone else that she sent out signals to stay away. I just don't remember. Who can really explain teenage chemical explosions – or fizzles?

So who was DeeDee? Her *Scarlet S* caption was spot on: "Whose brown eyes did flutter many hearts." One look at the photo above the caption testifies to the caption's accuracy. She just might have been the class's most beautiful girl. At least, I know one vote she would have gotten.

As to extracurriculars, DeeDee was sort of a slow starter, but that can be explained by the fact that she did not arrive at SHS until her sophomore year. She came to Shelby from nearby Mansfield. She did join the Pep Club right away, but the rest came later. She joined the Girls Athletic Association in her junior year. It was in our senior year, though, that DeeDee really emerged. First, she became a cheerleader. Now that may not have been without precedent but it was highly unusual. I mean, most of the cheerleaders got into that early in high school, even in junior high. But DeeDee's real moment in the high school sun came a few weeks later on September 11 when she was elected to the homecoming court.

After high school and earning a degree at Ohio State, DeeDee went off to live life and life smacked her hard. She had become an elementary school teacher. That was a good part. But when DeeDee walked into the K of C Hall for our 25-year reunion in 1988, she was arriving as our class's second widow. Her husband Terry had passed away just six months earlier, on January 29. We knew Terry's decline had been long and painful, and we were wondering how it might have affected her.

Well, when DeeDee entered the K of C Hall on July 16, 1988, my heart did the flip-flop it hadn't done 25 years before. I'm pretty sure what caused it. It was a combination of things – sympathy for what she had endured, admiration for how she had endured it, awe for how she had taken care of herself through adversity, or all of the above and something more. On seeing her, I experienced a powerful rush of emotion. I guess that's a genteel way of saying I could have stuck to her like glue for the whole evening. It was a hell of a chore not to. Fortunately for both of us, other classmates were just as eager to be close to her, and I really wanted to visit other kids or I might have followed her around like a puppy and embarrassed both of us.

When DeeDee and I first saw each other that night, we moved toward each other like water flowing over falls – naturally, smoothly, quickly. We embraced and hugged hard.

"DeeDee, it's wonderful to see you."

"Mike!" That's all she said.

As we pulled apart, it was clear that time and adversity had barely touched her face, etching just the very finest of lines around her eyes, and had not dimmed at all their luminescent brown.

"I was very sorry to hear about your husband."

"Thank you."

"It must have been very difficult – for both of you."

"Toward the end," said DeeDee, "he said he wanted me to put him in a nursing home. He said he was too much of a burden. I wouldn't do it."

Terry sounded like a man who would have been easy to like and respect. Multiple Sclerosis had struck him when he was 28 and he had endured it for 14 years. At one point, nearing his end, he sought a different kind of help. "He had hands laid on him," said DeeDee, "and hoped to be healed. His heart was but not his body."

Many years later, DeeDee shed more light on Terry with this story: "He would call me 'Fox' or 'Foxy Lady.' Remember that term from the '70s or '80s? Anyway, beginning in about 1983, the children and I would visit Terry's sister Vicki and her family in Corpus Christi (Texas) during our spring break. Kristin and Chad attended the Catholic School where I taught, so we had the same break. Terry's mother would come to the house and stay with Terry, since he was not only bedridden, but was beginning to not be able to move or talk. I would call him every day from Corpus and let him know what we did that day. He wanted so much to be part of our life, and we tried to include him as much as we could. Terry always encouraged us to visit Vicki. I think it was probably in 1987 that I called him one night. He could no longer speak, but I could hear his breathing over the phone telling me that he was trying to say something. Then his mother came on and said that Terry mouthed that he loved me and something about a 'fox.' After hanging up, I was crying and laughing at the same time. That was Terry, always trying to make *others* feel good, even to his dying day. He taught me patience, compassion, understanding, endurance, thoughtfulness, persistence, prioritizing, how to give and receive love, and the list goes on. Not only did I grow through him spiritually and emotionally, but others did as well. Especially my children, and we thank him for this."

If ever there was a woman and her ordeal that aroused a man's protective instincts, this was the woman. That July night in 1988, I wanted to embrace her and utter some magical incantation that would shield her from future adversity. That was *my* feeling. DeeDee's? Realistically, I think DeeDee's ordeal probably had toughened her. She may not have needed or wanted any protection. I said simply, "He must have had the most virulent form of MS."

"Yes," she said. "He just got worse and worse. He never had a remission. He was bedridden for the last five years. At the end, he couldn't speak."

Now, mind you, she was saying all this very matter of factly. No tears. No faltering voice. There was no hint of seeking sympathy which, of course, made my chest swell and fill with sympathy. Here was a classmate to be proud of.

"You're a hell of a woman. And the prettiest one here. If I didn't think it would cause hard feelings among the rest of the girls, I'd tell Ralph (Thauvette, master of ceremonies) to award you the prize for most beautiful girl in the class."

"No, don't." DeeDee looked slightly panicked.

"I won't but I'd like to. You're hands down the loveliest girl here."

Now, you don't have to tell me how syrupy all that sounded, but I was speaking from the heart. I'll tell you something; that night DeeDee was like a powerful magnet. Her mere presence just seemed to draw people to her. Classmates, men and women, clustered around her all night long. Good medicine.

As the reunion was winding down that night, Suzon "Mimi" Grove began working the hall. "They want us out of here at midnight," she was saying. "That's when they want to lock up. But," she added, eyes brightening, "if you don't want the night to end yet, come on out to my house." (Mimi is a nickname bestowed by a toddling grandson who couldn't pronounce grandma. The moniker stuck.) Suzon, or Mimi, was a sweet, warm-hearted blond who played in the band, was a member of the Girls Athletic Association, Pep Club, school newspaper staff and a YWCA-related club.

"Where do you live?" I asked.

"Out on Wareham Road, just past the city limits off Mansfield Road."

"Do you need anything?"

"No, I've got plenty of food and stuff to drink."

Warm hospitality seemed to come naturally to Mimi. Once years later she knew I was going to be visiting Shelby on a Friday night. "Why don't you stop by for coffee?" came her invitation.

I accepted. She poured two steaming mugs full, and we settled in at her kitchen table – and bore witness to a scene reminiscent of Chicago's O'Hare Airport on a Friday evening with weary travelers hustling to make connections while homeward bound after a week on the road. In the case of Mimi's house, the Friday traffic was her three sons coming and going in a seemingly endless bustle punctuated with *Be Home Laters* and *Don't Wait Ups*. "This is the way it usually is around here," Mimi smiled serenely. Not only did she remain unruffled amidst the hubbub, she was relishing it. "Just because they're all in college doesn't mean that they've left home," she laughed. "I tell them I'm tired of doing their laundry."

So anyway, at midnight about 20 of us, including DeeDee, began making our way to Mimi's home. It turned out to be a terrific way to cap a terrific night. Hours later, when we finally were breaking up at about 3:30, DeeDee and I came together as naturally and easily as we had hours before. But the hug was noticeably harder.

"Bye, bye, Mike."

"Bye, DeeDee."

I found myself hoping that some reasonable facsimile of Sir Galahad would come charging along and lift DeeDee onto his steed – if that's what she wanted.

1991

DeeDee's knight turned out to be Bob. They were married in March of 1991 and almost immediately relocated from Galion, Ohio to Aiken, South Carolina where Bob was being sent to manage a factory. In the south DeeDee didn't take to eating grits or drinking Dr. Pepper, but she did begin reading Southern Living magazine and sipping sweet tea. She also continued teaching – 3rd grade. With four teenagers and four cars, "I have to keep working," she related good-naturedly, "to pay for the car insurance and keep the kids in clothes." In a letter to me later that year, DeeDee seemed ecstatic but two years later, she did not attend our reunion.

1995

DeeDee and Bob had moved from South Carolina to northeastern Ohio where he had taken a new job. They didn't come to the class 50th birthday party barbecue in Shelby but, as planned, they were waiting for us in Cleveland when our chartered bus arrived at the East 9th Street Pier for the Goodtime III boat cruise.

We all were introduced to Bob who seemed really nice. And DeeDee – she seemed really happy and we were happy for her. For the first time, DeeDee's face was showing signs of aging, not much, but her brown eyes and her entire being still radiated high spirits. We were glad to have her back with us.

2002

DeeDee and Bob came to the 11-class reunion. Classmate Jeff Dawson cracked DeeDee up when he said if she looked any younger, he'd have to have her carded before letting her down a beer.

2003

DeeDee also came to our 40-year reunion in July of 2003. But the thing that really tickled me happened later that summer. In some email exchanging, I was telling her what I wanted to achieve with the video that I was producing for the 2004 SHS All-Alumni Weekend. The video would be set to music and shown on a big screen in the high school auditorium. I told her my goal was to have the video elicit a range of emotions – joyous laughter, thick throats, torrents of tears.

In the laughter category, I said I was planning to poke fun at myself by having me photographed batting – first "calling my shot" a la Babe Ruth, then in an exaggerated batting stance, then whiffing, then thrusting my left arm skyward with my forefinger extended in the "We're #1" sign.

DeeDee was game. She saw the fun in poking fun at ourselves and replied that she would have herself photographed doing a cartwheel – if she still could at age 58.

Well…In early November of 2003 came an envelope. It contained four photos. In them DeeDee was wearing a red top with a gray block S. The four photos:

- DeeDee standing perkily with hands on hips in a cheerleader's "ready" position.
- DeeDee cartwheeling. Not bad form.
- DeeDee doing an almost split – and grimacing funnily.
- DeeDee with her right arm raised skyward, forefinger extended in the "We're #1" sign.

Great stuff.

Then DeeDee had an inspiration. She connected with Connie Jones Glorioso, a first cousin, three years younger and also a former SHS cheerleader. They had not cheered together at SHS but now was their chance. They each took their big gray block S cheerleader letters and stitched them onto identical red sweaters. Then they put Connie's husband to work with a camera. The result: shots of them cartwheeling together, lifting each other (if only barely off the ground) and sitting perkily back-to-back on the grass. Priceless shots!

In August 2004 when that video was showing on that big screen and the song "All Star" was playing and those pictures – six in all in the sequence – began to appear, our schoolmates began roaring their approval. Know what else I'm thinking? In another 10 years, the loveliest widow still could be cartwheeling and fluttering hearts.

2007

In late 2006 in an email exchange with DeeDee, I said if she knew of anyone who might want me to do a program on my books, I'd be happy to do so. DeeDee already had bought five signed copies of *Warrior Priest* and had said she wanted to buy two copies of *Fate of the Warriors* when it first became available.

In January 2007 DeeDee emailed to say that a teaching colleague at her school in Hudson had asked whether I'd be willing to talk about World War II with some of her social studies students – 5th, 7th and 8th graders. I said sure and we worked out a date.

Upon arriving at the school and greeting the teaching colleague, I saw that we had a few minutes before I would be meeting with her students. So I asked the location of DeeDee's classroom. It was just around the corner and two doors down the hall. I arrived at her doorway and stood there only a moment before she saw me. I went striding forward and said to DeeDee's kindergartners, "You're going to see something you don't often see in your classroom – a man hugging your teacher." The kids were wide-eyed and DeeDee's teaching assistant at the rear of the room was beaming. DeeDee and I embraced. She introduced me to her class and teaching assistant and we exchanged a few words.

Then she asked if I had any extra copies of *Warrior Priest.* I said I had two. "Great!" she replied. "I want one for our principal (a nun, Sister Marie) and my teaching assistant." Then I was off to the first meeting with older students.

About 11:15 I was finished talking with the social studies students and per DeeDee's earlier invitation I returned to her classroom. "Nobody comes to my classroom without going to work," she said to me and her kiddies. And she put me to work on a project that had her charges drawing pictures of "Uncle Ugbee" walking somewhere. As I knelt beside a child, he or she would tell me where "Uncle Ugbee" was walking – to a store or baseball game or lake or wherever. I would then write – actually print, taking care to form the letters as they appeared atop the classroom's whiteboard – a matching phrase such as "walking to the lake." The child would then begin copying the phrase atop his or her drawing of "Uncle Ugbee." I soon learned that DeeDee makes this an annual project and that she compiles the "Uncle Ugbee" drawings into a booklet that is displayed at the front of the room.

After a few minutes it occurred to me that I was probably the first of DeeDee's SHS classmates to watch her in action. And it was action. She was stooping, squatting, kneeling, constantly on the move. She maintained order with quiet "shhhs." When a little boy asked to use the restroom, she waved him toward the door and said smiling to me, "When they are bobbing up and down, it's an emergency and you don't say no."

While in her classroom I also took a few minutes to write inscriptions in those two copies of *Warrior Priest* that she was buying as gifts. Having now bought seven signed copies, I said, "I should make you my Hudson sales agent."

At noon as she was putting on her coat, DeeDee said, "A couple years ago when I was doing the assistant principal stint, Sister Marie asked me to consider going back to grad school to get a master's and then become a full-time administrator. I told her that my body is tired. That at this stage of my life I just want to teach."

The weather that day was abominable. Snow had been falling since the early morning hours and while in DeeDee's room I could see that there was a whiteout. DeeDee had scaled back to teaching half days. Our plan had been to go to lunch together at noon, when her teaching day ended. I also had three more stops to make that day. The first was at the home of a *Warrior Priest* reader who had phoned me a few days before wanting to talk about the book. After a few minutes I had asked where he lives. "Hudson" he replied. When I told him that I would be in Hudson, he invited me to his house. My next stop was at the local bookshop to schedule a signing. Finally I needed to be at a high school near our North Canton home at 3:00 to pick up my wife Lynne who was subbing in Spanish. At noon DeeDee took a few minutes to confer with the teacher who would be working the afternoon "shift" and then took me to meet Sister Marie and give her the newly inscribed copy of *Warrior Priest.*

Afterward as DeeDee and I neared the door leading to the parking lot, I said, "You know, as much as I have been looking forward to having lunch with you-"

She cut me off and said, "Would you rather skip lunch?"

"I hate to because I was really looking forward to some one-on-one time but given my schedule and the weather, if we went to lunch we'd really be rushed."

"That's okay. Really."

"Good. Thanks. But there is another matter I'd like to discuss before we leave." I then asked if she'd join me and six other members of our class in signing letters that would go to others of our classmates in a campaign to raise $150,000 to upgrade the SHS Sciences Department. As I was articulating what I was asking her to do, I was removing from my briefcase a piece of paper with the names of our other classmates who had agreed to be signers. Last year in a phone conversation during the campaign's "quiet phase," DeeDee already had pledged a gift to the campaign. She looked at the names on the paper and said, "Sure, I'd be happy to."

"Good. Thanks."

Then she asked, "Do you remember when we first connected after high school? It was at a reunion..." and she paused, trying to remember the year.

"It was 1988," I said.

"Terry had just died."

"Yes."

"We went to Suzon's house after the reunion."

"Right. We stayed until at least 3:30. And I only left because I was driving a couple girls back into town to their parents' houses."

"That was such a nice night," she said wistfully. "I wonder why Suzon doesn't come to reunions anymore."

"I don't know."

"It's too bad. I really like her."

Then we pushed open the door and headed out into the driving snow. We waved goodbye as we headed to our cars which were going to require some serious brushing.

Once in my car I reflected on what DeeDee had told Sister Marie, that her "body is tired." Having had the privilege of the outside-in perspective, of watching DeeDee in action, I couldn't help wondering whether or to what extent she was aware of what she was achieving. I had watched her closely with those youngsters. She had shown strength, energy, patience, skill, understanding and love. I couldn't help thinking how many young boys and girls had begun building a foundation of learning under her tutelage. I don't know when DeeDee will stop teaching. But when that last day in the classroom does arrive and she has walked outside for the final time, I hope she reflects on what she has contributed to the lives of so many men and women who once were little boys and girls.

Two days later I received an email from her that read in part: "I do love my job!! Ever since I was five years old, I had wanted to be a teacher. My poor brothers and sister had to endure my 'instructions/bossiness' for many years. They were so glad to send me off to college!! I can honestly say that of all the 35+ years of teaching, there was only one in which I couldn't wait until the school year came to an end – 5th grade in South Carolina. The following two years I taught 3rd grade at the same school and loved it." It's clear she still does.

2008

On January 12 in my email in-box was a message from a woman who had just finished reading *Warrior Priest*. In reading the Acknowledgements section at the back of the book, the woman had spotted DeeDee's name as one who had participated in an email focus group to help me select the book's title. The woman told me that her youngest daughter, Jenny, had many years before been one of DeeDee's kindergarteners. "DeeDee was such a great teacher," the woman wrote, "and when you speak with her again, please tell her that that bashful little kindergarten student is now a grown woman with a husband and three sons – and also is a teacher in the Galion school system."

CHAPTER 13

DELIGHTFULLY DITZY AND ALWAYS HAPPY

During her SHS days Mary Ann Inscho Richards was occasionally ditzy and some things don't change.

She also was ebullient, always smiling, always sweet. She was tall, blond, slender, pretty and dressed to the nines. It didn't surprise me at all when in later years I learned that she was doing some modeling. We were good friends and kidded around a lot. As you will see, Mary Ann could be disarmingly candid. She possessed another trait – an admirable one seldom seen in teenagers – that was particularly endearing. She could – and did – laugh at herself easily and often.

It's funny the things we remember. Some of them are so damned insignificant and ought to be forgotten as soon as they are gone. But, for some inexplicable reason, they stick. My locker was always close to Mary Ann's – Inscho, Johnson – and one day she walked over to mine and without any preamble declared, "I love the way you look in your uniform."

"Huh?"

"I love the way you look in your football uniform. You're so handsome."

For a moment I remained speechless, mulling over my reply. "Mary Ann," I kidded her gently, "how can you say that? I'm wearing a helmet out there and it's got face bars." At a time in my life when my wit often crossed over into biting sarcasm, I could never be caustic with Mary Ann, not even in a kidding way. She always seemed so sincere and sweet and vulnerable that I couldn't bring myself to say anything even mildly stinging.

"It's the way you stand out there," she said. "Between plays you always stand with your hands on your hips. And I like the way you push up your helmet and spit under the face bars."

"Yeah? And?"

"It makes you look very handsome."

Believe me, there was nothing remotely romantic in this exchange. It was just Mary Ann being Mary Ann. I closed my locker and I squeezed her shoulder and went walking down the hall with her.

Well, like I said, Mary Ann was occasionally ditzy. Delightfully so. Now, that's not to say that she was a dum-dum. She just had a knack for sometimes putting her mouth in motion before putting her mind in gear.

On July 16, 1988, I learned that that part of Mary Ann hadn't changed.

I saw her enter the K of C Hall with her husband, Evan. Moments later, she saw me and came toward me, reaching out with her arms. I extended my arms, but then something, some random thought or memory, I'm not sure which, caused me to stop short. I dropped my left arm and extended my right arm as a restraint and placed it against her shoulder.

"You only get to hug me if you can tell me who I am," I said. Now, mind you, I was wearing a nametag that in inch-high letters read MIKE J.

Mary Ann didn't pause even a second. She looked me square in the eyes and cried, "Bill!"

"What? Mary Ann," I said with my voice full of clearly mock reproach, "try again."

"Aren't you Bill Anspach?" She was confused and there was more than a touch of embarrassment in her face and voice.

"No, Mary Ann, but Bill is here." I then pointed to my badge.

"Mike!" she cried. And then we hugged.

Now, after that embarrassment most classmates would have looked more closely at nametags. But not three minutes later Mary Ann looked at a boy named Bob – his name writ large on his badge – and said, "Hi, Jeff."

1993

Mary Ann's personality lights up any proceeding. When she enters a reunion hall it's as though someone has lit a dozen candles, making the room cheerier.

At the reunion dinner on Saturday night when I first saw Mary Ann, I stepped toward her and put my hands on her shoulders. "Mary Ann, five years ago when you saw me, I was wearing a nametag and you still called me Bill. I won't let that happen again. I'm Mike." She laughed her still girlish laugh and we hugged.

After chatting a couple minutes, I said, "You sound happy."

"I'm always happy." I believed her.

Later, as the humorous interlude I was emceeing was drawing to a close, I said, "Our next award will go to the classmate with the most youthful appearance and who is thus best able to represent our class as we move into our next decade. Now, I'd like to achieve a consensus on this, so don't start shouting out a bunch of names right away. First, let's take a minute to look around."

After 30 or so seconds of silence, a voice shouted, "Jim Starrett!"

"All right," I said as unemotionally as possible. Jim is a very handsome man who still had all of his hair which still was coal black. His face was virtually unlined.

"Dean Howerton" shouted a second voice.

"Okay," I said, "Dean still has all that blond hair. A solid nomination."

"Bob Lederer," shouted a third voice. As I glanced at Bob, I saw his eyes roll upward and his shoulders shrug as if to say, "Why me?" Bob, too, still had all his sandy-colored hair and a youthful countenance.

Then I spoke. "This is very interesting. Think about this for a moment. As things stand now, we could be writing a new chapter in the lore of Shelby High School class reunions. We have three candidates and all are men."

A brief silence. Then a female voice shouted, "Mary Ann!" There ensued cheers, laughter and applause.

"Okay, we now have three guys and a gal," I said. "I think we should close the nominations, or we may spend all night reaching a consensus. In reaching for this consensus, let's use the old applause meter. First, we'll test the sentiment for Mary Ann."

Resounding applause, hoots and hollers, filled the hall.

"Okay, now let's hear it for Jim."

Tepid applause – and more laughter. The fix was in and everyone knew it.

"Dean?"

Equally tepid applause but still lots of laughter.

"Bob?"

Ditto.

"All right, we have our consensus. And what a comeback! Mary Ann, congratulations! Mary Ann, would you please come forward." She rose, giggling, and started making her way between tables toward the front of the room. "Now, as the years roll on, Mary Ann may not always be our most youthful appearing classmate and she, like the rest of us, may begin to feel the effects of aging, such as poor circulation. So, Mary Ann, with all of that in mind, we have this for you."

I then handed her and she unfolded and held aloft a long, heavy woolen scarf, red and gray, naturally, and bearing the legend 'Shelby High School.' And she kept on giggling.

Though giggling and laughing have come appealingly easy to Mary Ann, as the years have unfolded, a serious side has shown through clearly – as a bright beacon for others. Caring and generosity are its luminous beams. This mother of two sons also devoted herself to working with underprivileged boys. In addition Mary Ann is a founder of an annual ball that benefits the American Cancer Society, and she serves on the board of directors of her local hospital's foundation. Betcha that in meetings her lightness of being brightens staid conference rooms.

CHAPTER 14

TRANSFORMATION

From high school onward some people may not change much, but others undergo major transformations. Ralph Thauvette was one of them.

Ralph's mom, Vera, taught English at SHS but Ralph was a lanky, curly-haired farm boy, and he was as quiet as a whisper on a windy night. Given his demeanor and heavy lidded eyes, his *Scarlet S* caption seemed appropriate: "Blessed be the man who invented sleep."

Sleepy-eyed, yes. A voice seldom heard, to be sure. But Ralph was not a man without passion, and his passion was music. He played in the perennially crack Shelby Whippet marching band all four years, and he was a four-year member of the Trombone Quartet. Everyone at SHS watched the marching band, but I'm not sure where the Trombone Quartet played or who saw them. Ralph also helped form a group of seven SHS boys called The Dixie Cats, and they were good enough to win an appearance on a weekly amateur variety show televised by a Cleveland station. I remember tuning in for that.

Although you barely knew Ralph was around the halls of SHS, somehow he and I got to be good friends. We didn't seem to have a lot in common. Certainly, any passion I had for music was limited to listening. Ralph didn't play on any of the sports teams. Maybe we grew close because he, like Mary Ann Inscho Richards, was another friend I just couldn't put down or make the butt of sarcasm, real or feigned. They were just way too nice. Our friendship grew stronger after high school when Bill Anspach organized a fast-pitch softball team that played during our college summer breaks.

At first I was shocked when Bill told me that Ralph would be on our team. Hell, I didn't even know Ralph liked baseball or softball, much less ever played it. But son of a gun, Ralph turned out to be a good player. He was fast and could field and hit pretty well. His throwing arm was weak but overall, Ralph's ability was an asset.

Few things help boys form bonds better than sports, and the bond between Ralph and me strengthened appreciably during those summers. Still, I would have characterized Ralph as reserved.

So, fast-forward 20 years and comes 1983 and our 20-year reunion. I'm in the American Legion Post hall, talking, listening, hugely enjoying myself.

Fred Mellick, the reunion planning team chairman, comes hustling up to me and asks, "Have you seen Ralph?"

"No, why?"

"It's almost time for our program and Ralph is emcee."

"Ralph?"

"Yeah," said Fred. "Well, see ya' later. I gotta find him."

"Yeah..." Ralph Thauvette, program master of ceremonies? Quiet, reserved, you hardly-knew-he-was-around Ralph. Curly-haired, bespectacled Ralph. I concluded immediately that the planning team couldn't get anyone else and, in desperation, had railroaded Ralph into the job. Oh, Lord, this was going to be embarrassing.

I spotted my buddy Bill Anspach and walked over to him. "Bill, know what Fred Mellick just told me? Ralph's going to be emcee."

Bill smiled at my incredulity. "Ralph's not the same Ralph you remember. When he went to Ashland University, I guess he really opened up. He joined a band and became real popular. Get this. Ralph became a ladies man. I heard he was one of the most popular guys on campus."

"Ralph?"

"Watch."

At our class reunions back then, the program really amounted to just a humorous interlude between dinner and dancing and chatting. It began about two hours after the reunion started. It was really a vehicle for poking gentle fun at classmates, for giving out joke gifts and bogus awards. It's the kind of thing that can be uproarious if pulled off smoothly and excruciatingly embarrassing if blown.

Fred Mellick had found Ralph and was introducing him. Despite Bill's assurances about a new Ralph, I braced myself and prepared to suffer acute embarrassment for me, Ralph, and everyone else in the room.

I needn't have worried. Ralph had hardly begun to speak when I knew Bill had been right. This was a different Ralph Thauvette. He

93

sounded like he had hired one of Johnny Carson's writers. Husky voiced, he was witty, glib, charming and polished. Very polished. I found myself admiring Ralph's performance as much as I was enjoying the substance of his program. By the time he had awarded a prize to the girl with the most last names since graduation and managed to do it without devastating her, I was in awe.

When Ralph was finished, I applauded with the rest of the class. Then I approached him, shook hands, and clasped his shoulder.

"God, Ralph, you were terrific."

"Thanks, Mike."

"I'll be honest. I just never expected you to get up in front of a crowd and look so comfortable."

"I've had lots of practice," said Ralph. "With my band, and with teaching." Ralph was teaching high school and living in nearby Crestline, Ohio.

"It's certainly paid off. Let's talk. I want to learn what's happened to you."

"Mike, I'm sorry, but I have to leave."

"How come?"

"My band is playing tonight. I'm sorry, real sorry, but it was a conflict that I couldn't avoid."

"You sure?"

"Yeah."

I blew out a breath. "I'm sorry, Ralph. Damn. You're absolutely sure you have to go now?"

"Yeah, really, I have to."

"Piss. Well, I hope we both make it to the next reunion, and I sure hope you plan it so you don't have to leave early."

"I promise."

1988

Ralph kept that promise. Five years later, on July 16, 1988, he arrived early and stayed until the end. Once again he had been tapped to be emcee, and he was as polished as ever. But there had been still another major change in Ralph, a change in priorities.

At the time of our 20-year reunion five years before, Ralph was divorced. On the night of our 25-year-reunion, I saw Ralph enter the K of

C Hall with a pretty woman at his side. Ralph and I shook hands warmly, clasped shoulders, and greeted each other. Then...

"Mike, I'd like you to meet my new wife, Patty."

"Very nice to meet you, Patty."

"Nice to meet you, Mike." We shook hands. "Ralph has told me so much about you." She was smiling. Outwardly, I was smiling, too. Inwardly, I was grimacing, not really sure what "so much" might have included.

"Ralph, I hope you don't have to leave early tonight," I said, smiling.

Ralph knew immediately that I was alluding to his early departure five years before. His eyes twinkled beneath their heavy lids and he smiled kindly. "No, not this time. I'm not in the band anymore. I finally decided that being out four nights a week isn't conducive to a happy home life."

"You'd like to stay married a bit longer this time."

"A lot longer."

1993

After emceeing the programs at the 1983 and 1988 reunions, Ralph was railroaded into chairing the planning team for our 1993 reunion. He did a terrific job of getting it on track and keeping it there. At planning committee meetings, themselves a series of mini-reunions, Ralph blended nicely the desire to reminisce and share with the need to develop and execute plans. From the earlier chapters on Jim Blair and Nancy Kuhn, you already know what a caring man Ralph is. I don't know that I've ever met a man more sensitive to the feelings of others.

Early on in the planning process for the 1993 gathering, Ralph had asked me to take over structuring and emceeing the Saturday night program with its humorous interlude. In its closing moments I said to my assembled classmates: "At the beginning of this program, I said that accepting responsibility for this part of the reunion meant that I also had some license. Now, I would like to do something we've never done before, but that's okay because having license means being able to set a precedent. So this year, for the first time, we are going to have a chairman's award. Ralph, please come up here."

Immediately, a rousing ovation erupted. Classmates stood and clapped and cheered. I shook hands with Ralph and presented him with a framed photo of Old SHS, a jigsaw puzzle showing three whippets, a tape cassette of rock and roll songs from the 1960s, and a wooden #1 hand identical to the one given John Crum. Ralph was much surprised and touched.

As to Ralph, perhaps the best thing occurred at the picnic the next afternoon. An hour or so into the picnic, Ralph and I were alone and I said, "You know, Ralph, we still haven't addressed the matter of chairing the next reunion."

"Hey," he said, "I would gladly hand this off to anyone, if someone wants it. But otherwise, I'd be willing to do it at least one more time – if I got the same level of support again."

That was music to my ears. With a single exception, all members of the '93 planning team were at the picnic. Upon hearing Ralph's offer, all pledged enthusiastically the same level of support for '98.

The 35-year reunion would be in very able hands.

1998

The 35-year reunion was the one I couldn't attend because of being at Stanford. But I was told that Ralph very ably led the planning.

2002

After Janet Page Whitehill from the class of '62 recruited me to help plan the 11-class reunion, I recruited Ralph. He was glad to pitch in. He took as a mission coordinating with the SHS Marching Band director and the Alumni Band to arrange a performance on the opening night of the three-day reunion. It was a job that required equal measures of persistence and tact. Ralph performed marvelously. That was the good news. The bad news: Patty had left him. I don't ever recall being with Ralph when he was so down. Patty's announcement that she was moving out floored Ralph. She had told him she wanted a lifestyle that she said Ralph couldn't provide. Exit.

Ralph's daughter Terra chose to continue living with Ralph, and that helped salve his wound. Later, she chose to attend Ohio University which pleased Ralph and he knew it would please me – a tireless OU advocate. (Lynne and I had met at OU and remained connected to the school. For six years, we served as co-presidents of an alumni chapter. Two of our three kids became OU grads. I had been guest lecturing there since

1990. We belonged to the athletics booster club, had been members of ad hoc committees, and once I served as the OU president's proxy at the inauguration of another college's president.)

2003

Ralph agreed to chair the planning team for our 40-year reunion. With me, he led the thinking to include the two classes that sandwiched ours – 1962 and 1964. And he was enthusiastically onboard with our theme: Honoring Our Teachers. Remember, his late mom had been an SHS teacher. He and I and Anne Lafferty Stock shared the emceeing, and we were a good team. Afterward, I recruited Ralph to team with me in putting together the school's first-ever All-Alumni Weekend, scheduled for August of 2004. I'm damned glad that Ralph transformed, and I'm hoping our teamwork continues for years to come.

P.S. Remember my surprise back in the 1960s when Bill Anspach told me Ralph would be on our softball team? In 2003 Ralph had become player-manager of an Age 50+ softball team. Still swinging.

2006

At a wedding, Ralph met a woman named Linda who is a cousin of Ralph's son's wife. They began seeing each other and then married. I visited Ralph at his home in the autumn of 2006 and he seemed very happy. He had reason to be. In addition to having a new bride, he had become a grandfather for the first time.

2008

Ralph led the organizing for our 45-year reunion which included a nice innovation – brunches on both Saturday and Sunday at classmates' homes. They turned out to be wonderfully warm, informal gatherings. The Sunday brunch was at his house, set amidst Ralph's seven acres with pond and pastures for his two horses. You just can't take the farm out of the farm boy. And my guess is that the farm boy will be shouldering the organizational leadership for our 50-year reunion.

CHAPTER 15

COLD CALLS FROM A WARM HEART –
AND THE LAST SPANKING

Jeff Dawson was one of our class zanies. Certifiably off-the-wall. If Jeff had inhibitions, he kept them well-hidden. Virtually no one was safe – or spared – from Jeff's antics. His *Scarlet S* caption was a bulls-eye: "Double, double, toil and trouble."

He lived his life as though he was on stage, which was as often as he could manage. At SHS Jeff acted in class plays for three years and was a member of the stage crew all four years. This thespian zest didn't end with high school. As recently as 2003 Jeff was on stage, playing an Italian grandfather, immigrant accent and all, at a regional theater.

Jeff and I weren't particularly close in high school and so I don't know whether he underwent a transformation or whether the real Jeff Dawson, or the rest of Jeff Dawson, was just slow in emerging. I do know that in the 15-year reunion booklet the comments supplied by Jeff suggest he still hadn't done much settling down: "Since our 10-year reunion, Jeff had a job with a bank for 2 months. Then he helped start a company which went under in 10 months. He was unemployed for one and a half years and then a year with Rockwell International at Pittsburgh as an exporter. He is presently employed as an International Transportation Coordinator for Babcock & Wilcox. At nights he works on Spanish in hopes of going overseas. He is looking for a beautiful girl with a rich father and a job earning enough money so Jeff doesn't have to work."

All of this wasn't entirely quixotic or even as dreamy as it sounds. Jeff majored in international business at Ohio State, and he got a master's in international business at the renowned Thunderbird Graduate School of International Management at the University of Arizona. Jeff's fondness for things international was manifested another way, too; after serving for a year with the Army in Korea, he stayed on to attend the Korean Language Institute at Yonsei University.

Jeff hasn't slowed down. In 1988 he was working toward a master's in business administration degree at the University of South Carolina. Part of the program would have him in Japan studying and doing an internship.

At the 20-year reunion Jeff had married a Pakistani woman named Anjum, and at the 25-year reunion in 1988 they had a five-year-old daughter, Amber. It was just before and just after that reunion that I began to see there was at the very least one other noteworthy facet to Jeff Dawson.

Toward the end of June in 1988 I picked up the phone and called a friend, a woman, to discuss my intent to write personal notes to a few classmates, encouraging them to come to the reunion.

"I know there's going to be a followup mailing in another week or so to classmates who haven't responded," I said. "What do you think about my sending personal notes to some of the same kids?"

"I think it's a wonderful idea," she said, "and you're not the first one to think of getting in touch with class members on a personal basis."

"Really? Who else?"

"Jeff Dawson. He was in town a couple months ago visiting his parents and he just stopped by my house. He wanted the addresses of classmates living in the area."

"That's great," I said. "Where does Jeff live?"

"South Carolina. He said he would even offer a ride to someone if it meant getting them here."

"Son of a gun."

On reunion night Jeff was a combination of loopiness and sensitivity. He was one who made a special effort to talk with John Crum, confined to his wheelchair, and DeeDee Milligan, newly widowed. The old zaniness was never far below the surface though. When I asked him and DeeDee to pose for a photo, Jeff went cheek-to-cheek with DeeDee, grabbed a bottle of booze and held it under their chins, closed one eye and let the other eyelid droop drunkenly. Hilarious photo. Vintage Dawson. Still the thespian – and comedian.

Later, he was one of 20 or so of us who drove out to Mimi Grove's house on Wareham Road for a reunion extension. We had barely settled in Mimi's family room, with several of us sprawled on the floor, when Jeff said, "Hey, Mike, I just remembered. I saw you on national TV."

"Under not very pleasant circumstances," I said dryly.

"One night," said Jeff, "I came home from work, ate, and sat down to watch the CBS Evening News with my wife. There was this story about TRW and then I saw this face on the screen, and I said, 'Hey, I know this guy. I went to school with him. That's Mike Johnson. Wow!'"

Someone else spoke up. "How did you get on TV, Mike?"

"I work for TRW in corporate communications. We've had some legal problems with our government contract work. Every once in awhile I have to explain our position. That time CBS asked us to film someone, and we were foolish enough to agree. The chore went to me."

"That's fantastic!" Jeff said. "My classmate on national TV."

"I assure you it didn't seem all that fantastic to me."

On Sunday afternoon, July 17, 1988, before I left Shelby to drive home to Lyndhurst, I phoned a classmate to double check some addresses. "Maybe next time, Jeff and I can write some more notes and maybe persuade some more people to come," I said.

"Oh," she said, "that reminds me. There's something else you should know about Jeff."

"What's that?"

"He got in town a few days early and you know how he spent his time?"

"No."

"He drove around the area and visited kids who had said they weren't coming or hadn't responded."

"Cold calls?"

"That's right, " she said.

"I'm impressed." And I was.

"So was I."

"Did he have any luck?"

"I don't think so but he did tell me one sad story."

"About who?"

"Do you remember George Parker?" she asked.

"Sure. We played baseball together."

"Well," she said. "Jeff went to visit George, and George told Jeff he was bitter at the whole class."

"For crying out loud, why?"

"George thinks the whole class looked down on him."

"Why?"

"Because of his weight."

"Oh, Jesus."

"I know," she said. "I feel the same way."

"The whole class didn't look down on George. I didn't. I *liked* George. Shit. What a shame that he has that perception. And to be bitter after all these years. Oh, man."

"George," she went on, "told Jeff the only reason he would come to a reunion would be to see who else was fat. Jeff told George, 'Well, come on and check them out.'"

I had to laugh at that, despite the sadness of the story. I could picture Jeff in George's house, listening to George, suffering with him, but with the Dawson wit poised to jump into the conversation to try to lighten George's load.

I was already experiencing a feeling of melancholy, a common feeling after a reunion, but this story hit me like a punch to the stomach. It was so sad. I could just imagine George sitting home the night of the reunion and feeling bitter.

I was so damned touched that two days after the reunion I wrote this note to George:

Dear George,

I was hoping to see you at our reunion. When the 30-year reunion comes along, I hope you'll come. One of the things I noticed was how youthful pretensions and prejudices had been left behind. Classmates at the reunion didn't much care what you were doing or how you looked but instead were much more concerned about <u>how </u>classmates were feeling. I was there with glasses and a lot less hair. John Crum was there in a wheelchair. Nancy Kuhn wanted to come but, as you may have heard, is in a hospital in critical condition. Jane Bell Henning couldn't come because of health problems. DeeDee Milligan was there as a new widow. Several people were there carrying more weight and several others, including yours truly, were there with bodies rearranged by time.

If anybody there cared about physical appearances, it didn't show. George, I <u>know</u> I'm not alone in hoping you make it to the 30-year reunion. I'll try my darndest to be there and I hope you're there to shake hands with me."

Very sincerely,

I didn't receive a reply from George and didn't really expect him to come, although I sure as hell hoped he would. But I couldn't stand the thought of his feeling bitter, of feeling so utterly apart from his classmates, many of whom no doubt liked George in high school. Shoot, he had been elected an officer for one of the high school clubs. When I returned home to Lyndhurst, I pulled my 1963 *Scarlet S* off the family room bookshelf. And when you look at the club's picture, there's George in the front row, and one thing is crystal clear. George Parker was *not* fat. No way.

1988

Soon after the 1988 reunion, Jeff Dawson and Anjum moved to Karachi, Pakistan. Afterward, he twice wrote the class long, witty letters on the country's history (politically tortured) and various aspects of life: diet (heavy on mangos – with frequent intestinal aftereffects), driving (no traffic regulations), education system (equal doses of Urdu and English), arranged marriages ("You marry whom Mama and Papa tell you to"), and divorce ("Under Islam a man can divorce simply by telling a wife 'I divorce thee' three times"). He also described long robes and a beard he sometimes felt compelled to wear to disguise his American heritage. Regrettably, Jeff was not able to make it for the 1993 reunion or the 1995 class birthday party.

2002

As part of the 2002 11-class reunion, we decided to include an old-fashioned assembly in the auditorium of Old SHS which since 1966 had been serving as the town's middle school. The assembly would include a guessing game based on songs from the 1957-67 period, door prizes, speeches by four former teachers and three alums, a specially produced video that recognized and honored the 11 classes, and some good-natured teasing by the emcee. I would be the emcee. As the assembly was nearing, I was experiencing a strong sense of déjà vu. I recalled that this wouldn't be the first time that I had emceed an assembly in that auditorium. I had done likewise in May of 1963, just before graduating.

In the weeks before that reunion, I heard that Jeff Dawson had returned from Pakistan and was intending to return to college to get a teaching certificate. Wow! I was impressed. Jeff already had bachelor's and master's degrees. Going back to school at age 57 told me that he was really determined to be a teacher.

So, once the assembly was underway and I was calling attention to certain alums, I mentioned that Jeff was back in the U.S. after 12 years in Pakistan and that we were darned glad to have him with us in the auditorium. The next day at the picnic, I talked with Jeff at length. Not only did he want to become a teacher, he was hoping to become a school principal. *Jeff as a principal.* Now that was a thought that, 40 years before, would have caused massive rolling of eyes among the SHS faculty and staff. Anjum and Amber were staying behind in Pakistan where Amber's goal was to enter medical school. Jeff's comments made it pretty clear that his marriage to Anjum had weakened if not ended. Anyway, Jeff surprised me when, with touching sincerity, he told me that my mentioning his return during the assembly had warmed him. "It meant so much to me," he said. "It really made me feel like I was back home."

It also whet his desire for more connecting because that autumn he quickly said yes to an invitation to join the planning team for the class of 1963's 40-year reunion. Like Ralph and me, he was four-square for inviting the classes of '62 and '64. At that point, little did we know that Jeff's involvement would give him an opportunity to once again display his thespian skills. But did it ever.

Here's how. After the planning team agreed to have a theme – Honoring Our Teachers – for our reunion, I had a little brainstorm. Why not have the reunion program include skits parodying some of our teachers from the early '60s? I bounced the idea off the team and they liked it. So, I set about scripting skits that would take fellow alums through a "typical day" at SHS in the '60s. That meant starting with homeroom and going to five or six classes. I picked six teachers to parody, four of whom wound up coming to the reunion.

At a subsequent planning team meeting, I read through the scripts. My teammates liked them. They poked fun at teachers and some fellow students. Irreverence would be in the air. And no one but the team would know in advance what we were going to be springing. Then I said to the team: "We need a cast. Volunteers?" The responses included averted gazes, foot shuffling, "not me's" and a plea from one teammate to delete her name from one scene where attention would be called in the "biology class" skit to her physique – which had been admirable and still was.

I said, "Okay, we'll hold off on casting to the next meeting. Between now and then, think about it. We'll need at least two volunteers – one to play teachers and the other students."

Sometime between that meeting and the next, I received an email from Jeff. "Mike, I've been thinking. I could do those skits as a one-man show. Play all the roles. JoAnn (the woman with whom he was then living and later would marry) said she could make masks that I could hold in front of my face whenever I switched roles. What do you think?"

It didn't take much thinking. I *loved* the idea. If Jeff had enough confidence in himself to pull it off, then I had enough confidence in him to give him the green light.

I sent Jeff the set of scripts, each of which would run three to five minutes. That meant a lot of memorizing. Via email, we talked about props that would help us carry this off. They would include a women's hairbrush, a toy frog, a necktie, a screwdriver, a football and the masks. We also would need a table to serve as a desk, as one of the teachers we would be parodying always perched on the front edge of her desk, legs crossed demurely – and suggestively. Jeff would be rehearsing at home, but he said he wanted to rehearse the skits in front of me since I had authored them and wouldn't hesitate to offer feedback.

Jeff was living in Mansfield and I in North Canton, and on the Friday morning of reunion weekend we met at Shelby's Rabold Park. I had suggested it because it is the most isolated of the town's parks. It's on the west end of town at the end of a quiet street and surrounded on three sides by farm fields. It also has a pavilion with tables and benches which themselves would serve as rehearsal props.

Jeff and I got started about 10 o'clock. For the next two hours, he rehearsed, I provided feedback, he tweaked his acting – both delivery of lines and mannerisms. We really wanted to "nail" the teachers. He was impressive. He was playing both teachers and students, and he pretty much had the scripts down pat. We agreed that during his performance on Saturday night, I would sit off to one side with the scripts just in case he needed any prompting. When we were finished, I said, "Great job, Jeff. I think you've got it licked."

"Not quite yet," said Jeff. "I want to go home and run through everything a couple more times. I need to get a little more comfortable with some of the lines."

Saturday Night Live! When it was time to begin honoring our teachers, Ralph handed me the microphone, and I told the audience that Anne Lafferty Stock would be teaming up with me as emcee for the rest of the program. Then I said, "There ought to be some rules. The first one is, 'We are not going to permit any undue rowdiness among the teachers.'" Appreciative laughter greeted that rule. "The second one is, 'The people in this room cannot applaud too often, too long or too loud.'"

Continuing, I said, "Once we decided to have a theme, we quickly and unanimously decided on Honoring Our Teachers. But it didn't seem entirely appropriate to treat them only with reverence." At this, there was laughter, but some of the teachers looked just a trifle apprehensive. You could see uneasiness in their eyes. "There will be some reverence, but we are going to do our best to *balance* it with irreverence. And you teachers are just going to have to live with it. The students are in charge. The inmates are running the asylum tonight. We thought we'd start with the reverential part. Handle that. Get it out of the way." More laughter.

So, first, Anne and I took turns saying something nice, sometimes funny, about each of the 15 teachers there. They ranged in age from 66 to 90. We called them forward to the microphone one-by-one – escorted by Larry Milliron, Doyle Minich or Jim Williams – to receive a personalized certificate of appreciation that had been signed by the alums in attendance. (Before opening the doors that evening, we had set up a table at the far rear corner of the hall. As alums arrived and signed in, we asked them to go right back and sign each of the 15 certificates. We asked them to include maiden names if appropriate and to put their class year – '63, '62 or '64 – after their names.)

It was touching. Most of the teachers did want to say something to the assemblage. But not all. One was just at a loss for words, and one, Karen Reimsnyder, had suffered a stroke and, although she could speak only haltingly, she was too choked up. Making it more touching was that her husband, Bob, also was one of the 15 teachers. Wife and husband, they came forward together, she clinging to his arm, Jim Williams holding Karen's other arm. Said Bob, "Normally, I'd have a lot of words to say.

But I'm just about out of words. My wife Karen has had a stroke. She has made good progress in the last year and a half." By this point, tears were streaming down Karen's cheeks. And lumps were forming in lots of throats. "We are enjoying life a little differently than we'd planned," said Bob. "We were going to go out and travel the world, but things can change very quickly. We are getting through it. We go other places – like here tonight. We enjoy it much. Thank you very much." Anne stepped forward quickly and hugged both of them. My schoolmates remembered Rule #2; their applause was loud and long.

There were also plenty of light moments. Doyle Minich escorted Edith Huston to the microphone. Now in her 80s and slowed by time, Edith uses a cane for support. That night, she used Doyle's arm. Her hair is white, and it was freshly permed. She is still bubbly and, as she approached the microphone, she girlishly scrunched her shoulders and smiled a huge smile at Anne. Anne recalled that Edith used to require memorizing 1,000 lines of poetry – a demanding assignment but one which helped her students realize their capabilities. Then Edith began to speak. "I love Shelby. And I certainly love my kids...The last one I paddled – Denny Lepp (a husky defensive lineman on the football team). Now, I'd be in prison. Anyway, I broke the paddle on Denny and I said, 'Now, Denny, you owe me a new paddle.'" Edith's eyes were mischievously alight at the memory. "And, you know, the next day he came in with a new paddle. He and his dad stayed up all night making it." Then, amidst the laughter of "her kids," Edith, with the timing of Bob Hope, added, "That's the influence of teachers." Laughter was rocketing through the hall and bouncing off the walls and ceiling.

Then we asked everyone – about 110 people – to stand and form an oval. I then announced that Harryet Snyder, biology teacher extraordinaire, had agreed in advance to let us help her celebrate her 90th birthday which would arrive exactly one week later. That was Bill Anspach's cue to wheel out from the hall's kitchen on a cart a huge birthday cake. Here is how it was decorated. Across the top was a range of mountains. They symbolized Harryet's love of mountain climbing which she often did during summer breaks. In the lower right corner of the cake was a pond with three frogs along the bank to represent the dissections that were part of her biology instruction. And there was a large football with both SHS and OSU writ large on it. Harryet likes to joke that she had come to SHS back in 1942 after a few years at another high school because SHS's school colors were the same – red and gray – as her beloved OSU.

Then I said to the assemblage, "We didn't want to mess up this cake with 90 candles, so...Larry, Doyle and Jim, would you please pass out the candles?" My wife Lynne had bought slow-burning, dripless candles. The idea for this lighting ceremony was Larry Reed's. I said, "Because we have so many brilliant people here tonight, we are going to do some multi-tasking." Some mock groans broke out. "You are going to do two things at once. The first one, you are already doing – lighting the candles. The second one isssssss...We are going to sing *Happy Birthday*." With each person lighting the candle of the adjacent person, it took only a minute at most to have all the candles aglow. Then we serenaded Harryet with *Happy Birthday*. Among the gifts we gave her were an Ohio State hooded, zippered sweatshirt and a roll of (late Michigan coach) Bo Shembechler toilet paper.

Then Jeff Dawson took over. End of reverence. As he moved to the microphone and began arranging his props, Jeff whispered to me, "I'm a little nervous."

"You'll be fine," I said.

He and I positioned two tables, one to serve as the "classroom desk" and the other to hold his props. I then took a chair, positioned it about a dozen feet to the right of Jeff at the microphone and sat with the scripts in hand.

Then Jeff cleared his throat and got rolling. For a good 20 minutes, his one-man show had fellow alums and the teachers alternately mesmerized and in stitches. As the teachers being skewered got over their initial discomfort, they seemed entranced by Jeff's dead-on portrayals. A couple of excerpts will give you the gist of Jeff's performance.

In his parody of biology teacher Harryet Snyder, Jeff used a true anecdote – a shipment of frogs that were supposed to be dead and ready for dissection but arrived very much alive.

Jeff as Miss Snyder struggles to open a container. As she removes the top, out jumps a live (toy) frog.

Jeff as student Susie shrieks with his voice pitched high.

Susie: *They are alive! Oh, my God!*

Jeff as Jeff: *This could be interesting.*

Jeff as Miss Snyder: *Someone get that frog.*

Jeff picks up the frog and shows it to Susie.

Susie: *Ewwww. It's slimey. How are we going to dissect it? It won't be still.*

Jeff hands the frog to himself as Miss Snyder. She holds the frog down with her left hand.

Miss Snyder: *We'll have to kill it.*

Jeff as Susie swoons.

Jeff as Miss Snyder then picks up a long screwdriver and plunges it into the frog's neck.

Jeff as Jeff: *I think I just figured out what biology is about.*

Harryet Snyder was laughing as hard as anyone in the hall. In the actual incident back around 1960, Miss Snyder had dispatched the box of live frogs with a series of injections.

The last of Jeff's six skits was a take on retired history teacher and football coach Don Monn, then age 77 and also in attendance that night. Excerpt from the script:

Jeff as Mr. Monn lowers his voice to mimic Don Monn's booming base: *Mr. Sarpa, Miss Bowman, Mr. Hay...they all teach history, too. But not like I do.*

Jeff as student Mary Ellen May Hall raises her hand.

Jeff as Mr. Monn: *Yes, Mary Ellen?*

Jeff as Mary Ellen: *How do you do it?*

Jeff as Mr. Monn: *With a vengeance. In my class, we are going to emphasize wars. The Revolutionary War...the Civil War...World War I... World War II...Korea...the war between students and teachers.*

Jeff as Mary Ellen: *Why not give peace a chance?*

Jeff as Mr. Monn: *When did peace ever win a war? Did peace ever change history?*

Jeff as Mary Ellen looks at him with deep suspicion.

Jeff as Mr. Monn: *Are you one of those hippies I've been reading about?*

Jeff as Mary Ellen: *A what?*

Jeff as Mr. Monn: *A hippie. You know, flower power. Purple hair. Guitars.*

Jeff as Mary Ellen: *I only play the flute.*

Jeff as Mr. Monn: *I was worried. Hippies could be a real threat to the American way. Let me ask you a question, Mary Ellen. Can you imagine Bill Anspach or Larry Milliron running onto the football field with flowers in their hair? Or Lybarger wearing beads and sandals? How about Coach Wilkins on the sidelines strumming a guitar?*

Jeff as Mary Ellen: *Gee, that actually might be kind of cute.*

Jeff as Mr. Monn: *Cute? Football players and coaches aren't supposed to be cute. You sure you're not a hippie?*

Jeff as Mary Ellen: *Maybe I could be one when I go to college.*

Jeff as Mr. Monn: *That kind of thinking is why there will never be a woman president.*

Jeff as Mary Ellen: *How can you be so sure?*

Jeff as Mr. Monn: *It's obvious, isn't it? Men are stronger. Men are smarter. Everyone knows that. Men are from Mars. I rest my case.*

And then Jeff Dawson rested.

So, unfortunately, did Don Monn when he passed away from cancer less than a year later in April 2004.

2008

Jeff was teaching and wanted me to know how he felt about his late-in-life calling. "I'm no saint," he said, introducing the topic. Who among us is? I was thinking. Jeff's passion shows clearly in an anecdote he related. "I try to influence every student I have. A boy whose mother died when he was five had his father drop him off at his grandparents, and the father went on to Tennessee. No one had ever told this boy how smart he is! He can make puns, has a great sense of humor and one day when I mentioned 'Let them eat cake,' he told me the whole story about how Marie Antoinette and her husband, Louix XVI, were caught when they tried to escape from Paris. Blew me away! This student is not dumb. He hasn't been motivated. When I told him he had a high IQ, he looked at me like I had lost my mind. Now he comes to talk with me every chance he gets because someone gives a damn about him. That's why I love teaching! If I can influence positively one student a semester, I can make a difference."

Sounds to me like Jeff Dawson is still making cold calls of a sort.

CHAPTER 16

Blessings to Jeanette Bly Egleston Allard, Wayne Potts, Joe Yohn
and other SHS teachers and staff who regularly endured the antics of

TWO CHILDREN OF CHANCE

Chance. To varying extents we are all children of chance. It begins with birth. Chance determines the continent where we are born, the color of our skin and our sex.

What else? As we move through life, the unexpected occasionally rises up. In some instances we can choose our response. In others there's no time to choose or even react. Unseen ice on a bridge in the dark of night sends your car into a 360-degree spin. That happened to me – with my wife and three kids in silent terror. A drunk driver barrels through a stop sign and broadsides you, a bolt of lightning strikes or a poisonous snake bites while you're ascending a Mexican pyramid. I know people – all women – who were on the receiving end of those chance happenings.

Chance holds the power to alter the course of lives. For Bruce Hunter I've often wondered whether it was a flu epidemic. Not one that laid him low but one that sent so many local teachers to bed that the administration asked high school students to teach elementary school kids.

Before elaborating let me set the stage with a reunion story. The 25-year reunion was the first for Bruce Hunter. It took some doing to get him there, and he was at least a trifle nervous when he arrived. That was obvious. The first few classmates Bruce saw he greeted stiffly: "Hi _____, I'm Bruce Hunter."

"Bruce," I said after listening to him about a half dozen times, "you don't have to say your name. Most everybody will remember you. And, here, you can put this name tag on."

He smiled and seemed to relax a bit.

At SHS Bruce had been both well known and popular. He played sports, was on the yearbook staff and acted in plays. Nonetheless, as I said, it took some persuasion to get Bruce back to Shelby. He was on the short list of classmates I wrote to about three weeks before the reunion.

I had written him to "bust a butt or two" to get back to the old stomping ground.

"Well," I said after we shook hands and hugged, "tell me, did my note help?"

"Absolutely," said Bruce. His eyes were alight with pleasure and excitement. "It did the trick. Your postcard was really responsible for getting me to attend. I looked at the card and when I read that John Crum was coming, I thought, 'Well, if he can make it, I'll go.' And then my boys said, 'Yeah, Dad, go. Ya' gotta go.' And then I paused and said, 'Nah, I won't go.' And then my wife said, 'Why don't you go? You'll have fun and it will be convenient. We have something planned for the weekend before and the weekend after the reunion, but we don't have anything going that weekend.' So I finally said, 'Why not?'"

Bruce and I were a pair in high school. We operated smoothly if not all that maturely. We jokingly called ourselves the "superior beings" and others the "lesser ones," and we were benignly mischievous. So much so that we often came to be suspected immediately when some prank was pulled off.

- One day we put an empty candy bar carton – the kind that held a dozen or two bars – under the padded chair seat of our homeroom teacher, Jeanette Bly Egleston. She was our favorite target. The sound of the crunch when she sat down sent her shooting up and sent us into gales of laughter. Of course, you should know that half the guys in homeroom were half in love with Miss Egleston who was a former SHS majorette and class of 1950. She was cute, shapely, spirited, and endlessly good-natured. We loved to tease her and she took it all with exquisite grace and good humor.
- Then there was the day we put a dead frog – one meant to be dissected in a biology class – in her desk drawer. For me and Bruce, that episode produced some delicious drama: *When would she open the drawer? This morning? This afternoon?*
- More than once we balanced chalk-filled erasers on top of the door to another teacher's classroom. He learned to look up when entering. Yes, I know, we were pretty juvenile, and we assuredly didn't score any points for imagination.

111

- Bruce and I cut up so much in Spanish that Wayne Potts, as excellent and patient a teacher as you could imagine, finally took us aside for a private, ten-minute chat during which he noted our penchant for purposely speaking fractured Spanish and asked us to try speaking a little more conventionally. He noted our entertainment prowess but good-humoredly reminded us that education also had its place in the classroom. (Mr. Potts and I stayed in touch for many years; he perished way too early from complications from Parkinson's Disease in 1996.)

- One of my favorite Hunter-Johnson escapades was the time we decided to make absent somebody who was present. We decided to do it after lunch during the afternoon homeroom period. Just before the end of homeroom, Bruce and I began edging toward the door. Miss Egleston ignored us. When the bell rang, we hustled across the hall to Miss Stroup's homeroom. We hung around as inconspicuously as possible, waiting for her to put the attendance slip in the little metal box attached to her door. Then when she walked back into her room, we quickly removed the slip from the box.

"Whose name should we put on this?" I whispered.

"Fred's."

We had to suppress giggles. It took only a scant moment. We wrote down Fred's name as absent and returned the slip to the box where soon a student-secretary would pick up the slip and take it with those from other homerooms to the attendance office.

Nobody noticed us, and nothing happened until the last period of the afternoon. Bruce and I were sitting in Royal Allard's government class when we saw Joe Yohn, assistant principal and attendance officer, appear at Mr. Allard's door. Mr. Allard left the room, and Bruce and I looked silently at each other.

A moment later, Mr. Allard re-entered the room, and we heard his voice. "Hunter, Johnson, would you please come here?" As we eased from our desks and started toward the front of the room, Mr. Allard said, "Mr. Yohn wants to see you."

We stepped by Mr. Allard and continued out into the hall. Behind us, Mr. Allard closed his door and resumed teaching. Mr.Yohn was a kindly, white-haired man and a friend. Besides being attendance officer, he was football equipment manager, the school's sports statistician and the golf coach. He was trying to look stern.

"Boys," he said, "do you know where Fred Vernier was this afternoon?"

Bruce and I both were trying to suppress smiles.

"Why?" I said.

"Because," said Mr. Yohn, "his name was on the absent list. I was concerned because he was in school this morning. So I called his home to check on him. When I asked his mother how he was doing, she was puzzled. She said Fred wasn't at home, that he must still be in school. So then I went to the study hall where he was supposed to be and he was there."

By now Bruce and I were struggling to stifle an explosion of laughter.

"So you thought of us," Bruce managed to say without breaking up.

"Naturally," said Mr. Yohn. I noticed a trace of a smile forming on his lips. "Your homeroom is across the hall from Fred's. Well, did you boys have anything to do with this?" He had no evidence, just well-founded suspicion.

Bruce and I looked at each other and then at Mr. Yohn and then spontaneously and simultaneously we each wrapped an arm around Mr.Yohn's shoulders and said, "Yes." And then we broke up.

So did Mr. Yohn, or nearly so. "Now, boys," he tried to say with some degree of dignity, "this is serious. Fred's mother was worried that something might have happened to him."

At which point, Bruce and I were laughing hard enough to produce tears. Mr. Yohn, now beginning to laugh himself, shook his head, eased from our grasp, turned and began walking down the hall.

One of the last times I remember Bruce and I operating together at SHS was during the winter of our senior year, but not as pranksters. As the winter of '63 was nearing its end, the aforementioned flu epidemic swept through the Shelby schools and decimated the teachers' ranks. Bruce and I were recruited as a team to teach an elementary school class – sixth graders as I recall – for a week. At the end of the week, we concluded that we had done a pretty good job when the kids announced that they had decided to rename their pair of classroom goldfish. The new names: Mike and Bruce.

It's too bad that Jeanette Egleston and Joe Yohn weren't there to see us in action. We used humor and we were patient and those kids learned. Bruce spent much time at the front of the room, working with the body of the class. He captivated and inspired them. You could see and hear their joy.

I spent much time sitting in the back corner with a girl who had been described to us as "slow." As the week moved along and I spent more and more time working with and encouraging that little girl, I could see a light beginning to shine in her eyes. She began to have fun, and she began to catch on. Back in those years, people weren't talking about learning disabilities. Students who failed to stay up with the rest of the class were labeled "slow" or worse. During the ensuing years I've often wondered what happened to that little girl.

I don't remember Bruce and I talking much about how that one-week stint affected us. But I do know that when Bruce arrived at our 25-year reunion, it was as a professor. He even looked the part – distinguished with a full head of gray-streaked hair. And if his work with those 6th graders was any indication, he likely was a stellar professor.

After graduating from SHS Bruce and I both headed off to college. After earning his bachelor's degree, Bruce moved south and eventually wound up working in public relations for a university. He very much liked the academic environment and, after a time, decided that if he were going to remain in academia, it might as well be on faculty rather than staff. He liked the flexibility that went with being on faculty, and he thought it would be stimulating to teach, do research and write. So it was back to college where he earned his doctorate. He quickly landed a teaching job at still another university where he excelled and rose to chair a department.

As you know, when you make a prediction, it's not very often that you can be really certain how it will work out. On the postcard that I had sent to Bruce before the reunion, I told him flatly that he would enjoy himself if he came. When I saw him enter the K of C Hall, I remember thinking, *Well, here goes; I hope I was right.*

This time I was. Afterward, Bruce said, "You were right. I really did enjoy it. I am planning on attending the next one as well."

114

The next one turned out to be just three months later. It was another mini-reunion. I had showing on my calendar a business trip to a destination not far from Bruce's school. I phoned him and asked how he felt about a visit. He was thrilled. He insisted that I come and stay the night at his home. In addition he arranged a mini-reunion over breakfast with another of our classmates who also was a faculty member at his school.

Bruce was in high spirits while we were together. His wife took a photo of the two of us while I was there. One glance and you can see that the prankster and the professor were glad to be together.

In later years, though, Bruce did not respond to any pre-reunion communications and did not attend subsequent class gatherings. Was his first reunion his last? Some months later I learned that Bruce, at the time of our next reunion, had been out of the country as part of his professorial work. Still, something inside was eating at me. Something that was causing me to wonder whether, had there been no conflict, Bruce would have joined us. I wonder if I'll ever know. Later I tried several times to reach him but failed.

CHAPTER 17

CHANNELING PASSION

Fred Eichinger immortalized me and hundreds of other alumni. So to speak. When Fred walked into the Knights of Columbus Hall for our 25-year reunion, I experienced a special feeling of warmth. More than anyone else in our class, Fred had undertaken a labor of love that will forever preserve a slice of SHS history.

During our SHS days, Fred was a member of the marching band for four years. He didn't play sports but I knew he was a sports fan. And a loud and supportive one. Fred's base voice easily penetrated the din at football and basketball games. Little did I know, though, that Fred's feelings for Shelby and SHS football would amount to a continuing passion and launch him on a mission.

What Fred did to channel that passion and record and preserve a segment of SHS's history may be unique in the annals of high school football. Not merely unusual but unique.

Here is what Fred did. In his spare time, when not serving as Shelby's police force captain, Fred poured *thousands* of hours into researching Shelby football, from its beginning in 1894 through 1985. He dug up and confirmed anecdotes and statistics. He collected photos, including one terrific action shot showing Charles Follis, the first professional African-American football player, breaking away for a long run for the Shelby Athletic Club in 1902 in a 48-0 romp over the Newark Athletic Club. That same photo resides in the Pro Football Hall of Fame in Canton, Ohio. Fred's research embraced all SHS football teams, Shelby amateur and semi-pro teams, and Shelby's early professional team, the Blues.

Here's an example of how hard Fred dug. It has to do with Follis. From 1902 through 1906 Follis played first for the Shelby Athletic Club and then the Shelby Blues. In his research Fred learned that Follis roomed at 16 Oak Street – and that another early pro football player, Branch Rickey, roomed at the same house. Rickey played for Shelby from 1900 through 1903. Ironically, that's the same Branch Rickey who in 1947 broke through major league baseball's color barrier by signing Jackie Robinson to a contract with the Brooklyn Dodgers. If we are in part a product of our experiences, you might find yourself wondering whether Rickey's time with Follis influenced his decision with Robinson nearly a half century later.

Perhaps this is the time to mention the nickname for SHS sports teams. It's a name that Shelbians are intensely proud of but which many non-Shelbians must puzzle over or snicker at. It's the Whippets. No, whippets are not something you stomp on or which slink off in the black of night. Whippets are a breed of sleek racing dogs that closely resemble but are somewhat smaller than greyhounds. The name was first attached to an SHS football team in 1928 and, as you might imagine, has spawned derivatives used in connection with other SHS activities and teams. One example: the school newspaper was called *Whippet Tales*. A second example: since the early 1960s, the name of the football team's defensive units has been the Hungry Hounds. A Google search shows that only eight other high schools use the Whippet nickname.

Back to Fred. In addition to his heart and soul and time, Fred poured $22,868 into his project. The result was a handsome, oversized hardcover book, *The History of Shelby Football, 1894-1985.* Between the red and gray school color covers, the book contains 372 coated paper pages of Shelby football history, including a photo of every team plus many other pictures. Fred had each book numbered and sold them for $35 each to recover his costs. I own number 455. Fred managed to make a small profit from the book and gave that to the SHS Athletic Department.

Fred served long as Shelby's police captain and assistant chief and, in retirement, worked as a bartender. He also worked as a disc jockey for dances featuring music from the 1950s and '60s. At our 20-year reunion Fred provided entertainment by doing a pretty professional impersonation of Elvis Presley. He was married and had two kids. I say all this just to let you know how impressed I am by Fred's dedication to undertaking and completing the football history.

If you ever visit the Pro Football Hall of Fame, you could check out the result of Fred's passion. The hall's library includes two copies of Fred's book.

Fred was the kind of classmate reunions were made for.

1993

Fred participated in the Saturday morning golf outing and joined us Saturday night. He was in great spirits and particularly enjoyed the Name The Tune contest. Small wonder. Fred's love for 1960s rock and roll is legendary among our classmates. He and Dennis Kidwell and Don Ralston were among top scorers in the Name The Tune contest.

Fred retired from the Shelby Police Department as a captain on March 1, 1993. Later, he wrote in our 1993 reunion booklet, "Could I be the first retiree from the Class of '63? Maybe not, there's always Jeff Dawson."

By then, Fred had transferred his literary passion from the history of Shelby football to Ohio Indian tribes and planned to write more books. Unfortunately Fred ran out of time. He passed away on February 12, 2006.

CHAPTER 18

FIRST FLYER, LAST BROTHER

Courage. Risk. Science. Adversity. Tragedy. All have been ingredients in Larry Reed's life.

Larry, who stands about six feet tall with black hair, was our class's first flyer and his family's last brother. In elaborating let me begin with this assertion: America is a smarter and safer nation thanks to Larry Reed. Did I imagine that while we were together at SHS? Don't think so.

From those years I remember most clearly two things about Larry, and they both had to do with biology. He was a member of the Biology Club for three years, and he served as my personal quiz alert. One year we both were taking biology with the same teacher, the late Harryet Snyder about whom you'll soon learn much. Larry's class preceded mine by a period or two. Each day I would see him approaching in a hallway. Before I could utter a word, Larry would smile knowingly, anticipate my question and say either, "Quiz today" or "You're okay, Mike. No quiz today." His alerts told me whether I would have to make time for some 11th hour cramming.

While still a child Larry developed a strong interest in science and airplanes. After graduating from SHS he wasted no time pursuing that interest. He joined the Navy and soon was taking flight training. In 1965 he soloed for the first time. Before much longer he was a member of a crew flying reconnaissance over Vietnam.

"We were based in The Philippines," recalls Larry. "On each mission we flew two hours en route to Vietnam, then we were on station (in the air) for eight hours, and then it was two hours back to base. Twelve hours in all."

Larry's plane actually was designed for anti-submarine warfare, and his crew spent considerable time tracking Russian submarines in the central and southern Pacific. Sometimes those subs sailed courses that were uncomfortably close to American bases. Once, just to let the Russians know they were being observed, Larry's plane dropped a small charge that pricked the skin of a Russian sub's conning tower. "It was about the size of a hand grenade," he chuckles. "We could have started World War III."

His military service fueled a fondness for California, and following discharge he settled there. Not one to let time slide by, he began building a remarkable career. To no one's surprise that career has centered around science and flight, first at Fairchild Semiconductor, next at Lockheed Missiles & Space Corporation and then with Lockheed Martin Space Systems Company.

Remember my assertion that America is safer and smarter thanks to Larry? "I worked as an electronics technician, a test engineer, product engineer and product line manager." In those positions he strengthened America's space presence and defense capabilities. Larry has worked on such programs as the Hubble Space Telescope, solar arrays for the International Space Station, the Airborne Laser and Missile Defense.

And, yes, he has continued flying. He possesses both private and commercial pilot licenses and teaches both pilot training and ground school.

His former teacher Harryet Snyder once observed, "Larry is a classic example of a young man who pulled himself up by his bootstraps. Nothing was handed to him."

Larry's passion for flying has continued unabated. In 1997 he was serving as president of the San Jose chapter of the Experimental Aircraft Association. In 2009 he was rebuilding an airplane – refurbishing and cleaning parts in his garage. "It's a 1949 Aeronca 7EC," Larry says. "It's a two-seater. 100 horsepower. An old trainer. It's what I learned to fly on years ago."

In 1998 I found myself doing something I'd never imagined – going back to school at age 53. My employer's CEO was a graduate of Stanford, and he offered me the opportunity to do the Executive Program at the university's Graduate School of Business in Palo Alto. I was flattered but accepting the invitation meant that I was going to miss our class's 35-year reunion. I hated that prospect. But given the intensity of the Stanford program, I knew I couldn't make it back to Shelby. Classes were held all morning every morning, Monday through Friday. Tons of reading were required. Afternoon lectures consumed more time. Presentations assigned one day were to be given the next. Study groups met Sunday through

Thursday nights. Stanford discouraged travel and visits by family and friends except during a mid-program three-day break.

Several friends including SHS classmates were living in the Bay Area. One was Larry Reed. Before leaving for Stanford I got in touch and asked if we could get together. His response was quick and enthusiastic.

Early one July Saturday morning, I rented a car and drove south to Larry's home on Alan Avenue in San Jose. Our reunion was delightful – and accented by the tumult attendant daughter Annika and wife Lorraine consumed with wrapping up last-day details for Annika's prom that night. Still, Lorraine made time to whip up a tasty lunch and take pictures of Larry and me.

Larry & Lorraine Reed

We spent all day catching up. When Larry and Lorraine wed in 1989, it was the second marriage for each. Their union produced an immediate brood of five. Lorraine's Annika and Andrew joined Larry's Laura, Robert and Richard. Laura, while living with her mother in Nevada, finished first in the state 400-meter dash finals. "She won a partial athletic scholarship to the University of Nevada," Larry related proudly.

Tragedy also had struck – and not for the last time. "My brother Wayne died in 1996 in Shelby. He was only 54. It was a military funeral and included an Ohio Air National Guard flyover. Several of our classmates attended."

Just weeks before Wayne's death Larry had his own health emergency. A foot of his colon needed to be removed. "Redundant. I was born with too much colon, and it was pressuring other organs. Luckily I've not had cancer – yet."

Larry has, however, had to contend with serious heart ailments and follows a healthy regimen.

His son Richard also had a near-death experience that shook – and angered – Larry and his family. It happened in August of 1997. "Richard was shot in a road rage incident. It took months but the perpetrator was finally arrested" – in late June of 1998, just weeks before Larry and I reunited.

Our reunion ended too quickly, but we have stayed in touch, exchanging emails and occasionally talking by phone. Unfortunately tragedy remained Larry's companion. In 2001 cancer claimed Donald, Larry's oldest brother who also was living in California. "My brothers dying in the last four years has been a little too much," Larry told me after the funeral. "I'm the last brother."

Still, Larry kept moving forward determinedly, and his progress included time in classrooms. "I have only four more classes to go to finish a degree," he told me in 2001. "I will finally, after all these years have a BS in professional aeronautics from Embry-Riddle Aeronautical University." The school has campuses in both Arizona and Florida. "Lockheed is paying for it, so I guess they will be happy too." Larry smiled and shrugged. "I have been a non-degreed engineer for a lot of years, but I will be official now."

He is. He is also another of those classmates who causes chests to swell with pride.

CHAPTER 19

THE FIRST HIPPIE – AND HIS BRIDE

Malcolm McKinney was the first hippie I knew. June Went was his mate. They were together at Shelby High, at Ohio University, on the road in Europe and in a primitive cabin in New Hampshire. Among members of the class of '63 they lived the most unconventional lives – and ones with unexpected twists. Two of those twists produced a note of sadness for me at our 25-year reunion in 1988 and a bigger note of surprise.

Back in high school I never would have guessed that Malcolm and June would embark on the kind of road they traveled. At SHS they were as conventional, or seemingly so, as local retail store clerks, machine shop lathe operators, or dairy farmers – of which there were small legions in semi-industrial, semi-rural Shelby.

Malcolm played in the marching band for four years, was on the *Whippet Tales* school newspaper staff for four years, was a member of student council for three years, ran track for one year, was my co-sports editor of the *Scarlet S* yearbook, worked the senior class concession stand selling candy, and went with me to Buckeye Boys State. Pretty conventional stuff. Malcolm was a brain, and his *Scarlet S* photo caption was an attempt to say so in a funny way: "He thinks too much; such men are dangerous." Given that Malcolm was the only member of our class to work four years on the school paper and that he decided to enroll at Ohio University which has a first-rate journalism program (E.W. Scripps School), I figured Malcolm's career would be spent in a newsroom, perhaps writing thoughtful editorials.

Malcolm had black hair, stood about six feet tall and had a tremendous facility for making people smile. He didn't have to work at it. Generally, he didn't say a lot but, when he saw you, his face softened into a wonderfully wide and kind smile. It was pretty darned impossible not to like Malcolm.

June was all bubbles and bounce, and I liked her a lot, too. Her *Scarlet S* caption was simple and accurate and it read: "Boundless energy and enthusiasm." Amen. Her walking was more like skipping. She was a member of the Girls Athletic Association and the marching band for four years each and the Pep Club for three years. She, too, worked on the *Whippet Tales* and *Scarlet S* staffs.

Slender, about five feet six with auburn hair, June always looked very sharp. She had a walk-in closet full of clothes and, during a school year, you didn't see her in the same outfit very often.

June Went – 1945-1995

She was always ready for fun. Once, June and I and Mimi Grove concocted a terrific plot to honor one of our favorite teachers, Wayne Potts. He had been our Spanish teacher for two years, and Mr. Potts was very cool, a word he used often and which always got laughs because it was obvious that whenever he used it he was poking fun at himself. Plus as I mentioned in an earlier chapter – *The prankster and the professor* – he showed remarkable restraint with mischievous students. Mr. Potts was terrific.

So anyway, one day the three of us went to Principal J.E. McCullough's office and persuaded him to tell us Mr. Potts's birthday and to let us have a surprise party for him. We wanted to decorate his classroom, have music and refreshments. The works. As our planning proceeded, June, Mimi and I began referring to it as our "Viva el Senor Potts Party."

Keeping this party a surprise for Mr. Potts wasn't easy. There were some 20 teenagers in that class. If you think only sieves and rusting sprinkling buckets leak, ask 20 teenagers to keep a secret. Plus we had to sneak everything into the school, hide it, and then get it all into Mr. Potts's classroom during a lunch hour and then work like mad to get it decorated and set up before his first afternoon class, which was us.

Well, incredibly, Mr. Potts didn't get wind of it. Either that or he masterfully feigned surprise when he entered the room. It all went terrifically, and we all cheered when Mr. Potts deemed it "cool." And the look on June's face? Well, her eyes were positively glittering.

June's wit could be described as extra dry. She once wryly articulated her life's goal: "End the arms race and floss." Of her relationship with her loving mom, she once remarked, "We incite each other by phone."

During our junior year at SHS, Malcolm and I were among four boys (the others were Rick Landis and Jeff Bricker) who were chosen to attend the American Legion-sponsored Buckeye Boys State for 10 days. Boys State was an annual summer program that taught the workings of government at all levels. At the time, Ohio University was hosting the event. While there we were quartered in Gamertsfelder Hall, Gam for short. We also learned that Gam – which during the school year housed some 400 guys – had a reputation for having the best intramural athletic teams, the best men's vocal group and the most active social program, which included Saturday morning "mixers" with women's halls and sororities and which were immensely popular with Gam men not hung over from Friday night boozing.

Well, after the experience at Boys State, Malcolm and Rick and I all chose to attend OU and to live in Gam. I don't recall seeing a whole lot of Malcolm our first two years at Gam. I was living sports as Gam's athletic director and player-coach of its football and softball teams (I surprised myself by hitting four homeruns in our first two games). I also was on the Gam senate. Mal was all but living with June.

But one day toward the end of our sophomore year Malcolm approached me. "You living in Gam again next year?"

"Sure."

"Going to room alone?" Malcolm asked.

"I don't know. I haven't thought much about it."

"Want to room together?"

Malcolm's question was as big a surprise for me as the birthday party had been for Mr. Potts. I never saw it coming. But my reaction was measured. "Mmm, I don't know. I suppose so."

"You can think it over," said Malcolm. "I just thought we might get along well."

"All right," I said. "Why not? Let's do it."

"You sure?" I think Malcolm was equally surprised by my fast decision.

"Like I said, why not?" The prospect of rooming with Malcolm seemed okay, but I was more than a little surprised by his proposal. If anything, I would have guessed that he and June would be shacking up together in an off-campus apartment.

During that summer of 1965 Malcolm and I both worked in Shelby in factories, but different ones, and we didn't see each other. The following September when I checked into Gam, boy did I get a surprise. When I arrived, Malcolm already was in the room we were to share, and what I saw and heard was something I never expected. Nor did it occur to me – even for an instant – that I was looking at and listening to a harbinger of Malcolm's life for the next 20 or so years.

The door was open and I stepped inside tentatively. Had there been a mix-up? Was someone besides Malcolm occupying the room I had selected?

"Hi Mike," I heard Malcolm say cheerily from the far end of the room.

I looked to my right. "Hello Malcolm," I said, and I'm sure my voice conveyed a trace of instant skepticism.

"Surprised?"

"Yeah."

"It won't be a problem," said Malcolm. "I promise you. When you don't want the music on loud, I'll turn it down. And when you don't want me to play, I won't."

"Okay, I think I can handle that."

Folk music was playing on a stereo. Malcolm was semi-reclining on his bed and playing a guitar and singing along with the record. He was wearing a flowery shirt and sandals and his dark hair was hanging to his shoulders.

"You've become a hippie." A statement of the obvious.

"I guess so." Malcolm smiled that wide, enormously friendly smile.

"You guess?"

"Does it bother you?"

"No." And I meant it. More than anything, I was curious. I had heard about hippies but hadn't seen any in the flesh, most definitely not in semi-rural Shelby which few would mistake for Haight-Asbury. Malcolm McKinney had become a member of OU's first hippie class which was a small one. And as it happened, he was perfectly cut out to be a member in good standing of early hippiedom. He was gentle, had learned to love nature, liked music and was determined to look the role.

As things turned out, his hippieness caused us a problem only once, and it was during that autumn of 1965.

"I'm going to Shelby on Friday," I told Malcolm, "to see the Shelby-Bucyrus game." Once again, perennially strong Shelby was contending for the Northern Ohio League football title. The matchup with Bucyrus likely would determine the champion.

"When are you leaving?" he asked.

"Right after lunch on Friday."

"You riding with Joel?" Malcolm asked. As I mentioned in the chapter titled *The bacon-saver's last reunion*, Joel Stentz was the only one of the nine of us who went to OU from the SHS class of '63 to have a car on campus. Joel used to provide rides to Shelby in exchange for gas money. In those days before interstates were completed, driving from Athens to Shelby took close to four hours.

"No," I said, "he's not going back this weekend."

"How are you going?"

"Thumbing." Hitchhiking in those years was generally safe, especially for students who carried signs such as *Student to Shelby* or *Student to OU*. Heck, a year earlier, I had thumbed home for the funeral of my maternal grandma. Some 150 miles. Got there in time. No problem.

"Mind if I go along with you?" Malcolm asked.

"Not at all...as long as you promise to wear shoes and get a haircut."

"What?!" cried Malcolm in a rare show of emotion.

"You heard me. I don't want people passing us by because you're a hippie." You may have forgotten but much of adult America viewed hippies not as gentle flower children but as serious threats to America's social fabric, whatever the hell they thought that was.

"Oh, come on, Mike," Malcolm pleaded. "If you carry the sign, they'll stop."

"Uh, uh." I was not giving in on this because I did not want to arrive too late to see the game. "And you'll have to tuck in your shirt."

I still smile when I think about this. On Friday after lunch, Malcolm and I each hefted a suitcase and started walking across campus to Court Street and then to the north end of Court to begin thumbing. Malcolm was sheepish. He had compromised himself and he wasn't happy about it. He was wearing shoes and his shirt was tucked in. But as to the haircut, I think he must have had June trim it lightly so he could honestly say it had been cut. It was still long, but I decided not to argue the point. Anyway, I carried the sign and had him stand behind me along roadsides. Everything worked out well, and I made the game on time. SHS won big.

I have two undimmed college memories of June. One night I was in a booth in my favorite Athens haunt, The Union Bar & Grill. Joel Forrester, Andy Blank (my closest college friend who was to die from cancer just nine months after we graduated) and I were surrounding a pitcher of beer. June and a girlfriend wandered in and squeezed into the booth with us. I don't know where Malcolm was, but the five of us had a rollicking time. If Malcolm and June hadn't been such a well-established item, I might have asked June for a date before she ever got out of the booth. Her joie de vivre was magnetic.

The other college memory goes back further to April of 1964 when General Douglas MacArthur died. Joel Stentz was driving some of us back to Athens after a break in Shelby. It was late and dark and June and I were in the back seat. We just sat there peacefully, leaning against each other in the blackness of hilly, rural Ohio while the radio announcer spent hours recounting MacArthur's life.

Malcolm and June were married on the OU campus in Galbreath Chapel and after graduation wound up in a cabin in the woods of New Hampshire. The cabin had neither electricity nor running water. Malcolm and June and Mal's younger brother Todd took to composing and performing folk, country and spiritual music. Once they recorded an album called *McKinney.* (In 2006, Todd released a fine album titled *Songs From Prospect Mountain.*) At this point, Malcolm and Todd looked like nothing so much as early American rustics. Long, unkempt hair, full beards and mustaches, plaid shirts. They also looked at peace with themselves.

In 1973 Malcolm and June journeyed to Europe in true McKinney style. They thumbed from Pittsfield, New Hampshire to Logan Airport in Boston. In Europe they traveled entirely by train and their experienced and talented thumbs. They started in Amsterdam, and in Barcelona they put on an impromptu concert in the city's main plaza. In Lisbon they played in subways, plazas and at universities. June played the autoharp and Malcolm guitar, and they both sang. Decades later in Lisbon, Lynne and I spent an afternoon lazing in the Plaza Rossio while an alternative rock band put on an impromptu concert. Very nice. Sitting there, it was easy to picture June and Malcolm doing the same thing 30 years earlier.

Their New Hampshire idyll lasted until 1979 when they moved to near Nashville where their life began conforming to convention. Oh, they still lived primitively in a rural cabin, and Malcolm still was writing and producing music, but June now took to working in the Vanderbilt University library. They were at our 20-year reunion in 1983, and all seemed well.

Five years later on July 16, 1988, amidst the chitchat during the morning set-up session for our 25-year reunion, I learned that Malcolm and June had divorced. I was surprised and hurt but more hurt than surprised. But that's the way I usually react when two people that I know and like split.

Oh, logically, I know that it may be for the best, but I still regret that they couldn't make it work. I learned that June had remarried in Nashville. But Malcolm had sprung the biggest surprise. Not only had Malcolm and June been just one of three pairs of our '63 classmates to marry, but Malcolm had remarried – and his new bride, Cheryl, was another girl from the class of '63.

I could only shake my head. Another reunion and more large surprises. To my great pleasure, Malcolm and June and Cheryl were at the reunion that night. I chatted briefly with Malcolm and June, and when I said something to June about her days with Mal and thought it might have embarrassed her, she was quick to be reassuring.

"Don't think a thing about it," June said. "Mal and I are friends."

"That's good. I'd like to talk with you for a while tonight."

"And I want to learn all about you."

I have another fond memory of June from that reunion, and this is one I can look at. I spent a half hour or so wandering around the K of C Hall with my camera and one shot caught June with John Crum. John is in his wheelchair and talking, and June is sitting and listening with a raptness that borders on adulation. Nice picture.

1993

Five years later the first hippie didn't make our 30-year reunion. His first bride did. The difference went far deeper.

A few weeks before the 1993 reunion, Malcolm was in Shelby visiting his dad who was ill. He left word that, after returning home to Florida, he would not be able to get back to Shelby for the reunion. Malcolm was still married to Cheryl – as he is to this day.

And then there was June.

After the 1988 reunion, June and I had corresponded and we promised ourselves significant one-on-one time with each other in '93. We kept that promise and I'm glad we did.

Our first opportunity came the Friday night of our set-up and decorating session. It was a gorgeous evening, sunny, about 80 degrees, low humidity. About 7 p.m., I was arriving at the K of C Hall. As I drove up the winding entrance road, another car was following mine. I parked, got out and waited to see who would pull in behind me. The other car parked and out stepped June. Quickly, we greeted each other with big smiles and no-holds-barred hugs. Immediately, I couldn't help noticing how much her appearance had changed. It was startling. Five years before, her hair had been brownish and pony-tailed. That night it was still long but now it waved up and out and in all directions. When June tossed her hair, it looked like it might fly away. All the brown was gone now and it was iron gray. All in all, quite becoming. Her face had grown noticeably lined, but her eyes still radiated expectancy and seemed to be saying, "I can hardly wait to see what comes next so I hope it comes fast." Her body still carried no extra weight. Her walk still had the old high school bounce. We were standing beside her car. A few minutes later, a station wagon pulled along side. David Studer got out.

From maybe 25 feet away, I said, "Hi, David. Good to see you again." We had seen each other just a few weeks before at the final planning committee meeting and had had a nice visit after it broke up.

Then June whispered to me, "We used to date."

My eyes blinked in surprise. Then I got my wits back. To June I said, "And that's the way you're going to greet someone you used to date?" I took June by her shoulders and began shepherding her toward David. They hugged politely and began chatting. Meanwhile, more than a few thoughts were racing through my mind. Such as: *June and David dated? I never knew David dated anyone in high school.* (He has never married.) *He was so shy. June was anything but. When was June NOT dating Malcolm? Whatever brought June and David together?* Later that evening I got to thinking more about David. Another surprise had been his choice of career – administration in a state prison. That too seemed at odds with his personality. I've a feeling he did his job competently and noiselessly. He was and remains unfailingly gracious, and he still corresponds with me from his home in California.

A couple hours later, after the set-up session, June wound up sitting across from me at our impromptu Pizza Hut party. About 15 of us were jammed elbow to elbow around small tables we had pulled together. Amidst the revelry was some serious conversation, but the best and most meaningful was still a day away. As the pizza party was winding down, I said to June, "Do you want to have breakfast together tomorrow? We don't want to waste any time."

"You mean just the two of us?" She seemed surprised, but more than that there seemed in her voice a hint of alarm. Puzzling.

I looked around at our group. "I mean anyone who wants to join us."

Well, as it turned out, between those planning to play golf, those wanting to sleep in, run errands and visit family, breakfast was June, me and Elaine Lybarger. I picked both of them up and we went to the Coffee Shop, one of only a handful of establishments on Main Street not to change names or disappear entirely since our teen years. (Years later it did close.) We lingered for a good two hours before leaving. Then I dropped off Elaine and continued on to June's mom's house.

She asked me to come in and see her mom. I was glad to. Goldie Went was 81 and white haired but you still could see where June got her bounce. After talking awhile, Goldie wanted me to see her backyard flower garden that was circular and something to be proud of. June soon followed us out back. She had been going through a box of memorabilia and had found a small, silver, heart-shaped locket. Inside were tiny black and white circa 6th grade photos of classmates Jim Henkel and Jerry Russell. Jim, as you might recall from earlier reading, was the one who had shanghaied me into first going to a class reunion. Jerry was our first classmate to die. More reminiscing followed.

As noon was approaching, June and I walked outside to the driveway and leaned against my car. We chatted idly for a few minutes. Then, in a quiet, reflective tone, words came pouring out. "I really hurt Malcolm. When I fell in love with John, I told Malcolm I wanted a divorce. He was so hurt, so upset. He even said, 'Go ahead and have an affair, but it doesn't make sense to end our relationship.' I said, 'I couldn't do that. I couldn't walk around with John and still be married to you. It wouldn't be fair to you or me.'"

After 18 years of marriage June and Malcolm had divorced, and June had married John Drury in 1986. June and John were divorced in May of 1992. June said she was glad for her years with John and credited him with awakening her politically.

As we continued chatting in the late morning sun, June was saying how very much she had come to value our reunions. That was a common enough sentiment, but she was expressing it with uncommon poignancy.

She was talking about how much she missed those who were gone and how much she already missed those she might never see again.

Beyond her words, my antenna sensed something else. Very gently, I said, "Just what are we talking about here?"

"I've had cancer."

"Oh."

"Twice."

"When?"

"The first time was back in '79. I had a mastectomy. I had a reconstruction in '85. Then there was a recurrence in '91. They think they got that with radiation. I haven't told Mom about that."

I couldn't help wondering whether the breast reconstruction in 1985 and her second bout with cancer were linked to her divorces from Malcolm and John. Did the reconstruction cause her to feel the need to have someone new, someone besides Malcolm, in love with her? Did the second cancer attack drive John away? I didn't ask.

We parted with a hug and then a few hours later, about 4:30 p.m., June showed up at Old SHS for a group tour we had planned. Again, she was all bubbles and bounce. "I feel like shouting," she exclaimed.

"Why not?" I said. "And how about sliding down the banister railings?"

"That, too."

Our group of 20 or so classmates plus some spouses first visited the old auditorium. It and the stage seemed so much smaller. I stood there, thinking back to when I had emceed assemblies while a senior. Back then, it all seemed so grand. As our group went moving through the school, floor by floor, hallway by hallway, we stuck our noses in classrooms and offices throughout the old three-story, L-shaped building. We were nearing the end of our tour of the first floor. The group was preparing to step inside what had been the vocational agriculture room but now was the middle school wrestling room. Suddenly, June moved to face me and said, "Here." And she slipped something into my hand.

I looked down. It was an old Christmas card with a larger piece of white bond paper sticking out. "What's this?"

As I was opening the card and unfolding the bond paper – which I have in my hand as I write this – the group gathered around and began to laugh. They weren't sure what they were looking at but it looked like fun was about to happen. The bond paper shows that, in 1965, two years after graduating from SHS, I had given June a homemade *Mike Johnson Good Gal Award* for "long-time friendliness and congeniality and in special recognition for sending me Christmas cards for the past two years when I, through my male forgetfulness, have neglected to send you one in return. This, I assure you, will be remedied next year."

True to my word, at Christmas of 1966, I had sent June the card she had just handed me. Inside, I had written: "Last year you were the recipient of my 'good gal' award for persevering in sending me a Christmas card every year, even though I was lax in reciprocating. This year, as a result of sending this card to you without your sending me one first, I must be completely exonerated from all past guilt. So it is with a clear conscience and a joyous heart that I extend to you a very happy Christmas."

Looking at the paper and card, I was touched. "Do you want me to keep this?"

"It doesn't matter," June said.

"Do you want it back?"

"It really doesn't matter."

The group around us was smiling, listening in silence to this exchange.

"Well, if I keep it," I said, "it will go in my memorabilia box."

"And if I keep it, it will go back in mine."

I kept it.

At the Friday night Pizza Hut party June had joked to the group, "I know I asked for more time together, but by Sunday afternoon, I'll probably be sick of you guys."

As the Sunday afternoon picnic was drawing to a close, June remarked that she was feeling tired. As farewells were being said, we hugged and I reminded her of what she had said on Friday night. Her reply: "Present company excepted."

As we parted, I was hoping there would be a next time for us.

Later, after the reunion, I closed a letter to June – I'm now holding it. Included is a paragraph that reads: *June, I was stunned to learn about your bouts with cancer. Stunned but not sorry. Actually I'm glad I learned. I realize my knowing doesn't change the past, but in looking ahead it will make me feel closer to you. Truth be told, I wish I had known sooner; not that it would have changed anything – except that it would have assured you another letter or two. Such a deal.*

I closed the letter by telling her that several of us were going to talk about organizing a class 50th birthday party in 1995.

1995

The news item was brief, just a single paragraph. It had appeared in the *Shelby Daily Globe*, and my mom had clipped and mailed it to me. I received it on Thursday, April 13, 1995, the day before Good Friday.

Reading that news item right away caused me to experience a sense of hollowness and dread. The paragraph said that June Went was "seriously ill" in Nashville, Tennessee and that she would like to hear from friends. That's all it said, but I was afraid I knew what it really meant.

That evening, I showed the news item to my wife and said I knew I had to phone June but that it wouldn't be easy.

After dinner that night, I used a step stool to reach a high shelf and pulled off my copy of the 1963 *Scarlet S.* Here is what June had written over her photo: *Mike – your personality is one I will never forget. No matter how much you change, I'll always recall now! We've really had riots, especially our viva el senor Potts party!! You're a great guy. Don't tear up OU too badly. Sincerely, June*

That had been 32 short years ago.

A couple hours later, I sat down at the desk in our upstairs den and picked up the phone. I sucked in a breath and pushed the buttons for June's number. I wasn't at all sure what I was going to say, and that made me feel awkward. I thought how easy it would be not to call. Her phone rang and rang again and then an answering machine clicked on. It was June's voice saying she couldn't get to the phone. But this was no ordinary recorded message. In words and tone, it was poignant. It encouraged the caller to leave a message, said how much it would be appreciated and said how welcome would be the sound of the caller's voice. To me, that message confirmed my worst thoughts.

So I left a message which said I would try again the next day, Good Friday. After hanging up, I thought June might not be able to take calls at all, so I decided to write a note which would tell her how much I had valued her friendship for the last 35 years. I wanted to write the note on special stationery, so I used a pre-folded Ohio University note card with a pen and ink drawing of Galbreath Chapel. That's where June and Malcolm had been married back in 1967.

But that thought occurred to me only after I had written the note and sealed the matching envelope. Then I had second thoughts. I began to wonder whether receiving the Galbreath Chapel card might upset or sadden June. I put it aside and then later decided to take that chance and mailed it the next morning.

Good Friday was a holiday for me so I was at home. About two o'clock in the afternoon, I took another deep breath and phoned June again. She answered on the first ring. The sound of her voice jolted me. It was just a whisper. A sickly whisper. My stomach tightened. I breathed in slightly and then I told June who it was and that I had phoned last night. She said she had gotten the message.

I still wasn't quite sure what to say, so I just spoke the thought that was running through my mind. "I assume there are times you just don't feel up to answering the phone."

"Or can't," June whispered. "I'm on oxygen all the time."

"My mom sent me the *Daily Globe* item on you. I got it yesterday and knew I had to call. I will tell you, June, it wasn't an easy call for me to make. I had to brace myself. I still feel kind of awkward."

"I understand, but I'm glad you did. My mom put that item in the *Globe*." Her voice was starting to become stronger, gradually sounding more like the June of old.

"You know, June, my guess is that lots of your friends want to call but just can't bring themselves to do it. Some of them may choose to write, but some won't do that because they just will find it too awkward. But that doesn't mean they don't care...that they aren't thinking of you."

"I know. I understand. But I feel their presence anyway. I really do. They seem so close. Do you know what I mean?"

"Yes, I think I do." By now, I was feeling more comfortable. It helped that June's voice seemed almost normal now and that she was grateful to be talking with me.

"June, when did you know something was wrong?"

"Last November," she said without any hesitation. "But I waited till December to see my doctor. You know, I've been through this twice before. It's hard, Mike." There was a noticeable catch in her voice. "My doctor told me the cancer was back and that it had spread to my lungs and lymph nodes and God knows where else."

I chuckled despite myself.

"I tried some experimental treatment," June went on, "but that didn't work. I did not want to do chemo again, so I decided to just let it run its course this time."

"I see..."

"Then I went up to Shelby. I saw Dave Studer (at this, her tone brightened) and I told Mom. It was hard on her."

An understatement, I'm sure. June's mom, Goldie, not only had lost her husband but also her only other child, June's older sister, Judie, who also fell to cancer. To have both her daughters precede her in death had to be excruciating. Now, Goldie would be alone. That visit to Shelby also had to be darned hard on June herself.

She continued speaking. "Malcolm came up to Nashville to visit me. Did you know that?"

"No. That was very nice."

"Yes, it was so sweet. And Suzon (Mimi Grove, a classmate I've mentioned several times) is providing support for Mom. And so is Karen (another classmate, now deceased). She is phoning me each week."

"Like I said, June, lots of people care about you."

She began to speak and again there was a catch in her voice. She choked it back. "I'm making my exit."

I felt a thickness in my own throat. "June, I want to tell you something. Last night I wrote you a note on OU stationery. It has a drawing of Galbreath Chapel. I thought it might upset you, but now I think I can stop worrying about that."

"Yes, you can. That's okay. No problem."

I decided to ask a question that had been going through my mind since I received the news item. "June," I said gently, "do you know how much time you have left?"

"No. I haven't asked yet. But not too long. I had to quit work two weeks ago. I quit driving about ten days ago. I'm on oxygen all the time.

I'm not seeing the doctor anymore. A hospice nurse comes to see me each day. So do friends. The hospice care is free. That's a big relief. When we figure it's down to the last few weeks, the hospice nurse will be here all the time. Maybe I should talk to her about that. I'm getting more tired every day."

"Yes…"

"I have an OU classmate in California. Melina Miller. She was my bridesmaid. When it gets down to the last couple weeks, she wants to come and stay with me. Isn't that sweet?"

"Yes, but not surprising."

"I know one thing," she said. There was a trace of the familiar feistiness working its way back into her voice now. "I'm not going to have a funeral or any of that crap." I laughed. "I'm donating my body to an organ bank."

I now spoke another thought that had been running through my mind for the last few minutes. "June, I think this call might have been better for me than you. I really mean that."

"I don't know about that."

"I do. You know, June, you'll always be in my thoughts."

"I hope so. Listen, Mike Johnson, when you are eighty years old and have Alzheimer's and you have a lucid moment, I want you to think about me."

"If I make it to eighty, you can count on that. June, there's another thought I want you to keep with you. I love you. I want you to know that."

"I know, Mike. I love you, too."

We both knew we weren't talking about being madly in love but about the love that can grow from common bonds, from a long and rich friendship. It did us both good to put that into words.

"Is there anything I can do?"

"Yes," June said immediately. "You can spread the word about me. I would appreciate that."

"Consider it done."

"And tell people not to send me flowers. I don't want a bunch of flowers sitting around. You remember the library in Shelby?"

"Marvin Memorial Library."

"Right. Tell people I would like it if they want to do something to give money or books to the library. Or they could make a gift to a hospice. The one here in Nashville or anywhere."

"I'll do that."

"Thanks, Mike. Thanks a lot. I'm so glad you called."

By now, after 20 minutes of talking, June was becoming weary. Her voice was growing weaker. Given my memories of June's seemingly boundless energy, that was hard to accept.

"Me, too, June. I'm very glad I made this call."

"Well, you take care of yourself."

"I will."

"Bye, Mike."

"Goodbye, June."

After hanging up, I didn't hesitate. Immediately, I picked up our SHS class directory and placed phone calls to the homes of some classmates I felt would want to know about our conversation, people I thought wouldn't hear about it from June or the classmates who already were in touch with her. Pat Papenbrock, an experienced hospice nurse herself. Elaine Lybarger and Denny Kidwell who were helping plan our class 50th birthday party for July 29-30. (June's 50th birthday would be June 15.) Rick Landis, Chris Straw, Randy Smith, Anne Lafferty Stock, Bill Anspach, Ralph Thauvette, Jim Henkel and others. One right after another. I reached only Rick and Randy. But most of the others had answering machines, so I left messages briefly summarizing what I had learned from June.

The next Monday morning, driving to work, I heard a radio ad for *Vermont Teddy Bears*. Teddy bears for all occasions, happy and sad. I pulled a note pad from my briefcase and wrote down the 800 number. That night I asked Lynne how she thought June might react to receiving a gift that seemed sort of silly and stupid. Especially with so little time left. Especially considering what June had said about flowers and giving to the library and hospices.

"I think she'll love it," said Lynne. So the next day I called the 800 number and asked that a simple, small teddy bear be sent to Nashville. I dictated this note to accompany the bear: *Dear June. Somehow – I'm not sure why – this seemed like an appropriate gift. You will be in my memories always – even when I'm 80 and doddering. With much love. Mike J.*

A few days later I received a phone call from classmate Elaine Lybarger. As things would have it, Elaine, a teacher, was to be taking nine students to a computer competition in Nashville in early May. She was going to try to visit June. I encouraged her to do so.

On May 10 Elaine wrote me this in a letter: *Called June on Thursday, May 4 around noon and she had just taken her medication and would not be up to visiting. Said between 10 a.m. and noon is her best time. So called Friday, May 5 and she said to come on out around 10:30. Got balloons saying 'You're special" across the street from the hotel and took a taxi to her house. Told the driver to come back for me in an hour, but she was only up to about 30 minutes of visiting. She wanted me to see her nice red brick house and pretty flowers. The hospice nurse visited with me until the taxi came.*

She had your teddy bear beside her in bed and hugged him when she told me about him and how much she enjoyed it.

She was able to laugh when I came in with the balloons as she said I have a place to tie them as she pointed to one of the posts on her four poster bed. She is only able to eat brown rice now. She wants me to visit her mother and only tell her the 'good things' about our visit. She talked so fondly of her work at the library and the fun we had in band. She laughed again when we decided you and Ralph (Thauvette) will still be planning 'reunions' in heaven! She said she knew it was hard for me to come but it meant so much to her. Our parting words were that she wanted to say hi to everyone and that she will be with us in spirit at our birthday events in July. I lost it some then, and then she hugged and kissed me and squeezed my hand. What a wonderful, brave lady.

On June 1 when I got home from work, there was a message from Anne Lafferty Stock on my answering machine. It told me that June had died at 9:00 that morning.

A day or so later I got a phone call from Elaine Lybarger. She and Ralph Thauvette were making a gift on behalf of our class to Marvin Memorial Library in June's name. The gift would be used for acquiring children's books.

June Went was a definition of life. For as long as I knew June, I saw in her an unusual combination of physical and intellectual energy. I and many others considered it a privilege to count ourselves among her army of friends.   She had our affection, respect and loyalty to the end.

When classmates gathered for our 50th birthday party, we raised our glasses to June.

1997

In March of 1997 my schedule included a business trip to Florida, specifically West Palm Beach. So I got out a map of Florida and my class address book to see if any SHS '63ers lived in the vicinity. I saw that Deerfield Beach was near by, perhaps only 25 miles south of West Palm. Deerfield was where Malcolm and Cheryl were living.

So just a few days before the trip, I phoned them. I got an answering machine and left a detailed message. At the end, I said I would phone again if I didn't hear back. But the next night, Malcolm called.

He was up for getting together, but we quickly realized that our choices would be limited. My business obligations would include dinners, and Malcolm had things going, too. We finally pinned down as a good time about 6:00 to 8:00 p.m. on a Thursday. I told Mal I would rent a car and drive down to Deerfield. But he said it would be easier all around if he drove up to the old Breakers Hotel where we were staying. I say we because my wife Lynne would be joining me on this trip.

On that Thursday, I was sitting in the Breakers lobby, reading *Newsweek* and watching for Malcolm. Without warning, I heard, "Mike." I looked up and Mal was standing in front of me. Quickly I stood and we shook hands warmly. "Mal," I said, "good to see you."

"It's good to see you, Mike."

"I think this is the first time I've seen you since the '88 reunion," I said. "I recall we talked on the phone a few years ago. I think it was before the '93 reunion. I was at Lucy Myers's house, and I heard you were in Shelby because your dad had been ill. I picked up the phone and called."

"I remember," said Malcolm. His hair, still flowing to his collar and a little beyond, was graying, but he seemed to still have it all, unlike me. He also had grown pudgy.

Our conversation bounced around a lot. "Mal," I said, "I remember hearing that you didn't graduate in '67 from OU. I heard that in your last semester, you basically bagged it and quit going to classes."

"That's right. I decided that what we were studying just didn't seem relevant."

I smiled but said nothing.

"I know," said Malcolm, "that seems kind of silly now. But I did get my degree."

"Oh?"

"When my dad was ill, he said he really wanted me to graduate. I told him I would. So, I got OU and a school here to let me combine my credits and get my degree."

"Congratulations! I'm sure that made your dad happy."

"Thanks. It did make Dad feel good."

"You, too."

"Yes," he smiled, "me, too."

"What are you doing these days?"

"I'm doing post-production work for a local TV station. Editing stuff. I enjoy it."

Malcolm still is composing and singing and you can check out his work at www.mjmckinney.com.

"That's great. How's Cheryl?"

"She's fine. She said to say hi. She had a meeting tonight and couldn't make it here."

"I understand." Right about now, I was thinking about June and Malcolm. I decided to say something. "Mal, when June was dying, she told me you had gone up to Nashville to visit her. That was very nice. June really appreciated it."

Malcolm smiled softly and nodded.

CHAPTER 20

"I THINK HE'S DEAD."

A pitched baseball can be a thing of beauty – or a fearsome projectile.

Barry Mettler and I had known each other since 1954 when we began playing Little League baseball. In 1959 when we were 14, Barry and I were playing Pony League baseball. I was a first baseman and a pretty good hitter. Barry was a good hitter with a rocket launcher of an arm who played third base and pitched for one of the opposing teams.

One evening early that summer our two teams were playing each other on a very soppy field. Heavy spring rains already had forced postponement of several games. Barry was pitching and without a doubt he was the hardest throwing pitcher in the league. He was right-handed and sufficiently wild so that most opposing batters rarely dug in. They preferred to stay loose, ready to bail out as fast as a feckless bridegroom-to-be at the first serious thought of his onrushing responsibilities.

When Barry and I played together on all-star or tournament teams, he usually played third or shortstop when he wasn't pitching. After taking a few of his cannonball throws at first base, my right or glove hand took on the hue of raw meat. We liked and respected each other.

I batted left-handed, and I liked to crowd home plate. Doing so, I believed, gave me a better look at pitches and enabled my bat to cover the entire plate. Early in that 1959 game, I stepped into the soggy batter's box, feet just inside the chalk line closest to the plate. Barry's first pitch was his usual scorching fastball, and it sailed inside and low. I tried to dance out of harm's way, but my spikes stuck in the spongy ground. The ball caught me on my right calf and stung as though a dozen darts had arrived in a tight circle. It was a painful price to pay for a ticket to first base.

The next time I batted, I got set. Barry's pitching certainly had my respect, but it didn't frighten me. Not sure why. Barry rocked into his pitching motion. He threw, and the ball shot from his hand and flashed toward the plate. In the next split instant, I saw the ball zooming toward my head. Now, batters are instructed to avoid such pitches by falling straight down. They are warned not to back away from home plate because a ball sailing inside is likely to keep tailing toward a retreating batter. In that sliver of time, I remembered that lesson and tried to throw my feet out from under me. But the gummy ground wouldn't release its grip on my spikes. In the next nano second, I tried backing away and ducking. Well, Barry's fastball wasn't going to wait for me to run through several dozen options. The ball seemed to be following my head like a heat-seeking missile zeroing in on a doomed target. The ball hammered my head just above and behind my right ear. It caromed off my red plastic wrap-around protector – no helmets then – and went rolling across the infield grass onto the dirt base path, stopping at the feet of the second baseman.

I'm told I went down with a certain lack of grace. The blow did what I hadn't been able to do myself; it ripped my spikes from the mud and threw my feet into the air. Strangely, I didn't feel any pain, but I did feel consciousness slipping away. It was a strangely peaceful sensation. I saw myself in a small, high-ceilinged room. It was dimly lit and the walls were black. Faint light filtered through the lone window that was a tiny aperture near the ceiling. Then an unseen hand reached up and slowly pulled down an opaque shade. Then there was total blackness.

I was supine and spread-eagled. After maybe a couple minutes, not very long I was later told, my eyes leaked a few tears but I didn't move. Three men stood around and over me – my coach, the umpire and my dad who had come rushing onto the field. Someone said, "Mike, can you hear me?"

I could but my eyes still were closed, and the voice seemed distant.

Near by, I heard a player say, "I think he's dead."

Barry had advanced slowly from the pitcher's mound toward home plate, and I could hear him sobbing. I felt sorry for him but still was unable to speak. Later he told me that he thought he had killed me. In fact, what he had done was give me a concussion and a hell of a headache that lasted for days. And today? Some of my friends would tell you I haven't been the same since.

The next time we saw each other we smiled and shook hands.

After that, we faced each other numerous times, and there was a difference, at least one that Barry and I were aware of, even if others weren't. I didn't crowd the plate quite as much, and Barry eased off a bit on his fastball. Call it mutual wariness. In the title-deciding playoff game, the last time we would have to oppose each other, I doubled, stole third and scored the winning run in a 2-1 victory.

In high school Barry was a hell of an athlete and he was troubled. He was built like a V, with wide, thick shoulders and powerful arms tapering to a narrow waist that separated his torso from muscular legs with lots of speed and drive. But Barry's mind seemed as confused as his body was sure.

After school we frequently used to walk together toward our homes. Slowly, just kind of shuffling along. I'm not sure why but he began seeking my counsel. Most of the conversations centered around Barry's future.

"I'm thinking of dropping out," Barry would say.

"You've said that before."

"I know, but I'm still thinking about it." You could hear the ache of uncertainty in his voice.

"What would you do?"

"Join the Marines, maybe."

My dad had been a Marine and proud of his service. And like Barry he had been a superior athlete, undefeated as a Marine boxer. "I think you'd make a heck of a Marine, but I think you should stay in school."

"That's what you always say," he'd smile.

"Hell, you know I'm not going to tell you to drop out of school."

"I don't like it. I'm dumb."

"Bullshit."

"I'm flunking most everything."

"Not because you're dumb."

"I'm not sure I can cut it."

"You should still stick with it – and pass. Get some help."

"I don't know…"

"Barry, you can join the Marines anytime, but you should graduate first."

"I guess you're right."

"Will you?"

"I don't know."

"You really should, man."

"I don't know."

Barry dropped out before our class graduated. He did join the Marines, and we lost touch. We kept including him on our class roster and invited him to our reunions but he never came. As one of our reunions was approaching, I knew I really wanted to see him. It would be nice – and overdue – to thank him for his service. So I decided to put him on that list of 10 or so classmates I would write to and encourage to come.

When I phoned a woman friend to get some addresses, I said, "Does Barry Mettler still live at the address listed in the old reunion books?"

"No."

"Where is he?"

"That's a sad story, too, Mike." In our conversation that night, she already had told me about Joel Stentz, his stroke and subsequent deterioration.

What now? I sighed. "Tell me about it."

"Well, you know, I tried to find Barry's address, asked several people, but I was told he wasn't in touch with his family."

"Man, oh, man."

"I know. Barry is one of only two people we couldn't locate."

After joining the Marines, Barry went to Vietnam. That much we knew. He was injured, although I'm not sure where or how seriously. I've no doubt he made a helluva Marine.

Once, in the mid-1970s, I took our young daughter to a Cleveland Indians game and saw a man I thought might be Barry. Same build, same blond hair, hauntingly similar face except with a jagged scar under the left eye. I wasn't sure and I didn't do what I should have done – what I would do today – and that was get up, walk back up the dozen or so rows where the man was sitting and simply say, "Barry?"

CHAPTER 21

LITTLE MISS LAUGHING EYES

"Little Miss Laughing Eyes" suffered a major injustice during our senior year, at least as far as I was concerned. Anne Lafferty Stock was one of my favorite classmates.

She was extremely bright, candid, quick-witted, blond and pretty. Her blue eyes radiated depth and understanding. You could have spelled the word energy, a-n-n-e. We used to enjoy each other's company, and I would occasionally walk her home after *Scarlet S* editorial staff meetings. Since she lived on the east side and I on the west side and the meetings tended to run late, I remember a couple times having to dash across town to beat the 9:30 p.m. football players weeknight curfew. It's a good thing I was in shape because I had to pick 'em up and put 'em down – across the Big Four tracks, down and across the Black Fork Bridge, up Whitney hill, up and across the Overhead Bridge, then around a corner and into the Auburn Avenue homestretch. There was plenty of incentive to keep moving: miss a curfew, get caught or just reported, and Coach Wilkins suspended you for a game. That had happened to my good buddy Bill Anspach when he got home late one night and his dad, Jim, reported the violation to Coach – just as Coach had asked parents to do. I wasn't sure if my dad would do the same, but I didn't want to chance it.

I remember dating Anne only once but, ironically, at our 25-year reunion, she remembered the precise occasion and recalled it right away: "The Snowball" in December of our senior year. We had a good time. In a yearbook photo of us dancing, you can see her smiling, perhaps suppressing laughter, because we did plenty of that that night.

So about that injustice. It had to do with the nomination of candidates for the homecoming court. At SHS in those days, the seniors nominated five girls for homecoming queen, and the entire student body then chose a queen from those five with the others becoming court attendants.

As you can imagine, homecoming and the homecoming queen election was a very big deal. If you were a reasonably attractive senior girl with a reasonably pleasing personality and were reasonably popular, you probably harbored at least a faint hope of being nominated.

Anne Lafferty Stock

Also, as you can imagine, there was a lot of spirited discussion among the seniors as to who should be nominated. It didn't take long for most seniors to settle on their personal favorites, and that was certainly true of me. And to me there was no doubt that Anne Lafferty should have been one of the five. I knew at the time that if Anne were nominated I would then have a tougher decision to make in casting my ballot for queen. In particular, if both Anne and Pat Papenbrock were nominated, then I would be facing a really tough choice. In fact, I was thinking of not choosing, just writing both their names on the ballot for queen.

Well, to my consternation, I wasn't hearing Anne's name mentioned much as a possible nominee. Not in the locker room among the guys on the football team. Not in homeroom. Not in hallway bull sessions. It was hard to believe.

Yes, Anne was in the girls Pep Club all four years, but she was never a majorette, and she was a cheerleader just one year – although to this day I wonder why. I know it didn't occur to me to ask her during the reunion, but I'm getting ahead of myself. Let's back up to the early 1960s. Anne was one of the two most athletic girls in the class. Believe me, Anne could easily have out-jumped and out-tumbled the cheerleaders and out-twirled the majorettes. Oh, well, maybe she just didn't want or care enough about having the spotlight.

But, hell, there was no girl in the class who gave more of herself to the school or who cared more about it. She was in the Girls Athletic Association all four years and an officer every one of those years. And as I said, she was in the Pep Club all four years. She was on the school newspaper staff and was co-editor of the *Scarlet S* (and helped produce SHS's all-time handsomest yearbook which you can examine at the town's library). She represented SHS at Buckeye Girls State and worked the senior concession stand. She sold programs with me at SHS basketball games, and we really hustled those programs. I remember even trying to sell them to the opposing teams' cheerleaders.

I started talking up Anne's qualifications for homecoming court whenever I thought I could do so without pushing so hard as to make it embarrassing for her or me. But I must admit that my lobbying met with little enthusiasm. I don't remember anyone actually putting Anne down. It's just that whenever I would mention her name, someone would say, "Yeah, but how about" and then rattle off the names of other girls. Anne deserved to be on the court, I told people, and one day I told Anne the same thing.

"Thanks but I won't be nominated," she replied.

"How can you be so sure?"

"I just am."

"You'll be nominated if I can help it."

"Don't worry, it's no big deal."

"It is to me."

"I have too many enemies."

"What enemies? Why?" What had I been overlooking?

"I say what's on my mind," she explained calmly, "and some people don't like it. I'm just not as popular as Pat or Shirley or DeeDee or some of the other girls."

I'll concede that Anne didn't mince words – she still doesn't – but that's another reason I liked her. Now, before reading further, pause for a few moments and think back to your youth. Can you remember a schoolmate whose outspokenness might have cost him or her popularity?

"You know you've got my vote."

"Thanks, I appreciate it. I really do."

Five lovely girls were nominated, but Anne was right; she wasn't among them. The five honorees were Chick Benedict Muenster, DeeDee Milligan, Shirley Mitchell Burrer, Pat Papenbrock and Diane Schull. Pat was elected queen.

If Anne ever minded this slight, she never let on to me. What she did confide many years later was her deep disappointment in not being elected a cheerleader after her one year on that squad. Each year girls – there had been no male cheerleaders at the school for many years – had to try out and she did so. The tryouts were held in the SHS auditorium. Here's how the selection process worked. A panel including former cheerleaders, teachers and coaches observed a tryout and narrowed the roster of candidates to 10. Those 10 then had to try out again in the SHS auditorium before the entire student body. "We had to do two cheers," Anne recalled, "and then the student body voted on the top five. My last two years I came in sixth. I really wanted to be a cheerleader. I felt worse about that than the homecoming thing."

Anne wasn't at our 20-year reunion but she was at the 25-year one. And I'll tell you, she still had her laughing eyes, she was still pretty, she still had her athletic body, and yes, I still think she should have been on that homecoming court. More important than all of that, though, it was obvious that Anne had taken on life and handled it with clear thinking and grace.

I had greeted Anne when she arrived, and she had introduced me to her husband, Mark, a graduate of Glenwood High School (now called Glen Oak) near Canton, Ohio. Several hours went by though before we began to talk and catch up. I saw Anne sitting with two other girls and I joined them. Pretty soon the other two girls were immersed in their own conversation, and Anne and I then had a chance to talk.

"In a way," I told her, "I'm kind of surprised that you're back living in Shelby, but in another way I'm not. You can sink some very deep and strong roots in a small town."

"Yes, but you know why I'm here? My husband is a school administrator."

I knew that from having browsed through the reunion book during the hours before the reunion started. And there was a touch of irony here; Anne's husband had become principal of Shelby Junior High, just as Anne's late father had done when we were at SHS.

"How do you like being back?"

"It's okay. I'm close to my mom; we're real good friends. And I'm involved in the community. I direct a preschool, and I've been involved with my church and the Y and the Girl Scouts."

None of this surprised me, that is, her getting involved. It was vintage Lafferty.

"You've been obviously taking care of yourself," I said.

"Thanks, I've tried." Then those eyes laughed merrily and she said, "I use Ron LaBarge's swimming pool a lot." Ron was another of our classmates who was at the reunion.

"Does he live near you?"

"Next door."

"It sounds to me like you've adjusted very nicely to living in Shelby again," I said. After graduating from SHS, Anne had gone to Northwestern University, an unlikely destination. Indeed, upon receiving a four-year scholarship, Anne had gasped, "But they only give this kind to boys." Her intent was to major in physical education. But after a year during which she felt "really out of place with all those rich kids," she transferred to Ohio State. After graduating, she spent most of the next 15 years as a phys ed teacher and secondary reading specialist. She and her husband had moved back to Shelby from Columbus where they had met.

"Where do you live, Mike?"

"Lyndhurst," I replied and told her how much I liked living in my community. I then added, "I loved growing up in Shelby, and I still feel very fond of it, but I think I'd have a tough time living here, at least for now."

"Too small?"

"Yeah, maybe, but more than that I think it's too homogeneous and too close. I think I'd feel claustrophobic. Too many people would know my business."

"You've gotten used to a little anonymity."

"Right. But it's more than that. You know when people ask me about Shelby, about what it was like growing up in a small semi-rural community, I tell them it was very sheltered and very homogeneous. I tell them that there were no blacks, that the Jewish community was a pair of old maid sisters who were school teachers, and that the Italian community was the town photographer and the shoe repairman and their families. Most everybody had English or German names like Johnson, Anderson, Williams, Yetzer, Metzger and Friebel."

Anne laughed. "It's not much different now." She then told me about the vast differences she'd observed living in Chicago, Columbus and Shelby.

"I didn't get to know a black person until I went to Ohio University," I said. "And that was funny. This black guy came out for our dorm football team. In September of my freshman year, I'd been named player-coach. He was tall and slim and I thought, 'I'll bet he's fast, so I'll try him at end.' Well he was slow and clumsy and couldn't catch. To top it off, I learned that he was a pre-med student. Another stereotype shattered. Today I think it's good for my kids to be exposed to a greater variety of people. I coach a youth soccer team and all the boys – 13 – live in the same school district. Besides my two Korean sons, there's a Chinese boy, a black, a Russian Jewish émigré – he's our top scorer – and the rest of them have names like Ricchetti, Bilinksi and Casiere."

"You know," Anne said, "we almost wound up living close to you."

"Oh yeah, where?"

"My husband was a finalist for a high school principal's job. It was a really large school district east of Cleveland. I can't remember the name."

"Mentor?"

"That's it!"

"I think it's the largest high school in the state."

"I think you're right. Anyway, he lost out to another guy."

"So you really don't know how long you'll stay in Shelby."

"No...Did you know I see your mother from time to time?"

"Where?"

"At Crestwood."

"What takes you to Crestwood?" Crestwood is a nursing home where my dad had been confined for a dozen years since suffering a debilitating stroke. He would pass away on Christmas morning that year, 1988.

"I'm a library volunteer and I take books to residents there."

"Hey, that's wonderful," I said. And Anne being Anne, I wasn't surprised. "You know, I have to gird myself to walk in there. It's really tough for me. And it's not just seeing my dad. It's all the rest of the people, too. It's very sad."

"I know," said Anne. "For so many of them – the ones with good minds who can read – it's very frustrating. I feel so sorry for them."

"But you keep going."

"Yes."

"I'm sure they love to see you coming." And I'm sure they did – with a stack of books and those eyes that could be laughing one moment and showing deep compassion the next.

1991

Anne was teaching pre-schoolers, ages 3 to 5, and once again her compassion showed through. More than half her kids had special needs or were at risk. Said Anne, "Never before have I been so challenged and so overwhelmed by the state of our children. What adults get from gaining power through abuse is one of the saddest situations in our country." And sadly, in the intervening years, not much has changed.

1993

During the 30-year reunion, from Friday evening through late Sunday afternoon, Anne seemed to be everywhere, talking with everyone. She clearly was having a fun time. We saw much of each other but because we had seen each other at planning meetings, didn't go out of our way to talk once the reunion got underway. Our first opportunity to talk at length, one-on-one, just sort of happened. It came as the Sunday picnic was nearing its end.

It was about 4:30, and everyone had left except Ralph Thauvette, Anne and me. We were tidying up the park pavilion. Ralph already had said he needed to get going so he could attend a softball function for one of his daughters. We hugged him and said farewell, and he climbed into his pick-up truck.

"Are you in a hurry?" I asked Anne.

"Nope."

Ralph maneuvered his pickup away from the pavilion and across the grass to the parking lot, and we waved as he drove off. Without any warning, I felt that familiar stab of post-reunion melancholy. Anne climbed on a picnic table and crossed her legs Indian style. I sat on the table across from her, my feet on the bench.

During the next 30 or so minutes, we both were in a reflective mood. She, too, was feeling melancholy. It had been a glorious 48 hours and we were sorry to see it ending. The park, Shelby's newest and on the edge of town, was surrounded by cornfields. Except for the breeze rustling through the corn stalks, the only sounds were our voices, and we were speaking too softly to disturb any small creatures in the vicinity. It was peaceful in the extreme.

A half hour later, as we were stirring to depart, Anne said, "I'm so glad I decided to be on the planning committee. I really enjoyed the meetings." Without another word being spoken, we stood and hugged, long and hard. I had a feeling she'd be on the planning committee next time, too.

1995

She was. On the planning committee, that is, for our class 50th birthday party. Anne took on working out arrangements with the caterer who would be providing the barbecue as well as the side dishes and dessert. She did her usual very competent, low-key job.

2003

In the early 1990s in connection with a job that I had taken, Lynne and I moved to North Canton, Ohio, a little more than an hour's drive south of Lyndhurst. This was very near where Anne's husband Mark had gone to high school. Once when visiting his family in the mid-1990s, Anne paid an afternoon visit to our home. It was wonderful catching up with each other. Anne is very well read, often having three or so books going simultaneously, and she's still as thoughtful and opinionated as ever. Talking with her is more than idle chitchat. She has well thought out, clearly articulated views on issues of importance. She is worth listening to.

In late 2001 some SHS schoolmates asked me if I would be willing to help organize a multi-class reunion that, in August 2002, would bring together members of 11 classes – 1957-1967. I agreed to join the planning team. Anne came to that reunion with her sister, a 1966 grad. That was good. But as things turned out, we had very little time to talk. We both were caught up in the rare opportunity to spend time with old friends from different classes. Most of them we had not seen in 40 or so years, and being together with them was a genuine thrill.

After that reunion our class of 1963 had to make a decision about our 40-year reunion in 2003. A group of us decided to invite the two classes that sandwiched ours – 1962 and 1964. Why? It was our experiences at the 11-class reunion that influenced our thinking. Ralph Thauvette put it succinctly, "At that multi-class reunion, class walls came tumbling down. We were not just classmates but schoolmates. Plus," said Ralph, grinning, "if we invite other classes to our reunion, maybe they'll invite us to theirs." Me? After reconnecting with friends at the 11-class reunion, I simply no longer had much zest for a reunion limited only to 1963ers.

I asked Anne to join our planning team. She accepted. It was good working with her again. Immediately, she took all responsibility for planning the Sunday picnic, and Ralph and I knew we could cross that off our task list. Handled.

One of the planning meetings was at Ralph's home, and Lynne came along. After the meeting, as we were driving back to North Canton, Lynne observed, "I can see why you like working with Anne. She's intelligent, and she likes to make decisions. At one point, when there was lots of talk but no decision, I could see her frustration. She looked ready to climb out of her skin."

"That's Anne," I laughed.

Leading up to the 40-year reunion there was a steady stream of email correspondence between Anne, me and other members of the planning team. Late in the planning, I had an idea. As at past reunions Ralph and I would be doing the emceeing. In fact, at the 2002 11-class reunion, for a good while, it looked like I would be emceeing all the events over three days. I thought that unwise and said so to my teammates. Late in the going, two friends – Dave Winans class of '60 and Steve Bell class of '64 – agreed to help. Still, I did much of it. Yes, it was fun, but it was tiring and left precious little time to hobnob.

Ralph and I were good at emceeing, and our planning teammates were always happy to see us take on that role. But, I was thinking, why not include a woman and why not Anne? It was way past due for her to be in the spotlight.

Once again we were hatching plans for a three-day gathering. Friday evening, we would set-up and decorate the K of C Hall and have pizza sent in. Saturday morning there would be golf, a group stroll down Main Street, a visit to the Shelby Museum and an informal afternoon gathering at Seltzer Park in a pavilion by a pond. On Saturday evening we would have our gala and on Sunday a picnic.

The Saturday evening gala would be very different, and I asked Anne if she would join me and Ralph as an emcee.

"I'd love to!" Her reply was immediate and enthusiastic. "Just tell me what you want me to do."

"I'd like you to work with me when we introduce and recognize our teachers and maybe run the 20 questions game."

"Sounds like fun."

Recognizing our teachers…At our past reunions, our class never had had a theme. For that matter, I know of no other class that used a reunion theme. That changed quickly at a planning meeting about eight weeks before our reunion. Classmate Mary Ellen May Hall earlier had agreed to handle reunion mementos and nametags, getting them designed and produced. At that meeting, I asked, "Mary Ellen, what kind of progress are you making?"

"I've been waiting for a theme. What's our theme?"

We all – there were 10 of us at the meeting – were a taken aback. We looked at each other mutely. Then Ralph said, "We've never had a theme, but maybe we should."

"What should it be?" someone asked.

"If we're going to have one," I said, "we need to settle on it quickly. As in right now."

"Agreed," said Ralph. "We need to include the theme in our communications with our classmates."

"Something just popped into my mind," I said.

"Uh oh," replied someone else to a round of easy, quick laughter.

"How about," I said, "honoring our teachers?"

Bingo!

"I like that," said Mary Ellen.

"Me, too," said Ralph whose late mom Vera had been an SHS English teacher.

And just that fast, we had a theme. Quickly, we moved to send invitations to all teachers who had been at SHS during our four years there. From that group, not quite half were deceased. The invitation emphasized the theme and said they could expect a blend of reverence and irreverence. To our delight 15 former teachers accepted. The youngest would be 67 and the oldest just a week short of 90. With her concurrence we decided to help her celebrate her 90th birthday at the reunion.

Back to Anne.

"It will be fun," I said. "We'll each introduce about half of the teachers. When we bring them up – one at a time – we'll say a little about each one. Funny stuff. Give them a chance at the microphone to say a few words. Give them a personalized certificate of appreciation that we all have signed."

"Great," said Anne, "I'll look forward to it."

"You know," I said, "we're going to play a couple games. We will make the teachers take a quiz that we students will grade, and then we'll have everyone there – teachers and classmates – play a version of 20 Questions based on our years at SHS. We each can administer one of those."

Came the Saturday night gala, and when Anne stepped to the microphone, she was just what I expected her to be – poised, warm and witty. Her eyes did a lot of laughing. And I've got the videotape to prove it.

A month after the reunion, one day I went walking down the street to our mailbox. Inside I saw this rectangular white package. My first thought was *Oh, it's Lynne's supply of drugs."* Back in 1995, Lynne had been diagnosed with an autoimmune disease that required a daily dose of medicine to keep the symptoms at bay. And her drug packages generally arrived in rectangular white packages. So, very carefully I inched the package from the box. When I glanced at the return address, expecting to see the name of the drug distributor, I thought, *Huh, what's this?*

I saw Anne's name in the upper left corner. Back at the house, I sliced open the package, and inside was a book, *The Da Vinci Code*, and a note from Anne, congratulating me on my retirement from corporatedom and wishing me well in my post-corporate phase. In return, I sent Anne an email: *After 58+ years, seldom am I bowled over. But that's precisely what I was last Saturday when I opened the mail. The book is a winner! My reading is eclectic –fiction, non-fiction and a variety of genres within each of those broad categories. Right now, I am reading a historical novel about the Korean War. Thanks much for bowling me over.* ☺

2004

When I wanted a reasoned opinion about whether and how to proceed with this book you are reading, it was Anne's thinking that I sought. Via email, I asked whether she would be willing to assess a non-fiction manuscript, one I didn't want to describe or discuss in email, only in person, face-to-face. "Interested?"

"I would love to meet" was her quick reply.

We met in Wooster, Ohio, midway between our homes, in a bookstore. After lunch in a restaurant next door we drove to nearby Christmas Run Park. There we set up a pair of lawn chairs in the shade of trees beside the quickly running stream.

First, I explained what I had written and why. Then I explained why I had sought her help. "You're brainy, sensitive and trustworthy. I know I can count on you for an intelligent reaction. And you're in the book. Your reaction will tell me a lot about how to proceed."

Then I handed the manuscript to Anne. Over the next five hours she read several chapters, asked incisive questions, and replied to my questions with deliberate answers, often after lengthy silences.

From Anne, I got precisely what I wanted, needed and, yes, expected.

Anne and I connected one other time in 2004. I was leading a team that was planning Shelby High's first-ever all-alumni reunion. It was to be a three-day affair that in the end drew more than 600 registrants. One of the weekend's nine events was to be an assembly in the high school's theater. There would be a specially produced video shown on a big screen, special recognitions, including those for SHS's oldest living alum (Margaret Weber

Hall class of '21 who died on March 11, 2005, at age 102), oldest living cheerleader (Helen Barkdull Freese class of '30 who wore a cheerleader's outfit and energetically led hundreds of alums in a 1920s cheer and who passed away on December 22, 2006, at 94), former Whippet band director Dwight Somerville and so on.

For this three-day reunion I recruited a cadre of emcees. One was Anne. During the assembly she had two roles: introduce the school system's superintendent, which she did warmly and wittily, and administer a series of quiz questions to three teams of three alums which she did with evident enthusiasm and good humor.

2005

Anne and Mark were divorced.

2006

Anne agreed to work with me as class representatives for the class of '63 in a campaign to raise $150,000 to upgrade the Sciences Department at SHS. The campaign succeeded.

2008

Anne, a grandmother now, came to our 45-year reunion, still looking and sounding like the girl with laughing eyes who should have been on the homecoming court.

Chapter 22

Coach

Moments of sharp, terrifying pain punctuated Bill Baldridge's life.

During our senior football season in the fall of 1962, Bill was our quarterback. When we ran out of the wing-t formation, Bill passed and ran very effectively. When we operated out of the antiquated but robust single wing, Bill's burly six feet and 185 pounds helped clear the way for our fleet of fast tailbacks.

Bill's zest for sports embraced all seasons. When not working out with weights and playing football, he played basketball and baseball. Bill wasn't a great athlete, but few worked harder. He was soft-spoken with a warm, ready smile.

My most vivid football memory of Bill goes back to 1960. It was our sophomore season, when we saw varsity action in a couple games but spent most of our time with the junior varsity or reserve team. During a practice we were doing one of those drills players detested – hitting and driving the two-man blocking sled. Under the best of conditions – cool, dry air and no coach standing on the sled – it was grueling work. But, boy, did it build leg strength and sharpen technique. In hot, humid weather with a coach and his 200 pounds perched on the sled, alternately grinning at our exertions and shouting at us to work harder, it wasn't far removed from hell's deepest chamber. Well, that day, when it was Bill's turn, he drove a shoulder into a sled pad, began churning his legs and then pierced the hubbub of practice with a primal scream. He collapsed to his hands and knees and began groaning and sobbing.

The other players and Coach Don Monn froze in terror.

"I can't move," Bill was saying, tears streaming down his face through the debilitating pain. "I think my back's broken."

That's what we and Coach Monn thought, too. Later, Coach Monn was to say that during those first terrifying moments he was so frightened that he was ready to abandon coaching.

Thankfully, Bill's injury turned out to be a pinched nerve. Serious but no permanent damage. It took a while for the excruciating pain to subside and to get a diagnosis, but it didn't take long for Bill to get back into action.

Bill was a fine player. Skilled, tough and poised. But he never struck me as a student of football, nor did he seem the kind of guy who would enjoy teaching. He was mediocre in the classroom. So much for my powers of observation.

Unbeknownst to me at the time, Bill knew he wanted to be a football coach, and he went at it with a single-minded determination. Bill went to Morehead State University in Morehead, Kentucky where he earned bachelor's and master's degrees. He bulked up while in college and made the rare switch from high school quarterback to college lineman. It paid off. He made second team all-Ohio Valley Conference after his junior and senior seasons. In 1966 he captained Morehead State's Ohio Valley Conference championship team.

Afterward, Bill quickly demonstrated his coaching prowess. As a high school head coach he fashioned a record of 72-20-1 and won numerous regional and state honors in Kentucky. Then at the college level he assisted at Murray State, Morehead State, the University of Cincinnati, the University of Kansas and was head coach for a year at Georgetown College in Kentucky. In January of 1984 he was named head coach at his alma mater, Morehead State.

In the fall of 1986 Bill brought his Morehead team to Akron to play the University of Akron, then in its first year under Gerry Faust who had been fired the previous year after an ill-fated stint at Notre Dame. Bill Anspach and I and two other Shelby friends decided to converge on Akron's Rubber Bowl stadium to cheer our classmate. Before the game we met with Bill Baldridge and all seemed well, especially since his team had gotten off to a fine start that year.

It was a night game and the weather was just plain miserable. Cold, wet and windy. Instead of sitting, we walked up to the top of the stands to gain the protection of the stadium wall.

During the game on the sideline, Bill was a picture of stoicism. He barely moved and said very little. He seemed to have picked a spot on the sideline and to have put his gearshift in park. He delegated offensive and defensive play calling to assistants and seldom spoke to anyone. Even as Akron began to pile up points and the game began to slip away from Morehead, Bill showed little emotion.

When the game ended, we all were wet and thoroughly chilled and headed back to our cars and on to our homes. It was another two years before we saw Bill – on the night of our 25-year reunion in 1988. Bill arrived with his wife Janie, a native of Bowling Green, Kentucky. At one point, I found myself alone with her.

"Did you know that Bill Anspach and I met in Akron to watch Bill's team in '86?" I asked.

"Yes," she said, "Bill told me about it. It pleased him very much."

"You know, there was one way that he really impressed me. He hardly moved or said anything during the game. I kept waiting for him to show some emotion. I coach youth teams and I'm frequently pacing and shouting."

Janie smiled knowingly. "I know he seems calm but I wish you could see what's happening inside Bill. Believe me, there's plenty going on. He just doesn't let it out very often."

Perhaps he should have. Barely two months after the reunion, on September 27, 1988, I picked up my morning *Cleveland Plain Dealer* and saw the following item:

Morehead State football coach Bill Baldridge, 44, remained in a hospital, recovering from chest pains he suffered after Saturday's game against Lynchburg University. Baldridge was moved Sunday from the coronary care unit to a semi-private room at Lynchburg General Hospital in Lynchburg, Virginia, and was in satisfactory condition, said Randy Stacy, Morehead's sports information director.

Two days later, *The Plain Dealer* published the following item:

Football coach Bill Baldridge of Morehead State underwent a cardiac test in Lynchburg, Virginia, and then was transferred to Lexington, Kentucky, where he was admitted to Central Baptist Hospital. Baldridge, 44, suffered chest pains during his team's game at Lynchburg. He is listed in serious but stable condition.

A few days later I was in Shelby, and Bill Anspach and I decided to let Bill Baldridge know that he was in the hearts and minds of his friends. We went to a local drugstore and bought a get-well card. Then we started hustling. We moved around town, telling Bill's old friends about his situation and hauling out the card for them to sign. Only a few of them had heard or read about his setback. A couple days later, when the card went into the mail, it bore numerous signatures, including those of two retired SHS coaches, four retired SHS teachers and these members of the class of '63: Bill Anspach, Susie Bell, Fred Eichinger (who had written the history of Shelby football), Jim Henkel, Anne Lafferty Stock, Mary Lou Laubie Lewis, Mimi Grove, Shirley Mitchell Burrer, Mark Wolford and me.

Retired SHS head coaches Bill Wilkins and Bill Varble both thought that this had been Bill Baldridge's second experience with serious chest pains, and both thought he should consider stepping away from coaching – just as those two driven and successful coaches had done at relatively early ages, Wilkins when he was just 49 and Varble in his early 50s.

1989

October 26, 1989. The newspaper headline read: *Baldridge resigns Morehead post.*

The article's second paragraph read: *Morehead athletic director Steve Hamilton announced the resignation Wednesday. Baldridge indicated his decision stemmed from health problems which have affected his family and job.*

The resignation took effect December 31 when his contract was due to expire.

1993

Bill Baldridge came to our 30-year reunion. It didn't take much conversation to see that Bill's passion for football still burned brightly. But following that bout with chest pains, Bill first underwent two angioplasties and then had undergone bypass surgery. After retiring from coaching at Morehead State, he and Janie moved farther south to Florida where he took a job managing a warehouse and distribution operation.

But that kind of work just didn't offer Bill the opportunity to experience what he still craved – teaching and prowling football fields. He began coaching youth football teams. After a while, as he was to tell us on that reunion Saturday night, "I figured I was driving all over Florida and working as hard as ever with the youth team. So, shoot, I figured I might as well get paid for it." So Bill headed back to Kentucky where he landed a high school head coaching post not far from Morehead.

During the reunion's humorous interlude, when we inspected birth dates that classmates had written down upon arrival at the K of C Hall, Bill won the award for being the oldest classmate in attendance. He came forward to collect his prize – a pair of heavy woolen socks emblazoned with a vertical red Shelby. As I handed him the socks, I joked that they would help combat the slowing circulation that accompanies age. Then Bill asked if he could take the microphone.

"After my bypass surgery, I was lying in bed, flat on my back." Happily babbling classmates and their spouses began to grow silent. "I got about a thousand cards and letters and most of them were from classmates. Janie would open a card and read it and tell me who sent it and I would say, 'That's my classmate.' And then she would open another and I would say, 'That's my classmate. That's my classmate. That's my classmate.' I can't begin to tell you how much all those cards and all those prayers meant to me." At this point, lots of lumps were forming in throats and tears were welling in eyes. Bill continued. "They really helped me pull through. A man couldn't have better friends, and I want to thank you from the bottom of my heart."

When Bill handed me the microphone, the complete silence was broken by a strong and prolonged ovation. We shook hands and hugged hard – football player hard. As Bill slowly made his way back to his seat, classmates rose to shake his hand, pat his back and hug him.

After resuming coaching, Bill said he let more of his emotions show. "I don't hold all of it inside anymore." A relief for his wife and his classmates.

CHAPTER 23

FEELING TRAPPED

The 25-year reunion was John Carner's first. We had gone to school together for 12 years, starting in the first grade at St. Mary's. We were never particularly close, I think in part because John wasn't much into sports. But I believe there was always a goodly measure of mutual affection and respect.

John was plenty smart and easy to talk with. He was about my height – five feet ten – and from childhood seemed to carry just a wee bit too much girth. Not really heavy but a tad overweight. He had come to the reunion from his home in Tipp City near Dayton, Ohio.

At the reunion that night, John was one of the last people I spent time with before the K of C staff chased us out of the hall and before some of us continued the reunion at Mimi Grove's house. John was sitting with a small group of other St. Mary's grads – his wife, Mary Jo, who is a year older and who used to live up the street from me on Auburn Avenue, and David Spangler and Mary Louise Hoehn. Everyone was in a jovial mood.

"We should have a St. Mary's reunion," John said. His first reunion, and he was already proposing another. I think he was hooked.

"That would be fun," I agreed. "Do you want to organize it?" We all laughed, John, too, and the idea was dropped.

The conversation got around to careers and work when we asked David about his job as an employment counselor.

"My feelings about work have really evolved over the years," I said, "especially during the last few years."

"How's that?" said John.

"Well, until a few years ago, I was ready to go almost anywhere at any time to pursue greater professional glory."

"And now you don't feel that way," John said.

"Well, now I've got three teenagers in the same high school, and I'd like them to be able to finish there. I know *they* sure would."

"Boy, I know what you mean," said John. "I really feel trapped. I've been with the same division of my company for 16 years, and I'm afraid to even apply for a job in another division." John was an accountant by education – University of Dayton – and began his career at Cessna Aircraft as head accountant, ultimately becoming chief financial officer.

"Don't want to be transferred?"

"Right."

"There's another thing, too," I said. "Where we live now is very livable. Our backyard backs onto a woods and we're not much more than twenty minutes from anything. I sure wouldn't want to wind up in New York or LA. I know both cities really well. Too much congestion. That sort of thought didn't used to bother me, but now, brrrr."

"I know what you mean," said John. "I have a son working in Cleveland, but suburban Dayton is about as big and congested as I want to handle. Just like you, nothing is more than a few minutes away."

"You know," I said, "a friend of mine from a different high school recently returned from a class reunion. He was telling me about a similar discussion about work that he had with his classmates. One guy simply said, 'I've reached the point where, if given a choice, I think I could figure out another way to spend eight or nine hours a day.'"

"He's got a good point," John laughed, "but I've got a little problem. With our twins at eighteen, I don't plan to be doing much different for a few more years."

"I can identify with that. My youngest is a ninth grader, which means I've got another eight years before I can think seriously about making that kind of choice. That would make me 51 – which is looking younger and younger all the time."

"Fifty sounds about right for trying something new," said John, and we both laughed.

2001

John no longer feels trapped. He tried something new, retiring from his corporate job. And to hear him and Mary Jo tell it, he's done an exemplary job of adjusting. They take daily walks, have morning coffee in the same neighborhood restaurant, do lots of bird watching and stay close to their growing brood of grandchildren. They also built a first-floor master bedroom and bath onto their house to help Mary Jo with life after she was seriously injured in an auto accident.

2008

John came to our 45-year reunion. He is reveling in his post-corporate freedom. These days he and Mary Jo enjoy traveling, and he does volunteer work for their church. John still is walking, bird watching and doting on his grandkids who now total 12.

CHAPTER 24

NOT EVEN THE BRITISH OPEN

When I learned about Randy Smith's situation, my memory flashed back to our days as Little Leaguers.

It was the day of tryouts for the Major League division of Shelby's Little League. Randy and I were 11. We had played the previous two seasons – 1954 and 1955 – in the Minor League division. We were ready to move up. We wanted to move up.

Most of the boys at the tryout were probably at least a little nervous. I was confident but still on edge. Randy? He was stone cold petrified. You could see fear in his awkward, jerky movements. You could see it in his dilated eyes. And, yes, even then, although just a boy, I knew the source of Randy's fear.

It was his dad. I knew almost nothing about Randy's dad, except that he had a good job with a local company – and that he was always on Randy to do better. My dad stayed away from the tryout. Randy's didn't. You could see his dad and, more than seeing him, you could hear him. "Come on, Randy, you can throw better than that." "Keep your eye on the ball. Smack it." "Oh, Randy, get your glove down." And so on and so on. His dad's pleadings and rantings had Randy wound tighter than the strings in a baseball. Poor kid. I felt sorry for him.

Randy didn't make the Major League division, and I think he might have been relieved. I don't know if Randy ever picked up a baseball bat or glove again.

What Randy did pick up were golf clubs. In time, he became a member of SHS's then perennially successful golf team. In fact, at six feet and slender, he developed into one of the team's best players. One reason he excelled, I think, was because his dad wasn't there to prod him while he practiced or observe him when he played in after-school matches. And it was Randy against a golf course, not against pitched and batted baseballs and the boys who threw and hit them.

Randy married Nancy in September of 1968, and they had two kids, a son and daughter.

Golf became Randy's passion and a lasting one. Even in his 50s and with way too much girth, he could still shoot in the 80s. He was good.

Randy was a regular at our class reunions, and over the years we had quite a few fun and insightful conversations. The last reunion he attended was the 11-class reunion in 2002. Late on the Saturday night of that reunion, he and I stepped outside the hall into the pleasantly cooling air.

"So what brought you back to Shelby?" I asked. Randy had spent the first 15 years of his career working for the United States Treasury Department in Cambridge, Ohio and the remaining 15 years with a bank in Columbus. He had retired in 1998.

He shrugged. "I wanted to be close to my mom and get back to the old hometown."

"Are you liking it?"

"Yeah. It's okay. There's not much to do, but I can still play golf."

Randy's wit tended toward drollery. In describing his work as a loan review officer, he once observed, "I'm still getting loan officers fired if they are booking lousy loans." Barely able to suppress a grin, he then added, "It's great to be a second-guesser."

As to Randy, the reunion that I remember most clearly was our class of '63's 50th birthday party in 1995. It was a two-day affair. On day one, we all met in the morning in Shelby where classmate Elaine Lybarger had chartered a bus to take us to Cleveland for a luncheon outing on the Goodtime II, a tour boat that plied Cleveland's lake front and the Cuyahoga River. The boat outing was fun, but what I remember most fondly were the bus rides to and from Cleveland. Randy and I were seatmates. The laughter on that bus was contagious, riotous and nonstop. And Randy was right in the thick of things. He was telling hilarious jokes and recalling one funny story after another from our SHS days. He and I and virtually everyone else onboard ached from laughing hard and long – so hard and so long that plenty of tears were coursing down cheeks. Those two bus rides were wonderful tonics. Turns out that Randy could have used more of them.

Randy was planning to come to our three-class – 1962/63/64 – reunion in 2003. He did come to a couple of the planning meetings and, at the last

Mike Johnson

one he attended, volunteered to get a large cake baked and decorated so we could help retired biology teacher Harryet Snyder celebrate her 90th birthday.

Randy wasn't at the next planning meeting. Before it started, Jeff Dawson, perhaps Randy's closest friend among our classmates, took me aside.

"Mike, Randy's not doing well. He won't be able to handle getting the cake done." Jeff was speaking very quietly.

"What's the problem?"

"Randy's going through a rough patch. Depression. It's really bad. He's just about dysfunctional."

"Oh, I'm sorry to hear that." I had seen up close a couple other people who had suffered from severe depression, and I knew how debilitating it could be. "How long has this been going on?"

"Off and on for quite a few years," said Jeff. "When I came back from Pakistan in 2000, he wasn't the same Randy I used to know. Stress is the real reason he got out of banking. He just can't stand pressure any more."

Jeff's comments caused me to remember email correspondence with Randy going back a few years in which he talked of the stress associated with working for a bank that was experiencing financial difficulties, was squeezing budgets and laying people off. I remembered Randy saying that he was glad he had dodged the axe but was stressed from working longer hours, many of them on the road. I also found myself thinking back to Randy's dad and the pressure he put on Randy when he was just a lad and wondering to what extent his badgering Randy had contributed to his problems later in life.

Randy didn't come to our 2003 reunion. Then in July of 2004 I received a distressing email from Jeff Dawson.

Saturday, July 17: *While visiting my parents today, Joanne, my fiancee, called and told me to get home. When I got home, I found out that Nancy Smith had called and Randy is in the intensive care unit at Mansfield General. On Wednesday he had some paralysis and he couldn't get up, but wouldn't see a doctor, and then Friday morning around nine, Nancy found him in bed foaming at the mouth and moaning. She called 911. I have just come back from the hospital. Randy is critical and on a ventilator.*

170

Nancy is doing fine, but Lisa and Brandon, his children who arrived from Columbus, didn't look good. I was real proud of myself and I think I held up well. Randy and I have been friends since we were three. My birthday is July 4 and his is the 11th. He's always been my best buddy. His son is my godson. Oh, he (Randy) *hasn't had a stroke nor a heart attack. They think it might be a combination of medicines. When Randy called me on Wednesday, he hadn't slept in 48 hours.*

Sunday, July 19: *Went to see Randy at 11:00. He is still in a coma. Nancy, his wife, was there. We talked to the doctor and he said that the seizure could have caused brain damage, but they don't know. MRI was negative. CAT was negative. I am still optimistic. I was hoping the British Open might wake him up.*

Tuesday, July 20: *It doesn't look good for Randy at all. He can cough on his own, but that is about it. We will get results today about his EEG or brain waves after they took away the sedative. Joanne and I go to see him every day. No change. He was taking two medicines – one for depression and one for seizures. They think maybe he didn't take the second medicine and then had a seizure. It was during the night so they don't know how long the seizure was.*

Saturday, July 24: *Randy will have his ventilator probably pulled by Tuesday or in two weeks, and he will be history. Another one of our classmates bites the dust. Learned a lot about comas and medicine.*

Sunday, July 25: *They are apparently going to pull the plug Monday before they would have to trachea him.*

Wednesday, July 28: Randy died.

Friday, July 30: *I saw Randy at 3:30 p.m. on Wednesday. He died shortly thereafter. When I was there, he was breathing very shallow and at 50 breaths per minute. He died about two hours later.*

Another good man gone too soon.

Chapter 25

Tin roofs and a ten-minute favor

1948. That's when it began. 61 years ago on Auburn Avenue. The longest and most meaningful of my friendships.

For the moment, though, let's fast forward to 1988.

At our 25-year reunion during the program, master of ceremonies Ralph Thauvette said, "Now we want to award a prize for the class member who has been married the longest. To the same spouse, that is." Chuckles all around. "I know some of you may *think* you qualify for this award, but we are interested only in longevity as measured by the calendar." The chuckles grew into laughter. "Okay, now who is it?"

There was a long pause as people were craning their necks and looking around the hall. Then a voice shouted, "Anspach!" There followed a ripple of cheering and good-natured jeering.

"Any other contenders or pretenders?" Ralph asked. "No? Going once, going twice...Okay, Bill – Bill and Toni – come on up and get your prize."

Twenty-five years earlier, I would have given you choice odds against that marriage of Bill Anspach and Toni Martinez lasting even five years let alone 25. And even today Bill would tell you the same thing; those early years of their marriage were difficult as he struggled to achieve maturity.

At age 17 Bill was no more ready for marriage than an aging and failing Fidel Castro is for a plebiscite. Bill was high-spirited, impulsive and about as mature as most 17-year-old boys, which is to say, his hormones were racing ahead of his rational thinking.

Toni was a year older and in her first year of college when she became pregnant. She was brainy, vivacious, sweet and pretty. Still is. Now at that time in that situation, young people didn't deliberate about options. They didn't think much, if at all, about abortions, adoptions, or having and keeping a baby without getting married. In the early 1960s there was only one generally acceptable course of action: get to the altar as soon as possible and hopefully soon enough so the bride could wear white without too terribly embarrassing herself and everyone else present, never mind those too mortified to come to the ceremony. At least that's the way it was in semi-rural, conservative Shelby. Bill and Toni rushed to the altar and were married in February of 1963.

By then, Bill and I had been next-door neighbors and best buddies for some 15 years. Today, though our lives took divergent paths starting when Bill got married during our senior year at SHS, we remain buddies. And there's no mystery to that. We each had fathers who were sticklers for things like talking straight and being loyal and honest. Some of that, a little anyway, rubbed off on Bill and me. In other words, it gets back to values and we share those in abundance. Now add some affection and respect and shared experiences to the mix and you have a lifelong friendship.

When I reflect on our relationship, it's as though my mind were leafing through a photo album.

- At about age 5, Bill and I and my sister Linda, younger by two years, are sitting together on the grass in my front yard. I'm holding my blond cocker spaniel named Lassie and all three of us are grinning at the camera. Naturally the snapshot is black and white.

- It's 1954 and we're nine years old and playing Little League baseball on different teams. Bill's team is doing fine and mine is doing miserably and I'm upset to the point of tears. Then we win a couple games and I'm feeling porky. Bill's dad, Jim, kids me about my sudden change in outlook and bets me a tin-roof sundae that we can't win the championship. My team stays hot, we win the title, beating out Bill's team, and Jim takes Bill and me to Isaly's ice cream shop for tin-roofs. What's a tin-roof? Ice cream, smothered in chocolate with chopped nuts, a cherry and whipped cream. It was delectable. But the winning was even tastier.

- Bill and I while away some lazy summer afternoons, reading comic books under a cherry tree in my yard.

- We put on oversized boxing gloves and go at each other. More than once.

- In the late 1950s, eager for baseball to begin, we play catch with each other in February with snow still on the ground. It's hard to find balls we drop.

- It's 1959 and we are playing PONY League baseball. Bill wins the batting title, and I finish fifth in hitting. Recollections of our hitting exploits are fun, but the memory that still causes us to smile most has to do with this: Bill was a crack centerfielder with a powerful and accurate arm – the best outfield arm I saw all the way through high school and American Legion ball. His team, Shelby Police, was short of pitching and Bill was pressed into service. From the mound, Bill couldn't locate home plate. He averaged a walk an inning, grew to dread pitching assignments and suffered the ignominy of losing six games and winning none. He had to endure considerable teasing.

- For the opening game of our senior football season we travel to Lakewood, Ohio to play St. Edward. Jim Henkel has received a St. Edward punt and is streaking toward the St. Ed goal line and a certain touchdown. No defender is near him. None will catch him. Then I see Bill getting ready to throw a meaningless block from behind on an opponent. "No, Bill, no!" I scream. Too late. Bill throws the block, and the referee throws his yellow penalty flag for clipping – or blocking in the back as they term it today. I cuss at Bill. No touchdown. We win anyway, 22-6. Neither Bill nor I ever forgets this – and today we joke about it.

- Bill and Toni's first baby dies at birth. Then in 1964 their daughter Lisa is born. Bill asks me to be godfather.

- In April 1965 Bill serves as a pallbearer for my maternal grandmother.

- It's the summer of 1966 and Bill and I co-coach a Little League baseball team to the city championship. Our biggest thrill: after the title game, one player's father – a very successful high school head football coach in a neighboring town – comes on the field and congratulates us on our coaching. His gesture made two very young men feel very good. I still have a baseball autographed by the boys on that team and given to me at a post-season team picnic.

- As a magazine writer for a management publication in 1977, I spend two days interviewing Bill for an article on how blue-collar workers view management. Bill is as thoughtful and articulate as I knew he would be. The editor-in-chief made it a cover story. Now, rereading the article, the thinking Bill expresses then is still relevant today.

- In 1976 I can't be in Shelby when my parents decide to move. Bill helps them and refuses to accept any pay. My parents insist that he take the money. Bill sends me a letter, explaining all this, and encloses the money that my parents had forced on him. He asks me to return it to them without their knowing it. Which I do by slipping cash into Mom's purse and Dad's wallet on subsequent visits.

- Bill's dad Jim dies on January 31, 1980, at age 63. When I was a kid, Jim was the only adult male I called by his first name and that was because Jim insisted on it. I drive to Shelby for the funeral. Afterward I receive a note from Bill's mom Phyllis. It reads in part: *Thanks Mike for being here for Bill. He really appreciated your visit. Bless his heart – he was holding up all the rest of us and had no one he could really lean on till you came. It did him a lot of good and I know he'll never forget it.*

- Bill has become a highly respected tool and die maker for General Motors. In May of 1986 I receive a postcard from Komatsu, Japan. *Half way into 3 weeks here for buying and checkout of transfer press for Mansfield plant. Visited this famous park in Komazawa. Picking up language. Communications OK. People friendly and helpful. Old part of Japan much more traditional than other side of island. Hope to talk when home. Love from your otomadachi. Bill.*

- On December 31, 1986, Bill writes me a long letter that includes this paragraph: *For almost forty years we have known each other. In that time many events and people have come and gone to influence our lives. It feels good to know that no matter how infrequent our meetings or letters are, there is someone you can write or call who shared your roots. It seems although we have gone in quite different directions, we still can communicate on the same wavelength.*

- Bill asks me to be his best man when he and Toni renew their wedding vows after 25 years of marriage. I'm honored and do it gladly. (They renewed their vows again on their 40th anniversary.)

- In the spring of 1988 Bill pays his first visit to my house since I left SHS in 1963. He brings his college son, and we go to a professional soccer game – their first. The home team treats us to a come-from-behind victory before a large – about 20,000 – and vocal crowd.

- In the summer of 1990 Bill drives to Mansfield to watch my son Ben's club soccer team play for a state title. We get our share of thrills as Ben has two assists and his team wins 4-3 in overtime.

- In the fall of 1988 we each take a day of vacation and meet in Shelby to do some serious catching up. We spend the day walking, talking, laughing, remembering, confiding and looking up friends. We have our picture taken, arms around each other, in front of Old SHS.

- In the summer of 2006 when I learn I've been voted for induction into SHS's Hall of Distinction, it takes me only minutes to decide to ask Bill to serve as my presenter. "I would be honored," he replies. Later my mom emails me: *Before Mass Bill whispered in my ear, wondering if I knew about your good news. I said 'yes' and he started to tear up. Then, really tearing up, he told me that you had asked him to be your presenter. He was definitely touched! I told him I thought you had made a great choice.*

At one point during our 1988 day together, Bill asks, "Do you remember if I came to your wedding?"

"To be honest, no." Lynne and I were married in 1969 by my late uncle, George Reinweiler, a priest in Arizona who flew back to conduct the ceremony and who later inspired my first book, *Warrior Priest*. "I think I was too excited to pay much attention to who came."

"You invited me but I didn't come," says Bill with a hint of contrition. "Boy, did I catch hell. Mom and Dad and Toni came but I didn't."

"How come?"

"I was hung over. I'd been out drinking the night before and I was feeling really punk. Mom and Toni were really pissed at me. Mom said, 'Mike's your best friend and you're not going to his wedding. How can you not go?' I told her, 'Mom, I don't want to go to Mike's wedding and get sick in church.' Afterward, Dad really tore into me."

I laugh and so does Bill. After 19 years he's still feeling guilty and still feeling the need to confide and clear the air.

As I said in the earlier chapter on Jim Blair, on the Friday night before our 25-year reunion, Bill and Jim and I went out for beers at the American Legion post bar. I was drinking on an empty stomach – smart, huh? – and it didn't take long before I began to feel woozy. Then I began to feel just plain sick. I finally said so and Bill said, "Let's get you something to eat."

"They don't have anything here I can eat." I was watching my cholesterol level and the American Legion bar menu ran heavily in the wrong direction. "Everything here is fried or loaded with fat."

"No problem," said Bill. "I'll order something. Could you eat a chicken sandwich?"

"Sure."

Bill backed away from the table, stood and went to a pay phone and dialed. I kept talking with Jim Blair. A couple minutes later, Bill returned to the table. "It'll be here soon," he said.

"I didn't know anybody delivered chicken sandwiches," I said. "Pizza, yes, but chicken sandwiches?"

Bill just smiled. "It will be here in a few minutes."

We kept on chatting, reminiscing, talking about the next day's reunion and the classmates we were expecting to see. After about 15 minutes, Bill's wife Toni came walking into the Legion bar with a bag of hot chicken sandwiches. To say I was surprised would be putting it mildly.

"For crying out loud," I protested, "You shouldn't have had Toni do this."

"Oh, that's all right," Toni said, smiling kindly. "I was going out anyway." She and I have been friends since our earliest days in elementary school at St. Mary's.

"Sure you were," I said, not trying to mask my skepticism.

"No, really, I was. I had to run an errand."

"Bill, we could have gone to get these."

"Forget it."

Yes, but I haven't. It was not a huge deal, far from it, but it was one of those little incidents that has become part of the "album" of mental snapshots I'll always have of Bill. We have lived for 64 years and been friends for some 61 of those. I'm keeping my fingers crossed that good health gives us time to take many more "snapshots" for that "album."

1990

- Two more "snapshots" for that "album." On October 1 of that year, I had started working with The Timken Company in Canton, Ohio. On December 5 I was in a meeting in someone else's office. The phone rang, the office's occupant picked it up and said the call was for me. It was news and it was jolting. Bill's mom, Phyllis, 72, had been killed in a car accident. She had been driving on a country road near Ashland, her hometown and about 20 miles from her home in Shelby. Her car had swerved left of center and struck a large truck head-on. She either was killed instantly or was already dead or dying. Phyllis had had heart trouble. She was a lovely woman with a rich voice that could be heard often performing solos at weddings – including Lynne's and mine – and funerals. Bill asked me to serve as a pallbearer, and I was honored.

- The second additional "snapshot" was cheerier and reminded me of Bill's capacity to laugh at himself. As 1990 was coming to a close, Bill converted to Catholicism. His kids joked that he should tape his first confession. I kidded him about taking out an "insurance policy" on his destination in the hereafter. Bill's quick reply: "I heard the bar is on the Catholic side."

1993

About two weeks before our 30-year reunion, Bill and I visited for about three hours in a suburban Detroit hotel room where I was staying the night while on a business trip. Why was Bill there? Technically, he still was employed at the General Motors plant near Shelby. But for the past five years, Bill had been spending four days each week at the GM Tech Center near Detroit, working on tooling and parts for advanced car models. This was a reflection of the respect Bill had earned as a tool and die maker, as were trips to Japan to study machinery for GM and to a California GM plant to troubleshoot machine problems. We had visited before when I had been in Detroit on business. We discussed much and both of us were looking forward to the upcoming reunion with huge anticipation.

Bill had a special reason for being excited. There was to be a golf outing on the Saturday morning of reunion weekend, and it was Bill's idea. He organized and ran the event and it was a sparkling success. The format was a "scramble" so that even the least skilled participants could have a fun time. About 20 classmates plus some spouses played.

As with past reunions, Bill and I spent relatively little time with each other. We were there more for others than for each other since we do a good job of staying in touch. But at the Sunday picnic, at one point we were sitting at the same table.

"Bill, I'd like you to do me a ten-minute favor."

"What's that?"

"Let's play catch." Several of us, as planned, had brought a variety of sports stuff – bats, balls, gloves, Frisbees, volleyball and bocce ball sets.

"Okay," said Bill.

"But no burnout," I joked, referring to youthful contests which had us competing to see who could inflict the most pain on each other's glove hands. Those matches, engaged in with gleeful and gritty determination, had been tests of endurance which strengthened our throwing arms and callused our glove hands. In fact, each summer our calluses became so thick and hard, we could – and did – stick sewing needles into them without feeling pain.

That Sunday afternoon we stood about 50 feet apart beside the picnic pavilion and began tossing lightly. It felt real good. As we threw, we joshed and reminisced. The hot afternoon sun was warming our shoulders and throwing arms. Vaguely, we were aware of being observed by classmates but, as in the "burnout" competitions of years ago, we didn't find our observers a distraction. We never did get to throwing really hard, but as the sun loosened our arms, occasionally we put a little snap on the ball. I could feel some sweat beading on my forehead and trickling down my sides.

Neither Bill nor I had thrown a baseball in several years. After about 15 minutes, we agreed that going longer might produce more soreness than either of us wanted.

Later, as the picnic was wrapping up, Bill and I shook hands. As always, we could feel the warmth of our long friendship in the hard grips.

"See ya' soon," I said.
"I hope so."
"We will."

1995

As I've written earlier in this story, Bill was the catalyst for our class deciding to have a group 50th birthday party.

1998

Once again, Bill organized a Saturday morning golf outing.

2002

For the 11-class reunion Bill again was the golf maestro.

2003

For our 40-year reunion, Bill expanded his role. Yes, once again, he organized a Saturday morning golf outing. But he also took it upon himself to secure the cake we wanted to have when we helped former biology teacher Harryet Snyder celebrate her 90th birthday. And he took on the chore of providing a keg of beer and ice for the Saturday night gala. He did all this with his warm smile and unprepossessing competence.

In my view, though, his finest moment in 2003 came when he phoned me and suggested that we take a...

CHAPTER 26

ROAD TRIP

It was the evening of Veterans Day, November 11, 2003. The phone in our family room rang, and Lynne picked it up. I was two rooms away in the living room, but I could hear her talking and laughing. Then I heard her call to me, "Mike, it's Bill Anspach!"

I walked to the kitchen phone and picked up the receiver. "Hey, Bill, what's up?"

"Hi, Mike. I hope I didn't disturb you or anything."

"Nah, that's okay."

"Good. There's something I want to run by you. I've been thinking about it for the last week or two. It's something I want to do. I want you to know that I'm not leaning on you to do this. It's just something that I think would be the right thing to do, and I wonder if you would like to go in with me. No pressure. None. If you don't want to do it, just say so. I know it's getting close to the holidays and you will have plans, be traveling, family." As Bill was speaking those words, I was thinking *What the hell is he leading up to? It isn't like Bill Anspach to tiptoe around things.* "It's something I'm going to do, even if you don't want to – or can't."

"What are we talking about?"

"A road trip to see Jim Blair."

"Oh."

"I know this is coming out of the blue," said Bill. "I just thought you might be interested."

"It's a great idea. When are you thinking of doing this?"

"Soon. Within the next few weeks."

"Yeah..." I found my memory flashing back to recent email correspondence with another of our '63 classmates, Margie Parsons Hoover Earick who lives in Bucyrus, Ohio. She recently had visited Jim and had provided me with details on his situation. That Margie had traveled to visit him came as no surprise. She was a long-time friend of Jim and a caring person. That trait had shown in another way when she served a four-year term as a thoughtful member of the Shelby City Schools Board of Education. Moreover she had had to deal with considerable adversity in her own life. Both of her husbands had died, and Margie had lost a hand in an accident. Through it all she was a picture of grit and grace.

"If we're going to do this," I said to Bill, "we need to do it soon. Margie and her sister Nancy visited him recently. They say he is declining rapidly."

"Right."

"You know, Bill, if you had called me about this a few months ago, before I retired from the corporate world, I would have said, 'Great idea, but I can't possibly take the time.' That was then. I would like to do it. Not just because of seeing Jim – we saw him last July at our reunion – but because I know I would enjoy the road trip with you. That would be fun. In fact, it would be great to have all that time together."

As I mentioned in the earlier chapter on Jim Blair, he had come to our 40-year reunion the previous July. A few weeks before that, he had written to Ralph Thauvette, alerting him that he might have Parkinson's Disease. At the reunion, Jim was visibly weakened. He couldn't stand for long, but his perpetually sunny disposition was firmly in place. Amazing. He had just retired in January from his longtime career as a civilian meteorologist for the Air Force. And a few weeks later, he had begun to notice ominous symptoms.

At the reunion's Friday night set-up and decorating session, Jim had pitched in as best he could. He helped to position red tablecloths and affix twisted red and gray ribbons to tabletops. The next morning, he went golfing. He fell down once but kept on playing. The next week Jim did undergo more testing, and he did get a diagnosis. It was worse than Parkinson's. It was ALS – amyotrophic lateral sclerosis or Lou Gehrig's Disease. A death sentence.

In October, Margie and Nancy drove to Columbus, Georgia to visit Jim and his sister Lynda Glover, a class of '68 member, who lives nearby, across the border in Phenix City, Alabama. Margie and her siblings and the Blair kids had been neighbors in their youth and had become very close. Upon returning to Ohio, Margie had emailed me. She reported that Jim was fully aware of his fate. Margie said that Jim observed that it would "take a miracle" for him to cheat death. The doctors were talking with him about inserting a feeding tube, and they had provided him with a rubber collar to keep his head upright.

Bill continued. "Toni doesn't really know Jim that well and doesn't want to make the trip. You and I go back to Little League with Jim. Like I said, I'm going no matter what."

"Bill, I want to go. Let me think it over. Talk it over with Lynne. I won't leave you hanging. I'll get back to you within a day or two."

"Okay," said Bill, "that's fine."

After hanging up the phone, I told Lynne about the conversation with Bill. She was immediately supportive. We didn't see a problem with scheduling.

The next evening I phoned Bill in Shelby. "Bill, it's Mike. I'll make the trip with you."

"That's great!"

"Let me give you a few things to think about. You know, Lynne and I are coming over to Shelby for Thanksgiving. As always. And I am staying overnight to take care of some things on Friday. How would you feel about leaving very early on Saturday morning? I don't see this as a lengthy trip. I don't think Jim is strong enough for us to be there very long, and we will have to gird ourselves emotionally for this. You remember what it was like emotionally when we went to see Joel."

"That's a great idea, leaving on Saturday," Bill said with enthusiasm. "And I agree that we wouldn't stay long."

"Just overnight. And then start back. By the way, I can tell you that from North Canton to Douglasville where Lynne has family is just about 700 miles on the button. We've made the drive many times. I've looked at my road atlas, and it looks like Columbus is another 60 or 70 miles southwest of Douglasville (a western suburb of Atlanta). If we get up and get on the road early, we can be in Columbus by early evening. Just make brief pit stops to piss and gas up. Take some food with us in the car."

"That sounds great," said Bill. "I can make up some sandwiches. Bring the cooler."

"Now I'd like to run an idea by you," I said.

"Go ahead."

"Diane Mowry. She had a stroke a few years ago, and she and her husband Keith live in Rome, Georgia, which is north of Atlanta. How would you feel about making a visit there?"

"That would be fine," said Bill. Diane also was a 1963 SHS alum. I sensed from email correspondence that Diane had made a good although not complete recovery. For example, she had written that she couldn't drive, that she had a companion to take her shopping and run errands.

"Have you spoken with Angie about your idea?" I asked.

"Not yet," said Bill. "But I will. Maybe I'll call her tonight."

"Well, while you are calling Angie – and she might say no if she thinks Jim is too weak now to receive visitors – I will send an email to Diane and Keith (a 1964 SHS grad). I'll tell her what we are up to and ask her how she feels about us paying a visit."

Within a couple days Bill had spoken with Angela. Immediately, she loved the idea of our visiting. Then she got Jim on the line with Bill and he, too, was fully in favor of our visit. "You've got to come," said Jim. A day later I received an email from Diane, saying she and Keith were excited about the possibility of our visiting. The Ohio to Georgia road trip was on.

In the predawn hours of the Saturday after Thanksgiving, Bill picked me up at my mom's home, and we set out from Shelby with the temperature in the 20s and snow falling. For several miles we got stuck behind a snowplow. We remained patient.

South of Mansfield, once we got on I-71, we picked up the pace. Through Columbus, Ohio to Cincinnati where we picked up I-75. Then through Lexington, Knoxville and Chattanooga. We stopped just three times, each time just long enough to use restrooms, gas up and for Bill to take a few drags on a cigarette. During one of our stops – in Kentucky – we still could see our breaths. But the sun was shining brightly, and the forecast was for warmer temperatures in Tennessee and Georgia. Along the way we removed sandwiches from baggies and washed them down with cokes. West of Atlanta, now on I-85, from Bill's cell phone, we called Jim and Angela to tell them we were about an hour away. Darkness had descended. Then we picked up I-185 and turned southwest toward Columbus. About 6:45 p.m., we pulled into their driveway.

Before we could ring the doorbell, Jim was opening the door. Our first impression: Jim looked much better than we had expected. Yes, he was walking a little less certainly and was using a four-footed cane for balance. But other than that, he looked about the same as in the previous July.

From left: Mike Johnson, Jim Blair (1945-2004), Bill Anspach

Angela was in the kitchen, preparing a sumptuous meal – a gorgeous salad, including avocado and pecans, chicken cacciatore with great side dishes and a glorious dessert. And wine.

Jim and Angela had invited their son Brady, then 31, and his wife, an elementary school teacher, to join us. They both seemed like young adults of the first rank. (Jim and Angela's other child is daughter Mandy, three years younger than Brady.)

Over dinner, Jim, at the head of the table, had some difficulty cutting meat and a couple times had difficulty swallowing. Brady was sitting next to him, was alert to his dad's needs but not overly solicitous.

Later, as the night wore on and Jim grew tired, he put on the collar to help hold his head up. "The first one they gave me was uncomfortable," he said matter of factly. "This one works much better."

The disease also had slowed and softened Jim's speaking. But his mind still was fully engaged. We talked about books, movies, global competition, sports and Brady's work. Jim had seen the film *Enemy At The Gates*, so had I, and that triggered discussion on history and politics.

Brady and his wife left about 10 p.m. A little later, after Jim went to bed and Angela saw that Bill and I had everything we needed, she and I chatted for about 20 minutes.

"I keep hoping the doctors will find that it's a nerve problem of some kind," she said. "We could deal with that, have some hope."

Hope can prove hard to kill.

The next morning dawned gloriously sunny. Angela was up early. Enticing scents were coming from the kitchen where she was fixing a southern-style breakfast that easily could have added two inches to our waistlines if we had eaten everything she put on the table. Pancakes, biscuits, fruits, coffee. We three guys ate heartily with a goodly amount of laughter between bites.

Afterward, Bill and I loaded our things into the car. Then the four of us went outside to take pictures. The air was just cold enough to have a bite to it, but the sun was rising and with light jackets we were very comfortable. While I was composing the first photo, Jim lost his balance, but Bill and Angela reached out and caught him. We all were laughing and joking. I took a photo of Jim, Bill and Angela together, then one of Jim and Angela. Then Angela took one of us three guys.

We said our goodbyes. Long, hard hugs. Those football player hugs.

"Mike," Jim said, "if you come to Douglasville to visit Lynne's family, please come see us."

"Yes," Angela echoed, "you are welcome any time."

"Count on it," I replied.

Then Bill and I got in the car, slowly backed out of the driveway, and took a couple deep breaths. "Well, my friend," I said, "I wonder if that was the last time we'll see Jim."

"I don't know," said Bill. "I'm glad we came."

So was I. We pointed the car north toward Rome.

Somewhere north of Atlanta, we pulled into a carwash to clean the Ohio road salt from the car. About one o'clock, upon approaching Rome, we phoned Diane and Keith. He answered and went over directions to their house. We arrived about 30 minutes later. And we were surprised.

As Bill and I eased out of the car, Keith came outside to greet us warmly. We could see Diane standing a few feet inside the door. She was grasping a four-footed cane. She was beaming but made no move to come toward us. Then as we approached the door, we learned why. She began closing the distance with us. Her walking was a slow shuffle. We spoke to her and hugged...and immediately could see that that her speaking ability was limited to a word or two at a time. The stroke clearly had done more damage to Diane than I had gathered from reading her emails.

Bill and I felt no awkwardness. Inside, Keith introduced us to his dad who had driven over from his nearby home for the afternoon. Then the five of us settled down to visiting. Most of the conversation was between Keith, Bill and me, with Keith's dad joining in on occasion.

Despite her limited speaking ability, Diane managed to communicate quite effectively. Not long after we had arrived, she spoke up. "Pop," she said and waved her arm and hand toward the kitchen.

"Right," Keith said immediately and got up to fetch soft drinks. "What'll you guys have?" He also offered us food. They had bought sliced roast beef, cheese and fine bread for the occasion.

Although Diane said little, she never stopped smiling. A couple times she tried to articulate thoughts and the words just wouldn't come. She sighed and grimaced in frustration.

Still, the conversation flowed on easily. Then, I said, "Diane, would you like to show me your computer? Perhaps we could send emails to a few of your friends. Tell them Bill and I are here today."

"Yes!" she said and immediately began to get up. Slowly, she led me toward a den. At the desk, I held the chair for her, then knelt on the floor beside her. She pushed a couple keys to get us on-line but had difficulty locating her computer's address book.

"Do you want me to ask Keith to give us a hand?" I was wondering whether Diane had authored emails to me, or whether she had gotten help from Keith. I chose not to ask. No need to ding her pride.

"Yes."

I got up and walked to the living room and spoke with Keith. He came in, did what was needed and left us alone while he returned to continue chatting with Bill. Keith's dad departed.

At the computer Diane and I picked the email addresses of several of our classmates and I tapped out a message, telling them where Bill and I were and encouraging them to reply.

Then Diane said, "Read?"

And I realized that her reading ability, like her speaking ability, was limited. I read the message to her and she beamed.

"How about a couple more?"

"Yes." She clearly was enjoying herself.

When we finished, I stood up. She rose. Then she said, "House" and waved her arm in a sweeping motion.

"Would you like to show me your home?"

"Yes."

We were standing by the foot of the staircase. "Upstairs?"

"No," she said decisively, and I smiled. I think her refusal had nothing to do with her disability. How many women of the house would want a tour to include an upstairs that wasn't immediately ready for viewing?

I followed her from room to room on the first floor. She obviously was proud of her home, and I felt good that she could show it to me.

In the living room, Bill and Keith were chatting easily. It was about 3:30 p.m.

"I guess we'd better get going again," I said.

"Right," said Bill.

First, though, Keith moved to the kitchen to make us sandwiches for the road. He also gave us a bag of pecans to munch on.

"Where are you guys headed now?" he asked.

"We're planning to head up to Knoxville and spend the night there," I said. "I think we should get there about six."

"I'll lead you out to the highway that takes you over to I-75," said Keith.

"Thanks," I said, "that would be helpful."

After assembling the sandwiches and handing them to us, Bill and I hugged Diane and then I said, "Pictures. Let me get my camera."

"I'll get ours, too," said Keith.

The four of us stepped outside into the bright sunshine. Then we arranged ourselves. Both cameras were put to use. Pictures of Keith and Diane. And then ones of Diane with Bill and me. Then we hugged Diane again and she turned and moved back into the house. Keith stayed with us.

Keith & Diane Mowry

He was a rock. He hadn't coddled Diane but was clearly caring and ever alert to her needs. He hires a woman to stay with Diane while he is away at work. As I mentioned earlier, the woman takes Diane shopping and runs errands with her.

"You know, we were planning to go to the reunion last July," Keith said, out of earshot of Diane. "Diane really wanted to go. But then at the last minute, she said no. She would be self-conscious of her appearance and she felt her classmates would feel awkward being around her."

"I hope she realizes now that wouldn't be the case," I said. "Heck, she could just sit and watch and have a great time. But the thing is, I know that the kids would sit down and visit with her." We had seen that when John Crum came in his wheel chair, when Joel Stentz was at a reunion after suffering a stroke, when Sam Elliott came, when Jim Blair had come and so on.

"I think there's a better chance she will come the next time," Keith said. "Your visit really helped her spirits. She was really looking forward to it."

"We're glad we came," said Bill.

"I hope you and Diane make it up to Ohio in August of 2004 for the All-Alumni Weekend," I said to Keith. "She would have a grand time."

"I know."

Bill and I shook hands with Keith and moved to get in our car. He stepped away toward his car, to lead us to the highway. But before getting in, he said, "Hey, guys, I'm really glad you stopped by."

Us, too.

During the ensuing months Jim Blair stayed in touch with several classmates via email. He remained consistently buoyant in his correspondence, though in her own emails, Angela told us that Jim had been having his share of tough moments. Understandably.

April 7, 2004. Jim sent me this email: *Mike, How are you doing? I got braces on and you ought to see me walk. I got a feeding tube in my stomach. I'm down to 150 pounds, and the doctor said I should take Endure. I take 3 every day and my wife pours it in a feeding tube. I hear crickets in my ear and every day I am weaker. I go back to Emory* (University Hospital) *April 25th. They have checked my breathing. I'm down to 50 percent in my lungs. Everyone is praying for me. I wish I could heal. I went to a friend and they laid hands on me and put oil on my head. I wasn't healed, but I thanked them. Bye. Your friend, Jim Blair.*

April 29, 2004. Jim sent this email to classmate Margie Parsons: *Dear Margie, I got a new wheelchair that goes up and down. Also bought me a* *typewriter that talks. Those ALS people take care of you. I feel blessed. Two nurses came from hospice today and I can count on them everyday. I'm down to 37% of my lungs, short breaths and I'm working not to go further. So pray for me. I love you, Margie, and you take care. Jim.*

Tuesday, May 4, 2004. I returned home late from a trip. Awaiting me were messages from three classmates – Margie Earick, Bill Anspach and Dick Shuler. They all bore the same sad news: Jim had passed away that morning.

His obituary remembered Jim as an Air Force veteran, a government meteorologist, an ordained Baptist deacon and a dedicated husband and father. Yet there was another way Angela was remembering Jim. After the funeral, she sent me an email. In it, she wrote: *Jim was so proud to be a Whippet. He remembered every play of every game he played in.* And that photo of Jim, Bill and me that Angela took with my camera as we were preparing to leave their house the previous November? Jim had had it framed and kept it on top of his computer.

Nearly five years later in March 2009, I spoke with Angela by phone. She told me that that photo still was sitting atop of Jim's computer. "You know, Mike," she said wistfully, "in that picture you can see how sick Jim was." And Angela herself? "I'm doing okay. Taking things one day at a time. But I still miss him terribly." As do I.

August 20-22, 2004. SHS All-Alumni Weekend. The Saturday night gala was held at spacious Fairhaven Hall at the Richland County Fairgrounds, about 10 miles southeast of Shelby. I arrived early to do a last check on arrangements. A few minutes later I looked outside and saw a man pushing a wheelchair toward the hall's entrance. It was Keith pushing Diane. She saw me, smiled and waved.

Within minutes after they'd entered the hall, schoolmates were clustered around Diane. I saw two of her friends – a man and a woman – dabbing at their eyes. But they also were smiling, and that seemed the perfect postscript to Bill's and my Georgia road trip.

CHAPTER 27

ROAD TRIP REUNIONS – FILLING GAPS FROM KOREA TO CLIFFSIDE PARK

Memorial Day weekend, 2007. Road trip. A 5:30 a.m. departure from North Canton, Ohio to Cliffside Park, New Jersey. 464 miles. Then on to Madison, New Jersey and the Pennsylvania towns of Downingtown, Lancaster and Harlansburg.

The roots of this road trip dated back to 1969 – in Korea no less. I'd arrived there in May 1968 for 13 months of military service as an Army correspondent and liaison specialist. In early 1969 with a few months to go on my hitch, Colonel Walter Moore, a gray-haired veteran and a decent fellow, came to my desk accompanied by a young Korean male, Kim Min Shik. Colonel Moore told me that Mr. Kim was representing a group of 20 or so students from Korean colleges who were hoping to find an American soldier willing to teach them conversational English.

Mr. Kim spoke up. "We have all been studying English since middle school," he said quietly, enunciating carefully, "but we have not heard an American speak it."

Colonel Moore continued, "If you agree to do this, it would have to be on your own time, at night."

I didn't hesitate. "Okay, I'll do it." At the time it didn't occur to me to ask the colonel why he picked me, but I'm darned glad he did.

A few days later, my first meeting with the group – about equally divided between men and women – was in a dimly lit tearoom in central Seoul. After Mr. Kim made introductions, I realized quickly that the students were understanding virtually nothing I was saying. So I resorted to pointing to objects in the room – chairs, tables, cups and so on – and pronouncing the words carefully and having the students repeat them. A goodly amount of laughter – some of it nervous – punctuated the session.

From that first night we progressed quickly and soon the group of bright, ambitious students and I were beginning to converse in English. Toward the end of my Army duty I began bringing to our sessions soldiers from other regions – Georgia, Wisconsin, Boston – so the students could hear other American accents.

The students, most just two or three years my junior, and I quickly grew close. Strong friendships formed. Two were with a man, Noh Sang Surk, and a woman, Won Chong Hee. Before I was to leave Korea, the group wanted to take me on a picnic. We scheduled it for my last week in Korea and we held it on the spacious and picturesque grounds of a palace in Seoul.

Right away that evening I could see that the students had gone all out. Most had little money and yet they had brought a delightful array of sandwiches, soft drinks and a basket of fresh strawberries, an expensive delicacy. As we started walking across the palace grounds, one of the women saw two young boys and said, "Would you please take these berries and wash them in that stream? I will pay you."

At that moment, I knew two things: within 24 hours I would be sick from the bacteria in the stream, and I nevertheless would eat those berries. I did and I was.

During the picnic the students gave me three gifts. Knowing I was planning to be married soon after returning to the States, they gave me two pairs of figurines. Each pair was carved from wood and depicted a Korean bride and groom wearing colorful traditional Korean wedding apparel. The third gift resulted from my answer to a question one of the students had posed during an English lesson: "Do you play chess?"

"No," I'd replied, "but I plan to learn."

The resulting gift was a chess set with the pieces carved from stone and contained in a lovely folding polished case which when opened forms a chess board.

I was touched. They had made financial sacrifices to buy the gifts that today can be seen in our living room.

As the picnic ended, we all walked back to the palace gate. There one of the students said, "We want you to write us letters."

I smiled, shaking my head slightly, and replied, "There are lots of you and only one of me. But if you write to me, I promise that I will answer your letters. Each one of them." Then I gave them my parents' address and told them to send their letters there because I didn't know where I'd be once back in the States.

During the next three or so years I received numerous letters from them. Noh Sang Surk and Won Chong Hee wrote more than the others. In one letter Chong included a photo of herself in her wedding gown and an invitation to the wedding. Today that photo and ones taken at the picnic are framed and displayed in our family room.

Gradually the correspondence died out as the students graduated, began careers and families and moved about.

Now, fast forward 25 years to 1998. I'm at Stanford's Graduate School of Business. One of my classmates is CK Choi from Seoul, Korea. One day during a class break, CK, a corporate chief executive officer, and I are sitting in the shade of trees, chatting about my soldiering days in Korea. I tell him about my student friends.

"Have you ever been back?" he asks.

"Yes, two or three times, including last year. And sometimes I think about those students and wonder what they have been doing. It would be nice to find out."

CK removes a sheet of paper from a notebook, hands it to me and says, "Write down their names." I write down just two, Noh Sang Surk and Won Chong Hee.

The next day during a class break, CK hands me the same sheet of paper, but this time I can see that it shows two phone numbers.

"CK," I say, surprised, "how in the world did you get these phone numbers overnight? There's a 17-hour time difference between California and Korea, and Korea is a nation of 45 million people."

CK smiles and says, "I phoned my secretary in Seoul and said, 'Find them.'"

Later that day back in my dorm room, I looked at the phone numbers. The one for Won Chong Hee was an international number. The one for Noh Sang Surk was a U.S. number and judging from the area code, one on the east coast. That didn't surprise me because he had said he wanted to work in an English-speaking environment, either in Korea or in an English-speaking country.

First I phoned Chong in Korea. She answered and was stunned that I had called. In broken, halting English she said that she was a schoolteacher, was married to a school librarian and had two sons. But, she said, she had not spoken much English in many years. There was a pause and then a young male voice got on the phone. He identified himself as one of Chong's two sons who happened to be visiting his parents. He stayed on the line, not so much interpreting but facilitating the conversation. It turned out that he and his brother both had received bachelor's degrees at the University of Washington. To describe Chong's and my conversation as heartwarming just might qualify as an understatement.

After hanging up, I phoned the second number and asked for Noh Sang Surk. The male who answered said he knew no one by that name. I asked if I had reached a business number. He said yes, so I asked a favor: please put down the phone and walk through your offices and say that Mike Johnson is on the phone. A couple minutes later, a husky male voice said, "Mike! This is Sang."

Why didn't the man who had answered the phone recognize the name Noh Sang Surk? Because Sang, in immigrating to the U.S., had anglicized – and legally changed – his name to Sam Noah, making it easier for Americans to pronounce and remember. Sam's story: After graduating from Kyung Hee University in 1969, he worked two years for a bank in Korea. Then he won a scholarship to study for a master's degree at Farleigh Dickinson University in Madison, New Jersey. That came about because Kyung Hee and Farleigh Dickinson were sister colleges, and Farleigh Dickinson's president had come to Seoul to interview Kyung Hee students for graduate programs.

While at Farleigh Dickinson, Sam grew fond of the U.S. A friend invited him to join a business and eventually Sam formed his own company, Noah Enterprises, which today includes an apparel manufacturing company with facilities in Korea and Mexico and an insurance brokerage. "I became the first licensed Korean insurance agent in northern New Jersey," Sam related with a measure of pride. In 1981 he married a woman eight years his junior and they have two children. Their son, a graduate of the University of North Carolina, has joined Sam's company and their daughter, a graduate of Wellesley College, is a financial analyst at Ernst & Young.

Since those 1998 phone calls, I've remained in touch with Chong via email and Sam via email and phone calls. In September 2006 I phoned Sam to wish him happy birthday. During that chat I said, "Emails and phone calls are good, but we need to see each other again."

"Yes," Sam replied earnestly, "we must."

"Then let's do it soon."

Almost immediately we began working to find a mutually convenient date. That wasn't easy as Sam's business career and family ties – three of his six siblings live in Seoul, three in the U.S. - have him traveling abroad frequently. We finally settled on Saturday, May 26 in Cliffside Park, New Jersey at the Palasadium Daewon which Sam described as the best Korean restaurant outside Seoul and just across the Hudson River from Manhattan.

Then I thought, okay, if I'm going to see Sam there, I could fly – or drive and try to see other friends in the area. I decided on the latter. I sent emails explaining my mission and received please-come-visit replies from Jodi Hutchison, one of my former interns from my years at TRW, and three of my SHS classmates – Jane Bell Henning, Jeff Bricker and Rich Mackey. After visiting Sam on Saturday afternoon, I would drive west to Madison, New Jersey to visit Jodi and her family. Then over the next two days I would drive south and west to Pennsylvania, visit Jane in Downingtown, Jeff in Lancaster and Rich in Harlansburg near New Castle.

On Saturday about noon I was nearing the Hudson River. By prior arrangement I picked up my cell phone and called Sam. He answered right away.

"Where are you?" he asked.

"About a dozen miles west of the Hudson."

"Good." He then told me which interstate exit to use. "At the end of the exit ramp you will see a Marriott Hotel. I will be waiting there."

"Okay. I'm driving a burgundy Lumina."

Moments later I came whipping off the near-circular exit ramp and could see easily the Marriott just ahead on my right. As I began looking for the parking lot entrance, I saw a man standing on a grassy strip between the street and parking lot. He was waving vigorously.

We hadn't seen each other in nearly four decades, but I recognized Sam immediately. He stands about six feet one inch with broad shoulders and a smile to match. I swung into the parking lot and wheeled around to where Sam was standing. He came bounding from the grassy strip to my car. I pushed open the car door, got out and we darned near crushed each other with bear hugs. Then we pushed back, hands still on each other's shoulders, and laughed joyously. The distance – and time – from Korea to Cliffside Park had vanished.

"I thought you'd be waiting in front of the hotel lobby."

"I was too excited to wait there."

Again we both laughed. Then, using my cell phone, I called Lynne so that she and Sam could at last hear each other's voices.

The rest of the afternoon flew by. First we drove to the Palasadium Daewon. Sam hadn't exaggerated. It's a spectacular restaurant – an ornate entrance, a sprawling dining room and a commanding view of the river and Manhattan beyond. Something more was also immediately clear; Sam had informed the staff about the significance of the occasion. We were greeted, served and cared for with genuine warmth.

Sam Noah and Mike Johnson

After our meal – a feast actually – we asked a staff person to take pictures of us. Sam then drove me on a leisurely tour of the area. Later we returned to the Marriott where I'd left my car. We went inside for drinks, and he asked me to inscribe four copies of my second book, *Fate of the Warriors*, much of which is set in Korea. He wanted to give them to friends.

In 1969 in Korea, Sam had helped me bridge cultural gaps. Now he had helped bridge a chronological one.

That evening I drove to Madison, New Jersey, checked into a hotel, and phoned Jodi Hutchison, the last of my interns – 1989-1990 – during my years at Cleveland-based TRW. Then I drove to her home, just blocks from the hotel. She and her kids, Libby and TJ, greeted me. I'd seen Jodi a few years before in Manhattan, but this was my first in-person look at her children. They were excited to see "Mom's old boss."

From 1976 through my departure from corporatedom in 2003, I employed more than 50 interns. None was more driven, more aggressive than Jodi.

"I want to be your best intern ever," she told me early during her internship, "and I want you to regard me as the best."

Brainstorm. Jodi's cubicle at TRW included a large whiteboard. Once when she was away I entered and wrote the names of 10 or so of her predecessors. I wrote her name at the bottom of the list. That was akin to dangling bloody bait in front of a starving shark.

As time passed and as she successfully completed more assignments, I kept on entering her cubicle, erasing her name and rewriting it higher on the list.

"You know," she told me more than once, "I won't be satisfied until I'm at the top."

After completing her internship – at the top of that list – she was the first of my TRW interns to be offered a permanent position with the company. She took it – even though it required moving to Berkeley, California. From there – not to my surprise – she has built a fine career that has seen her moving from California to Florida to New Jersey and rising to a vice presidency.

At her home in Madison, salad, grilled chicken, homegrown vegetables, dessert and conversation kept us up late. The next morning I checked out of the hotel and drove back to Jodi's house. She and the kids were waiting and ready to serve a delightful brunch. Afterward Jodi asked me to sign copies of my books for family members and friends. Next we headed outside into bright sunshine with the kids to take pictures. A round of farewell hugs and then it was back on the road.

On Sunday afternoon about 4:30, I arrived at Jane Bell's house, a handsome colonial with a woods at the rear of the property. Dick, her husband of 38 years, saw me walking through the open garage, waved me inside while on a phone call, greeted me warmly and then hollered upstairs, "Jane! Get down here. Mike's here."

She quickly descended, wearing a dark t-shirt and black slacks. Her feet were bare. We hugged and chatted and then she went about preparing a splendid meal: barbecued pork ribs, coleslaw and buttered garlic bread. Dick asked me for my drink preference.

"Red wine, scotch or diet cola," I replied.

"I have a nice 12-year-old scotch," Dick said.

"Scotch it is. Neat."

He retrieved the bottle and set it on the table with a glass. "Pour as much as you like."

I poured about two ounces.

"I think I'll join you," he said and retrieved a second glass. Then he excused himself to fire up the grill.

As Jane went about slicing and buttering small loaves of bread and sliding them into the oven, the conversation started steaming ahead. At one point I said to Dick, "If this catching up on Shelby stuff starts to bore you-"

"Don't worry," he smiled, "I'll just take a hike."

But for hours the three of us engaged in animated chatter, punctuated often with gales of laughter as we plugged in gaps in our knowledge of each other and our lives. After her freshman year at Muskingum College, Jane transferred to Ohio State. She told me she had gone to college mainly because her mom wanted her to. What Jane really wanted was to be an airline stewardess – as today's flight attendants were proudly known in that era. After graduating from OSU, she went to St. Louis-based TWA

Airlines' stewardess training center in Kansas City. "I asked to be based in New York because I wanted to fly international routes." Which she did, most often to London, Madrid and Lisbon. "It was hard work. I always had jet lag. But I loved my job."

But after 18 months, she had to quit because of a TWA rule: stewardesses couldn't be pregnant and Jane was.

She then described how she and Dick had met – in a bar in Manhattan. She talked about their kids, and she described the onset of agoraphobia.

"When did that strike?" I asked.

"When I was forty. It started with a panic attack when I was going to an appointment. So I decided not to go back there. But the attacks kept increasing and pretty soon I wasn't going anywhere." She was speaking matter-of-factly with no hesitancy or self-pity. "For three years I didn't leave the house. I couldn't even answer the phone. Not even to talk to my daughter."

"Fortunately," Dick interjected, "we found a psychiatrist who knew how to treat it. I had to drag Jane to see him. At that time many people with agoraphobia went untreated or treated ineffectively."

"Yes," said Jane, "and it took a while before I began to get better. When the doctor gave me the drug, he said it would take a while to take effect. Even so, the first few weeks I was worrying that it wouldn't work."

"Do you think the agoraphobia was in your genes?" I asked.

"Yes," Jane replied. "I think my dad might have had it. At least, he suffered from bouts of depression."

Our conversation also led to some interesting discoveries, just as had been the case during class reunions beginning with the one in 1983. For example, I'd known Jane had a brother, Todd, younger by five years, as I'd exchanged emails with him in connection with Whippet Echoes, our alumni email newsletter. But I was surprised to learn that Jane has a sister, Margaret Rose (Posey), younger by 14 years. Todd lives in Ohio and Posey in Florida.

"Whenever I was at your house in Shelby," I joshed, "you must have kept little Posey hidden."

Another surprise came when Jane volunteered, "It's tough being a teenager. I didn't have much self-esteem. Not until my senior year. Then I felt like I was on top of the world. I thought I knew everything, had all the answers. But if God said, 'You can live part of your life over again but it has to be your four high school years,' I'd say 'Forget it.'" It was difficult thinking that Jane had lacked self-esteem but there you have it – another Chris Straw-like masking job.

At one point we took a break and went outside to snap photos. I'd loaded my camera with black and white film which I prefer for close-up people shots. To Jane I joked, "I like black and white because it masks my wrinkles and age spots." For one picture, I had Jane don a Shelby Whippets ball cap that I'd brought along. Reason: Downingtown High School is, so far as we know after a Google search, one of only eight high schools that use Whippets as a nickname. Jane and Dick had moved to Downingtown in 1990 from near Chicago.

And so the evening went, conversation flowing comfortably. Then about 11:00 it shifted into talking about the kids Jane and I had known in our respective Shelby neighborhoods on opposite sides of town. Smiling at the memory, she told me she had had a dislike – "I can't remember why," she laughed – for a girl who lived near her and who had been one of my favorite dance partners during 7th and 8th grades. By contrast, Jane told me she had a fondness for one of the guys who lived just a street away from me. And Jane had this to say about another of her neighborhood girls, one you read about earlier – Pat Papenbrock. "Pat was so nice. And she was beautiful. But we weren't jealous of her because she was so nice. I loved her."

"Do you remember the only time you visited my house on Auburn?" I asked.

"Yes. It was after a football game. You were hurt and I came to see how you were."

"Right. When Joel Stentz brought me home, I was in so much pain that he and my dad couldn't get me upstairs to my room so they put me in the downstairs bedroom. The next morning I was to go to the hospital for X-rays. They thought I might have cracked my pelvis. But I didn't."

"A bad bruise," Dick observed.

"That's right. And," I said, looking at Jane, "do you know what I was thinking when you came into the bedroom?"

"I wish you'd leave," she laughed.

"Right. I was touched that you came but was in so much pain I didn't really want to see anyone or have to talk with someone."

"We went to the homecoming dance together," Jane recalled.

"Yes, I think we had a good time."

"We did. And recently you told me that guys wanted you to ask Pat but you asked me."

I laughed. "That's right. And I fictionalized that in my second book."

At midnight Dick said he needed to get some sleep. Jane and I remained in the family room, continuing our catching up. As the clock neared 1 a.m., Jane was showing no sign of tiring but I told her that I needed to hit the sack to get at least a few hours sleep before getting on the road again. We stood and hugged.

During our days at SHS, I viewed Jane as having "the package." To wit, brainy, witty, pretty and percolating with intellectual and physical energy. The passing years notwithstanding, she still has that package. Moreover, I now had a more complete picture that includes her being a heckuva wife and mom as well as a woman of remarkable resilience.

At 6 a.m., I was up and showering. By 7:00 I was sitting in Jane and Dick's kitchen, sipping juice and eating oatmeal. At 7:45 I was in my car, backing out of their down-sloping driveway, waving goodbye to both of them and heading to Lancaster to see classmate Jeff Bricker and his wife Sandy who celebrated their 30th wedding anniversary in March 2007.

Back at SHS, Jeff and I weren't buddies but we did share mutual respect and affection. The most time we spent together was on long drives to and from Ohio University in 1962 when we both were representatives of SHS at Buckeye Boys State.

Jeff was plenty smart and kindly. Recently, in recalling his teen years, he self-deprecatingly said, "I was probably a little geekie back in high school." He was more than that. Yes, while at SHS he was a member of the Biology Club, Radio Club and Hi-Y. But he also was lanky and a skilled golfer. So in exchanging emails to schedule this mini-reunion, I wasn't surprised to learn that Jeff and Sandy were living in a condo complex that is part of Bent Creek Country Club. What did surprise me was learning that they had been living there 10 years.

A bigger surprise came later. Meanwhile, when I rang their doorbell, Jeff had company – plenty of it – as he led me into the foyer. Two extremely curious and friendly golden Labradors and two mildly curious cats greeted and inspected me with noses damp and sniffing and tails wagging furiously.

A few moments later, Sandy, who had been showering, joined us. She laughed at the pets and said, "We have no kids; these are our kids." Then we moved to their patio where they laid out a nice spread of fruits and pastries. It began sprinkling but we sat there anyway under a large umbrella. Then we began catching up. Jeff and Sandy had lived the early years of their marriage near Chicago. Then Jeff found himself out of a job. Meanwhile, Sandy, a consultant, was growing weary of heavy travel. In 1986 they learned that a small assisted living home was for sale in Pennsylvania's Lancaster County where Jeff's family had settled in 1732. "We felt an affinity for the area," said Sandy. "Yes," Jeff added, "it felt like home."

They decided to take the financial plunge and buy the assisted living home. "We had enough money to last for about seven months," said Sandy. "We knew we had to make the business grow or we'd be in deep trouble fast." She was smiling at the memory.

They did make it go, expanding that first home and adding a second.

Jeff strikes me as just the right kind of person to own an assisted living home. In my view, having visited such homes as well as nursing homes way more often than I like to remember, a topnotch owner needs to combine a strong business sense with compassion and courage. Why courage? How often have you visited assisted living or nursing homes?

Jeff and Sandy got their camera and I readied mine and we took a round of photos. Then they had me inscribe copies of my books.

When it was time to move on, I asked Jeff the location of the nearest gas station.

"I'll lead you there," he said immediately. "And from there I'll lead you onto Route 283 which takes you back up to the Pennsylvania

Turnpike. I'll get off at the first exit but you keep on going." That was the best road to…

Harlansburg to see Rich Mackey.

Back at SHS, Rich, a solidly built six-footer, was the student manager of our baseball team and a three-year member of the Future Farmers of America. For two of those years Rich was an FFA club officer. His family owned two mid-sized farms.

"I was pretty much an introvert in high school," Rich reflected.

"You were one of the quiet ones," I concurred, smiling.

Rich nodded. "But I wasn't afraid to speak my mind."

Forty-four years later he still wasn't. More on that later. After graduating from SHS, Rich went to Ohio State. During two of the summers when we were in college, Rich and I played on a fast pitch softball team organized by Bill Anspach. We entered tournaments, and I have two particularly strong memories: those summers brought Rich and me closer, and I learned that I was a better baseball hitter than fast-pitch softball hitter.

After college Rich entered the Army as an ROTC-commissioned second lieutenant. Sent to Vietnam, he served as an advisor to South Vietnamese Army troops.

"Infantry?" I asked.

"No. Armor." Then he laughed, "But they quickly made me infantry." He saw plenty of action which, he said, "I'd rather forget."

"Did you plan to be a farmer?"

"No, not really. I majored in ag-econ." That degree led Rich to a career with two organizations that provide counsel to farmers.

Then came Rich's big news. "I've joined you," he smiled. "I retired three weeks ago."

"Congratulations!" We shook hands. "I think you'll find the post-business phase of life has much to recommend it."

Rich smiled. "I've liked the first three weeks." The day after my visit Rich turned 62. "I really wanted to retire at 62, but my last supervisor was the worst I ever had."

As Rich described that supervisor, the man seemed rigid and petty – and Rich wouldn't abide his small mindedness. As with his high school days, Rich again showed his willingness to speak his mind. "I called him out – in public and in front of his boss and his boss's boss. We were in a meeting. He was supposed to have a brochure ready long ago for farmers. I asked him, 'When are you going to have that brochure ready?' 'Soon' he said. 'That's what you said two weeks ago, a month ago, a year ago.' He didn't like it."

"I can see tension building," I laughed. Rich laughed too. "Did you think he might fire you before you retired?"

"No. I didn't think he was man enough."

During this chat, Rich was grilling lamb and chicken kebobs while his wife Jamie was laying out a mouth-watering array of salads, side dishes and desserts. We filled our plates in the kitchen and then moved to tables outside to eat. With us were their two daughters, one a schoolteacher like Jamie had been for 34 years and the other an accountant, and their beaus, one a husband and the other a boyfriend.

The first six years of their marriage, Rich and Jamie lived in an apartment. The house they live in is one they built in 1976. It's comfy. Lots of rich paneling, antiques and Ohio State memorabilia. "We built small and kept adding on," Rich said.

It was time for more picture taking. Afterward we walked to the garage, a large three-bay one that was added on to the original which now serves as a work and storage area. In the far bay sat a beige SUV, Jamie's vehicle. In the center bay sat what Rich wanted to show me - his retirement gift to himself. "It's a 2005," he said as we stood by the gleaming red Mustang. "I thought about getting a 2007, but it really wasn't what I wanted. So I went with the 2005 – which got me what I want and saved a few bucks." He was smiling.

"Your late-in-life toy?"

"Sort of. Well, not really. It's really my car. I plan to drive it regularly." Then he pointed to a big green pickup truck. "That's my only other car."

"Looks really clean." It too was gleaming.

Rich smiled. "It's a 1979."

"You're kidding."

"No."

"How many miles?"

"About 85,000."

"On a truck almost 30 years old."

"It belonged to my dad. It wasn't driven much on the road. Just mostly around the farm."

The truck looked solid, just like Rich. And the sporty Mustang? That was a surprise, just like Rich could spring.

When I returned home 63 hours after my predawn embarkation for New Jersey, my odometer read 1,064 miles. Stiff and bushed though I was, every hour and mile had been worth the effort.

Two weeks later I was on the road again, this time driving south with Lynne and daughter Andrea whom we picked up at her home in Columbus. Destination: Douglasville, Georgia for a visit with Lynne's sister and brother-in-law, Dianne and Dick Vots, and numerous other family members, including my fourth goddaughter, Julia Vots Hatfield, herself now the mother of two daughters, and nephews John, Alex and Thomas and their spouses and kids.

A few days before embarking I emailed classmate Diane Mowry and her husband Keith - whom you've read about earlier - in Rome, Georgia. I asked if they were up for another visit. Rome is only about a 75-minute drive northwest from Douglasville. Keith's reply was quick in coming and enthusiastic. "Great! How about Monday? If you can be here early, we can buy supper."

"What time is good for you?" I replied. "I'm flexible."

"About 5:30," Keith emailed.

That Monday, entering Rome, I cell phoned Keith. Talk about serendipity; he was driving home from work and was just a few blocks ahead of me on the same street. Moments later we pulled into their driveway just seconds apart. We parked, exited our vehicles, shook hands and hugged.

Inside their house Keith walked through the spacious kitchen and headed down a long hallway. "This way, Mike," and he led me into Diane's bedroom.

She was sitting in a large upholstered chair, holding a laptop computer and looking at pictures on the screen.

"Hi, honey," Keith said. "Mike's here."

Diane was beaming. "Hi."

I walked to her, bent down and kissed her cheek.

We began this reunion by watching *Shelby – A Place In The Heart*, a DVD that I'd had produced back in 2004 and that Diane and Keith hadn't seen, on a large-screen TV in her room. She was smiling throughout the 22-minute video with Keith providing commentary, identifying SHS alums and town buildings and parks as they appeared on screen.

As the video ended, Diane said, "Pictures, me."

"Would you like a copy of Mike's DVD?" Keith asked.

"Yes."

"I'm sure Mike could burn a copy for you."

Actually I couldn't burn the commercially produced DVD, but I said, "Sure," thinking I had an extra copy or two back home that I could send Diane. And a week or so later, after returning to Ohio, did so.

"Are you ready to eat?" Keith asked Diane.

"Okay."

Keith then helped Diane shift from the upholstered chair to her battery-powered wheelchair. Next he went outside where he helped Diane into their mini-van. Then he pushed the chair to the van's rear, raised the door, removed and positioned a pair of homemade, hinged wood ramps and maneuvered the chair up and into the van.

We ate at a local steakhouse and covered a lot of ground. Keith was excited because the following weekend he would begin fulfilling a boyhood dream. "I'm going to ride my motorcycle out west." He'd been riding scooters and cycles since age 12.

"How long will you be on the road?" I asked.

"A month."

"Are you going with a group?"

"No. Alone. I just want to be on my own."

"Sounds like the perfect stress reducer."

Keith smiled. "Right. My kids said they were worried I'd feel lonely."

"You could use some time alone," I observed.

"Yes. Every day I've got my company to run. And I've got Dad (age 83) and Diane to take care of. Dad had some health problems but we've got those under control. And Diane's doing pretty well now, and she really likes the woman who looks after her. I figured at my age it's either do it now or forget about it." Then he looked at Diane and smiled. "She told me if I'm going to be away for a month she wanted her own vacation. So I sent her and the woman on their own vacation to Savannah for a week. They had a great time."

Diane nodded her confirmation.

Keith remains a rock. He is attentive to Diane's needs but doesn't overly coddle her. That she remains spirited is, I think, a result of Keith's approach. During dinner Keith and I talked quite a bit about tragedies and coping. We agreed that it is the truly lucky family who can get through an entire generation without a member suffering a serious illness, disease or accident. "I think the way we grew up in Shelby, a small town, teaches us something about being responsible and loyal," Keith observed.

We finished eating and drove back to their house. As Keith was helping Diane from the van into her wheelchair, I said, "You two stay out here for a minute while I go inside and get my camera."

"I'll get mine too," said Keith and followed me inside. A round of picture taking ensued. Then it was time for farewells. I kissed and hugged Diane, and Keith and I shook hands and hugged.

"Enjoy the heck out of your journey out west," I said.

"I will."

Then I got in my car, backed down their sloping driveway and began driving south and east back to Douglasville. During one stretch I found myself driving parallel to a long fast-moving freight train. That sight and rumbling sound carried me back to my youth in Shelby. That set me to thinking about the kids I'd grown up with, and I couldn't help wondering about our final reunion. It already had come and gone for too many of our classmates. When would it arrive for the rest of us '63ers?

CHAPTER 28

INSPIRATION FROM A FROG KILLER

I can't close this account without commenting on our SHS teachers. They have become central to our reunions.

Back in the day, some of them inspired terror. Some were inspiring. Some were both. Some you saw for the last time on your last day of high school. Some you stayed in touch with. Amazingly, after decades, you reconnected with a few. Sound familiar? The SHS teachers of the early 1960s were a memorable bunch.

Leora Kuhn could inspire terror. Think of Miss Kuhn as a grandmother with too much makeup. She had the face and hair of a lioness, and she taught 9th grade English with bared feline incisors. I liked her. But poor Mary Longo. Mary sat beside me and she was cute. But each day that she entered Miss Kuhn's room, Mary must have felt her stomach tighten and rise, anticipating Miss Kuhn's claws closing on her throat. When Miss Kuhn began asking questions, Mary corkscrewed in her best effort to become formless and invisible. Rarely worked though. With unfailing instinct Miss Kuhn knew which students were prepared and confident and which weren't and she showed no mercy. When Miss Kuhn called on Mary, she swung her head toward me, eyes wide in panic.

Mary didn't graduate. For her, I think entering SHS each day might have been the equivalent of a daily trip to the Colisseum as a doomed Christian about to become food for the beasts. I'm pretty sure she saw Miss Kuhn as one of the beasts and a heartless one at that.

How did you regard your teachers? What did you think of them then? And now? How do you regard their role in helping you form the foundation of your life? How grateful are you? If at all?

At SHS in the early 1960s we were blessed with a cadre of teachers who were well grounded, high-minded, dedicated, skilled and hard-working. Many were wonderfully creative and witty. Were they all tutorial stars? One was a dud. He was a history teacher who could have authored a treatise on how to induce sleep – and how to crudely wake students who had dozed off. Then there was an English teacher who kept a bottle of booze in her desk drawer – and who fooled no one. Still, amazingly, she managed to be engaging and effective, and most students liked her. Including me. One year they dedicated a Scarlet S to her. Then, too, there was one teacher who was just downright mean. As seniors, we were at war with him, with each side only occasionally granting quarter. They were the minority.

As a group those SHS teachers worked hard to help us learn to think, to study, to achieve. As former biology teacher and football and track coach Bill Varble said in 2003, "Our programs were successful, our students went on to become doctors, lawyers, successful business people and good family people. We teachers must have been doing something right." They helped us build self-esteem and self-discipline.

In earlier chapters you read about Spanish teacher Wayne Potts, dead from Parkinson's Disease at 74; civics teacher and football coach Bill Wilkins, dead from cancer at 77; and office practices and homeroom teacher Jeanette Bly Egleston Allard, still going strong at 77. So many others distinguished themselves. To cite just a few:

- Dora Summer who was able to make studying Latin a pleasure and who taught us how to think. She was a 1912 SHS graduate and taught at SHS from 1916-1964 – 48 years! She died in 1983 at 88. During my SHS days I was Dora's "boy Saturday." After her sister died, she continued to live alone in a large house on West Main Street. Most Saturday mornings found me there, mowing the lawn, washing windows, sorting attic contents, painting the garage, whatever Dora needed.

- Mel John who made sense out of algebra, demonstrated wit and patience in doing so, and also managed sales of athletic tickets and programs. Now 82, he co-manages the database for the 1,700-member SHS Alumni Email Network and is on the SHS Alumni Association Board of Trustees. In 2006 we surprised Mel with a framed certificate proclaiming him an honorary alumnus of Shelby High (he had graduated from Bellaire High). In 2007 he was voted for induction into the SHS Hall of Distinction.

- Don Monn who taught American history with the same gusto he brought to coaching football and baseball. He also was an SHS alum, class of '44. He passed away in April 2004 at 78. How respected was he? Some people who came to visiting hours at the funeral home to pay their respects had to park several blocks away.

- Ward Holdsworth, in 1961 just out of Muskingum College, already balding and the epitome of cool. He taught biology and coached football and track. Girls adored him and guys liked him. Now 70. In 2004 he came from his home in New Philadelphia, Ohio, where he concluded his stellar teaching and coaching career, to the All-Alumni Weekend to salute Miss Snyder. He did the same in 2008 when we were announcing the successful conclusion of the $150,000 Harryet Snyder Memorial Science Center fund-raising campaign.

- George Shuler who surprised me by helping me realize I could enjoy geometry.

- Lowell 'Mac' McMeeken who helped a student with zero mechanical aptitude build a three-tiered table that, 46 years later, still graces our family room. He taught at SHS from 1941-1974. Warmly witty, he passed away at age 90 on June 1, 2007, in Bellevue, Ohio.

- Joan Arrington who was a taskmaster and English teaching zealot. One of Joan's admirers tells the story of her son who when entering college realized quickly that he wasn't sufficiently grounded in English. Says the woman, "My son contacted Joan who tutored him during Christmas break – at no charge." One of Joan's former students has this to say: "Miss Arrington was unquestionably the most influential teacher I ever had. If it hadn't been for the writing skills I honed under her strict eye, I'd never have made it in advertising." In 2006 after reading my first historical novel, Joan phoned me. "I've read your book," she said, "and I'm calling to tell you what I think about it." I could feel my stomach knotting and my armpits leaking as instant anxiety began attacking. I held my breath, waiting for her next words. "I really, really like the book. I've loaned it to a friend, and I'm telling the library to buy lots of copies." Whew. Passed the test. I could feel my anxiety draining and a sense of exhilaration building. And then, dammit, a few months later on September 3, Joan died. She was

79. She had fallen and broken her hip on August 11 and seemed to be recovering well. When she fell ill, she was rushed to an emergency room where she died hours later from a blood clot. When Mel John phoned with the news, I felt as though I'd been punched in the gut.

- Lillian Rae Bowman who taught world history with an obvious relish and who founded *Whippet Tales* – the school newspaper – in 1954 and who served as advisor for the Pep Club and cheerleaders. On April 24, 2003, at age 78, she passed away after suffering a slow, painful death from cancer, strokes and pneumonia. Her passing elicited tributes from several former students which we published in Whippet Echoes. A sampling:

  o Michelle Black Abrams '69: "Miss Bowman is one of the teachers I have often remembered through the years. In fact, I think Miss Bowman is one of the original 'Steel Magnolias' role models."

  o Dr. Jim Hennessy '61: "Miss Bowman was a gem, and I remember her classes well that I had in world history in 1958-59. She gave me some special encouragement on a report project. She was a gentle soul with a delightful personality. She was the best example of a kind, human spirit."

  o Elaine Lybarger '63: "Rae (no one called her Lillian) was our mentor when the band members in 7th grade were the only 7th graders at the high school that year, and everyone else was at Central Junior High. We all were in her homeroom. She 'protected' us from the upperclassmen."

  o Pat Gates Saltzgaber'63: 'I have the same memory as Elaine of Miss Bowman protecting the only class of 7th graders that year at SHS. Also for being the Pep Club advisor. She deserved another star in her crown for that one."

  o Colleen Henson '55: "Miss Bowman was my cheerleading advisor and also my advisor on Whippet Tales. After I graduated, I always went to her apartment for a visit when in Shelby. I always remembered her saying that her grandmother's family was attacked by Indians on the way to Illinois. The grandmother was just a tiny baby and survived scalping. The Indians only got a bit of skin."

o   Byron Wagoner '59: "She was one classy lady who has left her imprint on all of us who had the privilege of attending SHS while she was there."

o   Nancy Nicholson Yoder '60: "This is my last year as a history teacher. I've done it for 28 years and loved it. Miss Bowman is the reason I chose history. My one hope throughout my career was that I was half as good as Miss Bowman and the other excellent teachers I had in Shelby. We were lucky to have known such teachers."

Then there was Harryet Snyder. Yes, Harryet, not Harriet or Harriette. As she once explained to me, her dad had been hoping for a boy. When Harryet turned 90, you'd not likely have guessed her age. Yes, her face was lined and spotted with age, but her voice still resonated strength and energy and her gait was reminiscent of a New Yorker late for the afternoon train. Her specialty and her love was biology, though early in her career, she also taught Latin and English.

Harryet was born and raised in Norwalk, about 30 miles north of Shelby. She always remembered clearly her first trip to Shelby. It was about 1928, and she came to Shelby with a Baptist Bible study group. In the late 1920s, 30 miles still was a considerable journey – in both physical and mental distance. Harryet used to laugh about that visit. She remembered seeing the white-painted, six-story Moody & Thomas Milling Company building and thinking it a skyscraper. She was surprised to learn that Shelby had a main street. And little did she dream that she would one day return and want to stay.

After high school Harryet wanted to go to Ohio State University in Columbus. But her family deemed it too distant and too expensive. Instead, she went to Bowling Green where she achieved a dual major – biology and French-Latin. After getting her bachelor's degree there, she concluded that she could go to Ohio State to pursue a master's. She did and began a lifelong love affair with Ohio State, including Buckeye football. Especially Buckeye football.

213

In later years, had you visited her home, you would have seen Buckeye football mementos throughout her house. But in her downstairs bathroom, you would have seen virtually every inch of every surface covered with Buckeye stuff – photos, program covers, pennants. On the floor was a rug in the maize and blue of the "hated" University of Michigan. And thanks to members of the SHS Class of '63, she also had a roll of Bo Schembechler (the late Michigan coach) toilet paper. I wouldn't have been surprised had she drawn her last breath while watching her Buckeyes, especially since she said that watching made her "so nervous."

After completing her master's degree in biology at OSU, she took her first teaching assignment at the high school in Butler, Ohio. To her chagrin there was no opening for a biology teacher, so she taught Latin and English. After four years at Butler she accepted an offer to come to SHS. Why? "Because," said Harryet, eyes full of mirth, "the school's colors were the same as Ohio State's."

Norwalk and Shelby both compete in the Northern Ohio League. Although Harryet was a Norwalk grad, it didn't take long before she was throwing her full allegiance to Shelby. She put it this way: "I have re-established my roots in Shelby." In the autumn of our sophomore year, 1960, Norwalk and Shelby both were undefeated as they prepared for a showdown at Skiles Field in Shelby. A couple days before the big game, my buddy Bill Anspach was in Harryet's biology class. Harryet noticed Bill peering at his book with uncommon intensity. She walked back to him. He looked up sheepishly. Between Bill's eyes and the biology book was Bill's copy of the football scouting report on Norwalk. He expected a dressing down and possibly a trip to the principal's office. Instead...

"Are we going to beat Norwalk?" Harryet asked calmly.

"Yes," said Bill, "we are."

"Are we *really* going to beat Norwalk?" Harryet said with narrowed eyes.

"Yes, we are really going to beat them."

"I hope so," said Harryet, "because I have a bet with my family in Norwalk that Shelby will win. If we don't," she said, eyes again narrowing, this time with a hint of playfulness, "you will get a demerit."

Bill was quick with his reply. "If we win, do I get extra credit?"

Shelby triumphed 16-14 and won the NOL title. Says Bill, "I don't remember getting extra credit, but I did pass the course." (Bill's telling of this story is captured on videotape.)

In addition to high intelligence and high humor, Harryet could be highly decisive. One day SHS Principal J.E. McCullough came to Harryet's room. "Your new shipment of frogs is in," he said.

"Good," said Harryet. She and her biology students each school year went through hundreds of frogs as the kids learned dissecting. The frogs arrived from a commercial laboratory in packages of 50, smelling of formaldehyde and ready for dissection. "I'll send one of the students down to pick up the box."

"I think you'd better come," said Mr. McCullough. "These frogs are alive."

"Oh my," said Harryet. Off she went to inspect her 50 very alive specimens. Then her decisiveness kicked in. She recruited a couple of her students. Following her instructions, she and they proceeded to dispatch the frogs. "It's called pithing the frog," Harryet told me early in 2004. "I learned it at Bowling Green. We made a tiny cut across the back of each frog's neck, then injected a syringe. It was very quick and humane," says Harryet. It's one of her favorite stories and her telling it in her own words also is captured on videotape.

One of her former students, Sharon Dillon, remembers a dissection that didn't happen. "The Friday before we were to dissect frogs I jokingly announced that I was going to be sick the next week. Well, wouldn't you know it. Sunday afternoon, I came down with a whopping case of the flu and was out all week. Needless to say, I failed the test. I don't think Harryet ever believed that I was really sick."

Harryet's teaching provided direction and determination to some, including Gary Page, SHS class of 1964. "When I took biology class from Miss Snyder, I was a confused, lazy kid. But somehow Miss Snyder saw something in me. She inspired me, got me interested in biology, seemed to have confidence in me. I stayed with biology in the general sense and went on to become a veterinarian. Oh, and coming from someone who spent eight years at Ohio State University, I would like to tell her, 'Go Bucks.'"

Adds John Arntz, "What a gem she was. Her enthusiasm encouraged me to pursue a bachelor's degree at OSU in biology and biochemistry."

We also published those encomiums in a special memorial edition of Whippet Echoes.

For decades Harryet's summers were spent working in Yellowstone Park, where she also went hiking and mountain climbing. She credited that summer regimen with her enduring physical strength. Her companions each of those summers included a teacher friend from Cleveland and Lillian Rae Bowman. For decades Harryet and Rae shared a home. While I was at SHS, there were rumors – and frequent expressions of hope – that Harryet and Wayne Potts would marry. But Harryet, Wayne and Lillian Rae all remained single.

While at SHS, Harryet and I did not forge a lasting friendship. In fact, after taking Biology 1 my sophomore year, I doubt if I ever said more than "Hi" to her in the hallway. Why? I can't say. We got on well in class, and I was one of her better students. After graduating from SHS, I wasn't in touch with Harryet again until 2002. And that reconnection, while memorable, wasn't overly warm or encouraging. Here is what happened.

In the spring of 2002 the team planning the 11-class reunion decided to invite all remaining former teachers from our years at SHS. I mailed letters to them and promised to make follow-up phone calls. Some already had attended previous reunions, and we were confident that they would accept our invitation. But not all. On my list were Harryet Snyder and Lillian Rae Bowman. When I made the follow-up call to their number, Harryet answered. I introduced myself. Before I could say much else, Harryet said icily, "We don't go to reunions. Never have. We aren't going to start now." The conversation came to a rather abrupt end.

About a dozen other teachers from that era did accept our invitation, and four of them agreed to speak at an "assembly" that was part of the three-day gathering. Former biology teacher and coach Bill Varble, also an inductee in the school's Hall of Distinction, was the last to speak and while on stage told us, "Miss Bowman is in very poor health and is in a hospital in Columbus." Between the end of the assembly that afternoon and the gala that night, one of our schoolmates, Dave Mellick of the class of 1960, dashed to a drug store and bought 11 get well cards. At the gathering that night, he circulated the cards, one for each of the 11 classes represented. Signatures crowded all 11 cards which were then mailed to Miss Bowman.

In February 2003, I decided to contact Harryet and Rae again. I wrote a long letter to them, describing how things had gone at the reunion and expressing hope that Rae would regain her health.

A few weeks later, to my surprise, I received a note from Harryet, saying, *Your letter couldn't have arrived at a better time,* she wrote. *Miss Bowman has had a setback. She came home 2/17 from Oak Manor and was finishing her chemo treatments when she developed pneumonia. She was in the hospital 4 days. She came home and the next day she had a stroke. Today, 3/24, she is being released back to Oak Manor. It's a day-to-day situation.* She closed by expressing appreciation for the letter which she said she would read to Rae.

A week or so later, I found myself pondering that icy rejection from the previous year and contrasting it with Harryet's note. It seemed to suggest a thawing. I sent off an email to former algebra teacher Mel John who, along with wife Anne (SHS Class of '51), was a longtime close friend of Harryet. I asked him how he felt about calling Harryet and inviting her to a meeting a bunch of us were holding on Saturday, April 12, 2003, to kick off planning for the school's first-ever All-Alumni Weekend in August of 2004. "What," I asked Mel, "do you think are the chances that she would accept?" We also were planning an indoor picnic to follow the meeting.

"I think she just might accept the invitation," said Mel. "And I think you should make the call. It would carry more impact than if it comes from me."

That exchange was on the Wednesday before the Saturday meeting. So, on Thursday at about noon, I picked up the phone in my office. I found myself feeling again like a teenage boy who is about to ask a girl for a date after she already has rejected him once before. I dialed Harryet's number. It rang only once before she picked it up.

"Harryet, this is Mike Johnson." I braced myself for her response.

"Mike, I want to talk with you, but I am running for an appointment. Could you call back at, uh, uh…"

"Harryet, you don't have to be precise."

She laughed. "Okay, how about four o'clock?"

"That's fine. Talk to you then." We hung up. I was encouraged but, since I don't believe anything is a sure thing until after it's happened, there still was a measure of suspense.

About 4:20 p.m., I rang her again. She picked up the phone.

"Hello," she said.

"Harryet, it's Mike. How are you hanging in there?"

That simple question unleashed a torrent of fun conversation, peppered with laughter. We reminisced happily for about 40 minutes – and that was remarkable because I'm not particularly good at phone chats. At one point I said, "Harryet, I have a question. Please be honest with your answer. Harryet, do you remember me?"

There was no hesitation. "No, I don't," she said.

I laughed. "Well, I'm neither hurt nor offended. I know I got an 'A' in your biology class when I was a sophomore, but I don't recall that we ever spoke again."

"You weren't into the sciences," Harryet observed.

"No," I said, laughing, "my interests lay in other directions."

Finally, it was time for me to administer the test. "Harryet, I have another question for you. You can answer right now or just say you'd like to think about it."

"Go ahead," she said.

"How would you feel about joining a group of your former students at Sally and George Hays's house on Saturday for a picnic?"

Her reply was immediate. "That's a delightful idea. I would love to."

Whew! Now, I felt like a teenage boy who had just landed a date. I decided to press my luck. "You know," I said, "there is a planning meeting before the picnic. Would you like to go to that as well?"

"I think I'd better just do the picnic," said Harryet. "That might be all I can handle."

"That's fine," I said. "How about if I pick you up about noon?"

"That would be fine. But you know about Rae..." By this time, Rae was on a feeding tube and weakening steadily.

"Yes, if you get a call about Rae, we will all understand."

Over the next two days I hoped that Ray's condition wouldn't prevent Harryet from joining us. My wife Lynne and I arrived in Shelby in time for the 10 a.m. meeting. After the planning meeting, while the rest of the team headed for George and Sally's house, Lynne and I drove to Harryet's home. I rang her doorbell and she quickly opened it. As she pivoted to lead us into her house, she said, "You know, now that I see you, I think I do remember you."

"Harryet," I said, smiling, "you don't have to stretch it."

She laughed.

After helping Harryet put on her coat, Lynne and I walked her across the street to our car. It was about a 10-minute drive to George and Sally's. Harryet was ready to party. On the way we talked nonstop. She brought us up to date on Rae. The previous night, Rae, in frustration and discomfort, pulled out the feeding tube that had been sustaining her for the last 10 days or so. Now, she was getting only water. In addition to cancer, pneumonia and the stroke, now Rae was suffering from shingles.

At George and Sally's, Harryet was in fine fettle and was a very good sport – especially when I asked her to be part of a photo that would become part of a video that I was producing for the 2004 All-Alumni Weekend. I positioned Harryet, with former teachers Bill Varble and Mel John flanking her. Then I handed each of them a big red and gray pompom and told them to smile. Snap. After the first shot, Bill swept his pompom toward the ceiling and plopped it on top of his head. Harryet looked up and laughed – and I snapped again. Priceless shot. Then I asked the former students if they would like to be in a shot with the three teachers. Immediately, they crowded around Harryet, Bill and Mel. Snap, snap, snap.

A couple hours later Harryet was still having a grand time. At one point I showed her a video that had been shown at the 2002 11-class reunion. Among the images were photos of Harryet and Rae. She watched raptly. When it ended, she said, "That was very professional – and a wonderful trip down memory lane."

As the picnic was winding down, Harryet was chatting with Dr. Jim Hennessy '61. I saw them and walked over. I waited while Jim and Harryet finished talking about diet and exercise. As I began speaking, my left hand took hold of Harryet's right arm. For me, it was a natural move, and I wanted the contact. Harryet showed no discomfort.

"Harryet," I said, "when I phoned you two days ago, I had a question for you: Would you consider coming to this picnic? Now, I have another question."

"Okay," said Harryet, "go ahead."

"Well, you know about the 2004 All-Alumni Weekend that's in the works. But this summer, the class of '63 is having a reunion and is inviting the classes of '62 and '64. Would you consider coming?"

"Yes, I would love to. If I'm alive."

"Oh, you'll be alive," said Jim, a pediatric cardiologist.

"What are the dates?" Harryet asked.

"July 18th to the 20th. There will be several events, including a dinner and a picnic," I said.

"Oh, I'll still be 89," she said, smiling.

"When is your birthday?" I asked.

"July 28."

"Harryet," I said, "would you be uncomfortable if our reunion included a birthday cake for you?"

"Not at all," she said, smiling. "But 90 is a lot of candles."

"Harryet," I replied, "90 candles is a challenge."

As you now know, Harryet did come to that reunion. On Saturday night we presented her with a beautifully decorated cake – mountains, frogs around a pond, a football with the OSU and SHS logos. More than 100 of us stood in an oval, lit 90 candles and sang *Happy Birthday*. Jeff Dawson parodied her, including the frog-killing episode. We gave her gifts, including a porcelain pig figurine that I had purchased in France for her collection, a bag of red and gray M&Ms, a new OSU sweatshirt selected and purchased by Jim Williams, and the roll of Bo Schembechler toilet paper. She was one of the last to leave.

Her reservoir of energy had not run dry. The next morning she was one of the first to arrive for the picnic. A few hours later, as the picnic was winding down, Harryet was saying goodbyes and preparing to leave with Mel and Anne John. I walked over to her. She looked up at me and said, "I'll be forever grateful to you for nagging me. This reunion was the best party I've ever attended."

Afterward, Harryet became a regular at our planning meetings and the group lunches and picnics that followed. She told me and others that she regarded her former students as her "kids" and loved being with them. "All of this," she said, "has given me a new life."

I continued to press my luck with Harryet. About a week before Thanksgiving 2003, I phoned to ask what plans she had for the holiday. I learned that Harryet – at age 90 – would be hosting a dozen or so family members for dinner.

"Harryet," I said, "Lynne and I will be in Shelby for Thanksgiving. Would you be available for a get-together the day after? Will your family be gone by then?"

"Oh yes, they will be leaving Thursday evening."

"OU and Marshall are playing on TV on Friday afternoon. How about if I come around and we watch together?"

"I would love that."

Marshall jumped out to an early lead and was so embarrassing OU that we turned down the TV volume so we could concentrate on conversation.

"Harryet, there is something I would like to propose."

"Oh, oh." She smiled. She had long ago caught on to my game.

"Our All-Alumni Weekend will begin with an event on Friday evening at New SHS. You taught at Old and New SHS from 1942 through 1980. Most of the folks who come either had you or knew of you. Can you think of anyone more appropriate to take the stage to do the official welcome?"

"Oh my," she said, "I don't know what I would say." We had come a long way from that icy rejection.

I laughed. "Harryet, I think we've got plenty of time to figure that out." And we did. But on Friday, August 20, 2004, Harryet didn't make it to the SHS theater for the weekend's opening event. Unexpectedly she had begun to weaken and the day before the big weekend she was hospitalized. I had recruited her former biology teaching colleagues, Bill Varble and Ward Holdsworth, to escort her down the aisle to the theater's stage. Now, with Harryet hospitalized, they came to the stage and took turns saluting Harryet with poignant and funny stories.

2005

In 2005 our SHS Alumni Association inaugurated the SHS Hall of Distinction to honor both distinguished alumni and former teachers and administrators. That first group of inductees was to include seven alumni and three former teachers and administrators. In voting that was open to alumni and former and current faculty and staff, Harryet was voted for induction.

On the evening of October 8 I drove to Crestwood Care Center nursing home to pick her up to drive to Hunsinger Park, a party center located east of Shelby. Harryet was in high spirits. That night when presented with the framed Hall of Distinction certificate, she strode to the stage and spoke spiritedly and wittily.

After the ceremony I drove her back to Crestwood. Upon entering the nursing home, she immediately went to the nurses' station to show off the Hall of Distinction certificate.

Six weeks later on the evening of November 22, Mel John phoned me. His news: at 7:30 p.m. the SHS community had lost one of the brightest stars in its galaxy. Harryet had died peacefully. Mel told me that Harryet, always a planner, a year earlier had picked seven of her "kids" – seven not six in case one couldn't make it – to serve as her pallbearers. They were Lowell Jarrell '56, Dave Winans '60, Jim Henkel '63, Mike Johnson '63, Butch Biglin '66, Steve Stover '71, Dave Finn '80. To a man, on learning she had selected them, they were stunned, touched and honored.

Harryet also had selected the decorations and music for her funeral – the 1960 Scarlet S yearbook that had been dedicated to her, Ohio State Buckeye football mementos and a tape of the Buckeye marching band playing the school's fight song and its signature rock song, "Hang On Sloopy." No surprises there; at the funeral of her great friend Lillian Rae Bowman, Harryet had placed an arrangement of purple and white flowers – Northwestern University's school colors – on the casket and played a tape of the Northwestern band playing the school's alma mater.

Then came the encomiums from Harryet's "kids." Here is a small sampling:

- "She is a great loss to the community. Biology was fun and painless because of her. She will be missed." Tom Whitacre '64, Walterboro, South Carolina
- "Miss Snyder was one of the best teachers I had at SHS. She got me interested in the natural sciences. She will be missed." John Stevenson '59, Boulder, Colorado
- "We were all very lucky to have this wonderful woman in our lives. Each time she attended an alumni meeting, she brought such joy and fun with her. We truly lost a 'shining star.'" Cathy Dodge '65, Shelby, Ohio

- "She was one of God's great gifts to us all. She will always be part of my heart and soul." Mike Armstrong '66, Lexington, Kentucky
- "This is a loss for all those who were privileged to meet and know her, especially for those of us who were blessed to have had her as a teacher." Fred Lightfoot '56, Mt. Pleasant, South Carolina.

Harryet never took to using a computer and so email never supplanted her zest for writing letters. The last one I received from her was dated November 5 and arrived just a couple weeks before she died. In it she wrote, *I'm so glad you 'kids' 'pushed' me into the activities in a nice subtle way. I had two times when I was very doubtful about finishing October let alone the current football season. Now I am so glad I made it. It was so good to see my big family (*at Alumni Homecoming*). Each one of them is special. And a big Thank You for my award (*Hall of Distinction induction*). I couldn't ask for the great memories that brings back.*

Chapter 29

Man of Steel

"Shit."

That's the first word that came to mind – and escaped my lips – when I learned that Larry Milliron had died. Why shit? Two reasons. The first was shock. I knew Larry had been struggling with serious health problems for several years. But deathly ill? That I didn't know.

On a Thursday in early June 2008 I received an email from his wife, Kathy Ryland Reed Milliron, a darling woman three years younger than Larry. She wanted to buy three inscribed copies of my third book. One would be for her and Larry, a second for her older brother and the third for a work colleague. Kathy and Larry worked for the same company. In replying I asked how Larry was doing. Her answer jolted me: *Larry was admitted to Case Western Reserve's University Hospital on May 27. He is battling pulmonary hypertension along with a disease called crest and trying to get well enough to be put on a lung transplant list. Right now his heart is too weak to do that, but they are trying very hard to make his body strong enough for this.*

A serious situation to be sure but one that bespoke a measure of hope. My wife Lynne and I were due to leave the next morning for a drive to Georgia to visit family and before departing I did two things. I sent an email to our classmates, forwarding Kathy's email and adding their street and email addresses so classmates could send support messages. Then I wrote a note that began: *Dear Larry, We are pulling for you.* I inserted it in a mailbox on our way out of town.

That was the last I thought about Larry for the next six days. Then the following Wednesday afternoon in Georgia, using my sister- and brother-in-law's computer, I logged onto email. One message was from Connie Jones Glorioso, one of Kathy's 1966 classmates. Connie told me that Larry had died that morning about 1:00. I was stunned. From his getting strong enough for surgery to death in six days. "Shit." I said it loud enough for Lynne and her sister Dianne to hear me and they were startled. Before they could say anything, I said, "Larry Milliron died this morning." My lips pursed and my head shook in dismay.

The second reason for uttering that word – sadness. I liked Larry. A lot. My fondness for him came later in life. In high school, although we were football teammates – he a left tackle to my left guard – we weren't buddies. I regarded him as arrogant and he might well have seen me the same way – in a mutually unflattering light. In fact, Larry was the only classmate with whom I ever got physical away from the football practice field. It happened during a lunch hour. In a hallway near the cafeteria, Larry and a bunch of guys were talking girls. Nothing unusual about that. I was standing a few feet away, talking with someone else. I overheard Larry making disparaging comments about a girl. They happened to be about a girl I liked, and I was darned sure he was spewing garbage. Typical teenage machismo running amuck. He hadn't dated the girl and I had.

A hot surge of anger went flashing through me, and without thinking I stepped in front of Larry, shot my arms out against his shoulders and pushed hard, slamming him back against a locker. The crash was loud. "If you ever say anything like that again," I hissed, "you'll have a Roman nose. It'll be roaming all over your face."

To say Larry was startled qualifies as an understatement. His eyes bulged in shock. He wasn't expecting an attack. If I'd thought before assaulting him, I probably wouldn't have. For starters Larry was two or three inches taller and weighed about 195 pounds to my 180. And as much as I enjoyed physical contact on the football field, it just wasn't my nature to pick fights in school. Through my first eight grades I can recall only getting into one fight and that was in 7th grade. It happened when an 8th grader was tormenting a smaller boy on the playground.

As I write this I can't help wondering whether Larry took my attack to heart. Did it create a lasting memory or was it quickly forgotten? Neither of us ever mentioned it. To be honest, I hope he did forget. I certainly had moments best deposited in my brain's dustbin of shameful memories. Many of them had to do with barely tamed arrogance.

After leaving high school I didn't see Larry again until 1973. I was attending an industrial trade show at the Convention Center in downtown Cleveland. After walking the show floor for an hour or so and feeling the need to stand on something besides concrete, I decided to drop into the carpeted hospitality suite of Shelby's Copperweld Steel. After a few minutes someone simultaneously called "Mike" and tapped me on the shoulder. It was Larry. I was surprised and delighted, and we had a terrific catch-up chat, covering both our personal and professional lives.

Another 10 years went by until we saw each other again at our 20-year reunion. From that point on our mutual vibes were good and strong, and genuine friendship took root and blossomed. What nourished it were occasional phone conversations that centered on business. Larry built a solid career in the seamless steel tube industry. He was knowledgeable, dependable and widely respected.

From 1990 onward I worked for a company whose product lines included seamless steel tubing. In periods of high customer demand, when our company maxed out its seamless tube making capacity, we outsourced to Larry's company, confident that the product would be made to our own exacting standards. We enjoyed talking about economic issues, financial performance and politics as it affected the business environment. I found Larry knowledgeable and incisive. He laughed easily and often was self-deprecatory. He was easy to like and respect.

Leading up to our class's 2003 Honor Our Teachers reunion, I asked Larry if he would serve as an escort for retired teachers. "I would be glad to," he replied. He took on the roll with a quiet dignity and was all smiles that evening. As a teacher was introduced, Larry would spot him or her in the audience, go forward and gently lead the teacher to the microphone. Larry looked and sounded terrific. You can see that on the videotape made that night.

Over the next few years Kathy bought numerous inscribed copies of my first two books. Whenever I was scheduled to head to Shelby soon after one of her orders, I would hand deliver them to her office – just one floor below Larry's. After dropping off books with Kathy, I would go upstairs to see Larry. It was during that period that Larry told me about his precarious health situation – serious it seemed but manageable. Or so he said and thought. Or hoped.

When chatting about his health problems I never heard Larry utter these two words or any variation of same: "Why me?" Perhaps on occasion he did to himself. I mean, it's entirely understandable that someone who has taken care of himself might wonder, at least fleetingly, "Why has my

Larry & Kathy Milliron

body betrayed me?" In Larry's case, even privately, I wouldn't be surprised if he avoided engaging in self-pity. Publicly Larry carried on with courage and grace, working his job until virtually the very end. Just as I would have predicted.

During those visits in his office we also would discuss business and do some reminiscing. A favorite memory was Shelby's 1994 Centennial of Football celebration. During the Saturday afternoon parade down Main Street, Larry and I rode side-by-side with other class of '63 footballers on a flatbed truck. It was an ideal occasion for further strengthening the bonds of friendship. We'd had great fun, waving at parade spectators while I held up a large homemade sign reading:

1962 team

Points scored – 302

Points allowed – 26

We could hear occasional comments from parade watchers. One said to a companion, "Man, that was some team." It was.

Larry was a caring man and in 1990 he demonstrated his leadership ability by chairing Shelby's United Way campaign. Under his guidance the campaign exceeded its goal.

When Larry died, I felt really sorry for Kathy. Her first husband had been stricken by a heart attack at age 36. He survived but then died two years later while doing maintenance on a Lake Erie cottage.

"I thought my life was over," Kathy reflected years later. "I didn't think I could go on. Except for going to work, I didn't go anywhere. I just sat in my room and watched TV. That went on for nine months. Then my 21-year-old daughter Michelle who was in college came home one night and said, 'I almost killed myself today.'"

Kathy sputtered, "What are you talking about? What do you mean?"

"I mean," Michelle replied, "I almost pulled in front of a truck on purpose."

"Why?"

"Well, you don't seem to care about living, so why should I?"

"That was a real wakeup call," said Kathy. "I knew I had to get going. I had a family. I had to pull myself together."

After Kathy and Larry began seeing each other, she was reluctant to wed again. Eventually they took to living together and did so for 11 years before marrying. Larry passed away just two months before what would have been their fourth wedding anniversary.

Following Larry's unexpected death, Kathy offered this perspective. "As bad as it was losing him, I knew I would get through it. I don't miss him any less. I don't love him any less. But I know I'll get through it."

In inscribing my third book for Kathy, I took special care to write a message that paid glowing and deserved tribute to Larry.

Classmate Jim Williams drove up from Columbus to attend Larry's funeral and later sent the following email to classmates: *I attended the funeral as did many others. The eulogy would have made Larry proud. It emphasized that Larry was a giving, caring and friendly person who loved life, his family and his job. He will be missed.*

Yes, Jim, he will. Indeed, he is..

CHAPTER 30

SUPER GLUE

"I'm still waiting."

Those few words, always spoken impishly, became a refrain that helped to keep glued a half-century of friendship.

Diane Schull and I didn't meet until we were 9th graders. Ironically, the man, Tom, she later would marry had been my neighbor and good friend since early childhood. He was three years our senior.

Diane and I became friends, good ones. In my eyes she was – and remains a half century later – a picture of sweetness, kindness and serenity. Those were the appealing components of her visage. Still are.

But a central component of our friendship was joshing each other. A running thread of that joshing wove together her home's backyard and my baseball batting prowess. Diane lived on South Gamble Street which was at a decidedly higher elevation than the neighboring high school campus, including its baseball field. Beyond right field rose a slope that led up to the rear of Diane's house.

During my 11th grade baseball season Diane and girlfriends took to sitting on that slope during our games. One spring day in school, Diane asked, "When are you going to hit a ball up to me?"

"You keep sitting up there," I replied, "and sooner or later it might happen."

We both knew that my achieving that feat would be a long shot – literally.

Relevant facts: I batted left-handed which meant that most of my longest drives were to right field – toward her backyard. But although there were no posted distances, for a ball to reach even the bottom of Diane's slope would require baseball's equivalent of the perfect storm. Every facet required for success would have to come together flawlessly and simultaneously. The delivered pitch would have to be approaching home plate at a level just below my belt buckle and from the center of the plate inward. Pitches in that location were the ones I usually hit most solidly.

I would have to hit the ball just before it reached home plate, and I would have to connect at the bat's "sweet spot," just beyond its Louisville Slugger trademark. A dry day – low humidity – would mean less resistance, helping the ball to carry farther.

Early during that 11th grade season I hit some long drives but nothing that approached the slope. Often in school when my path crossed Diane's, she would smile sweetly and say, "I'm still waiting."

During high school summers I played American Legion baseball, and our home games were contested at the high school field. In addition to Legion games and practices, often a few teammates would gather for informal practices. One summer day Denny Kidwell and I were among a gang who met for extra batting practice. Denny, our best pitcher who would go on to star at Defiance College, was throwing when it was my turn to hit. Before one of his pitches, I called to him, "Throw me a fat curve."

Denny obliged and *Perfect Baseball Storm #1* materialized. His slow curve bent deliciously over home plate just below my belt buckle and slightly toward the inside. I connected solidly at that sweet spot. The crack of bat meeting ball resounded like an echoing gun shot. The ball went soaring toward right field on an arc that resembled nothing so much as that of a swelling rainbow. It carried far up Diane's slope. But there was no waving, no cheering. The slope was unoccupied. The only ensuing sound was Denny's voice. He chuckled huskily and said, "Got all that one, didn't you?"

Came May 15, 1962. The day was gloriously sunny, and after school our Whippets were hosting Mansfield Senior High School's Tygers. Yes, not Tigers. Unlike football, in baseball we didn't have an archrival. But games against Mansfield Senior seemed to get everyone's competitive juices flowing a tad stronger. It was a much bigger school, and baseball was the only sport in which we competed.

The Tygers had their best pitcher, George Haag, on the mound. Denny was pitching for us. My first two times at bat I had popped out and grounded into a force out. When I came to bat the third time, the situation was ripe for drama. The score was tied 2-2. The bases were loaded and there were two out. Emanating from the fans was an expectant buzz. In attendance was Don Zeiters who for two years had been my Little League coach, and he was one of the best teachers in or out of a classroom. He had brought with him his current team of youngsters to watch.

I stepped into the batter's box, drew a deep breath and got set. Haag's first pitch was a scorching fastball. Right down the middle. A pitch meant for crushing. I swung hard – a confident well-timed swing – and fouled the ball back to the screen.

"Good cut, Mike," I heard Don Zeiters shout.

Strike one.

Haag's next pitch made me look take-your-pick comical or pathetic. It was a slow curveball and I swung way too early, darned near corkscrewing myself into the ground.

"Oh, Mike," Don groaned loudly, "You can do better than that." I'm sure I blushed.

Strike two.

Batters don't like to guess what kind of pitch might be coming next, but they nonetheless often do. At that moment I did. I guessed that Haag wouldn't waste a pitch outside the strike zone, hoping that I might chase it. Instead I guessed that he would come at me with another sizzling fastball. Put it by me, strike me out, strand three Whippet base runners, keep the game tied.

Haag rocked smoothly into his throwing motion and unleashed a missile, one that was zeroing in on home plate's center and just below my belt buckle. Because I had guessed fastball, I started my swing a split second sooner than usual.

Perfect Baseball Storm #2. The ball rocketed off my bat on a low trajectory. No soaring, dazzling arc. But I'd hit the ball so hard that it kept on carrying – easily reaching Diane's slope. A grand slam homerun. When I stepped on home plate, those three base runners were waiting excitedly to greet me with happy "way to go's" and slaps on my back. Fans, including Don Zeiters and his young players, were cheering lustily.

My day wasn't done. In my next at bat I slashed a drive to right field, driving in two more runs, and we wound up winning 10-4. Denny Kidwell went the distance.

The next day in a school hallway Diane saw me approaching and, with eyes signaling delight, exulted, "You did it!"

"But you weren't there to see it." And she hadn't been. The slope had been unoccupied.

"I know," she replied apologetically. "Hopefully next time."

There was no next time. During the remainder of that 11th grade season, during the ensuing American Legion summer season and then during my 12th grade season, there wasn't a *Perfect Baseball Storm #3*. In a Legion game I did hit a soaring drive to left center that landed in a plowed field. But there was no slope and no Diane.

In the autumn of our 12th grade year Diane was elected to the homecoming court. I don't think anyone was surprised. Yes, she was pretty and a cheerleader. But to me what cemented her place on the court were her unfailing and genuine sweetness – and the wide respect it earned. Other girls in the class were aspiring to be a teacher, nurse, stewardess or secretary. One was aiming to be a psychologist and another a lawyer. But Diane was dreaming of becoming a missionary. That seemed consistent with her essence. Reach out to others, selflessly. But Tom, her husband-to-be, would become a petroleum geologist, a career that led to multiple postings in the U.S. and abroad. "I still hold some disappointment that that dream never came to fruition as I had envisioned it," Diane said decades later. "However, the Lord showed me that the mission field He had for me was different – amidst family and friends. Over the years the Lord has richly blessed me" – just as her friendship has enriched the lives of so many others.

Her deep faith and positive outlook have remained unswerving through the years – years during which she lost older sister Judy, at Diane's home, back in April 1992 and subsequently both her mom and dad.

Her recollections of our mutual high school experiences embrace more than baseball. Back in 1991 she asked me if I remembered studying *The Lady of the Lake* in freshman English with the aforementioned and singular Leora Kuhn. I did, vaguely, and not altogether pleasantly. For Diane the memory was sharper: "I thought that book was going to be the end of my sanity."

Fast forward to 2008. Diane wrote a letter for insertion into our 45-year reunion booklet. Before reading it you need to know that our graduation ceremony in 1963 took place not in our high school but in the spacious gym that was part of the adjacent building that accommodated grades 1-8.

Her 2008 letter: *May 1963. Graduation ended and I found myself back in the school where I attended grades 1-8, taking off my graduation gown and thinking, "I may never see many of these friends again – friends that I had known since I was born and had shared my life with till then." Now 45 years later, I know that indeed I have not seen many of you, especially when I take a tour through our yearbook. I hold a high regard for how each of you have influenced my life. In fact, unlike most people, I am greatly saddened when I listen to the songs of those years – sad that what was, will no longer be. I have been back to Shelby many times to visit parents and friends, but my life has never returned to Shelby, the place where all my training and dreams began.*

Except for reunions I've not seen Diane since that graduation ceremony. I did get to see Tom in 2007 when he attended one of my book programs in Ohio that coincided with a visit he was making to his mom. Diane and I have occasionally emailed each other, but those reunions have kept our friendship glued. When we do see each other, we happily recall our joshing, especially her afternoons spent on her backyard slope, waiting expectantly for the ball I never hit while she was sitting there. In the years to come I expect that reunion glue to keep our friendship firmly intact.

CHAPTER 31

STRANGERS NO MORE

"Why," an alumnus asked dubiously, "would anyone want to attend a reunion with people not members of their class?"

"No one would come," asserted another.

"No thanks," a third said curtly. "Count me out."

At least three more commented similarly.

Massive resistance. That's what Janet Page Whitehill, SHS class of 1962, met when she began advancing the concept of a multi-class reunion for our hometown. Surprised?

Several more alumni Janet approached voiced similar opposition. So why on earth did Janet broach that apparently unwelcome idea? It was far from hare-brained and unprecedented. In fact, at her husband's high school alma mater in eastern Ohio, multi-class reunions had become traditional. Janet had attended them and witnessed how alumni from different classes took joy in mixing with each other.

After those early rejections Janet easily could have thrown in the towel. But Janet has pluck. Looks can be deceiving and in Janet's case they are. Signs of pluck aren't what you first notice. She is willowy and pretty with full lips and doe eyes that crinkle warmly when she smiles. She is in fact a gentle woman – who can be doggedly persistent and not easily dissuaded. She kept asking and eventually spoke with three alums – two women and a man – who said just maybe it could work in Shelby.

So at this juncture, let's pause and ask: how does the multi-class reunion concept strike you? If invited to one, would you dismiss it as ill-conceived? Or would you be inclined to give it a go?

Janet's thinking was to invite members of 11 consecutive classes – hers and the 10 that sandwiched it – five older and five younger. She was thinking kids in those classes had friends in other classes they'd not seen in decades, and she knew that numerous high school dating relationships had led to wedding nuptials.

Janet and her intrepid threesome kept phoning more alumni until they found about 20 who agreed to attend an initial planning meeting. They met for the first time on the first Saturday of September in 2001 – just days before 9/11. Eleven months later, 400 people converted Janet's persistence into a three-day love fest – punctuated by piercing shrieks of recognition, gales of joyous laughter, scores of misting eyes, endless rounds of hugs. And not just among alums from the same classes. There was instant bonding that sliced right through the boundaries that had separated classes.

That's the macro description. Here's the micro and it is more telling. Bill Wilkins and I were at SHS at the same time, but we were strangers. Ditto Connie Jones Glorioso, Jodi Seaton Lowery and Dave Spangler. Why? Bill was a 12th grader when I was a 9th grader, and how many stud seniors paid a whit of attention to gawky freshmen? And when I was a full-of-self senior, Connie and Dave were wide-eyed frosh.

After the 11-class reunion? You could say things had changed. We were strangers no more. Before elaborating, though, clarification is in order. Bill, a retired U.S. Coast Guard officer, is a son of the aforementioned Coach Bill Wilkins, and this Dave Spangler is unrelated to my classmate David Spangler.

Curiosity can be magnetic, intrigue an incentive and shared vision can fuel sustained effort. Curiosity and intrigue drew Bill, Connie and Dave to that first multi-class reunion. Shared vision led these heretofore strangers to first become members of the alumni association's planning team and eventually members of its board of trustees. Before Janet's mind-opening efforts, who woulda thunk it?

Along the way Bill initiated – and subsequently shepherded – the previously mentioned drive to raise $150,000 to upgrade science education at SHS. He graciously accepted the chairmanship of the board's special gifts committee that spearheaded the campaign and later agreed to stand for election as the alumni association's vice president. He is easy to like and respect.

Then there's Connie. The main agenda item at the first planning team meeting she attended in early 2003 was the first all-alumni reunion that had been scheduled for the summer of 2004. Right. All alumni from all classes. (Planning team meetings are open to all alumni as well as retired and current faculty and staff.) Except for identifying herself during roundtable introductions at the start of the meeting, Connie had remained silent. Then when we began brainstorming ideas for reunion content, she spoke up.

"What do you think about having an Army band?" she asked semi-diffidently.

Her question was met with a long moment of silence. Then someone asked, "What do you have in mind?"

"Well," Connie said evenly, "my son Josh is in an Army band. I know they do performances all over, and maybe they would do one at our all-alumni weekend."

"Great idea," someone said. "I know from seeing military bands that they are crack outfits. Are you willing to invite the band?"

"Yes," Connie replied. "I think we should do it with a nice letter."

Everyone at the meeting agreed that such a band might be a big reunion drawing card.

A year later on the Sunday morning of our all-alumni weekend – attended by 600 visibly excited grads – that U.S. Army band, with Connie serving as a polished emcee, put on a rousing performance in the SHS theater that had emotions on the loose.

Immediately preceding the band's performance was a moving memorial service for deceased and troubled fellow alumni and former faculty and staff. As the service closed with a blessing, the stage curtain began to open slowly to the strains of *Taps*. Audience members began reaching for tissues. Then the band, with Josh a percussionist and an Ohio State University band alum, played the *Star Spangled Banner*. Afterward the band played several patriotic songs and a "Bob Hope Medley" (songs that Hope liked to include in the many shows he had presented abroad while entertaining troops). Two Army band vocalists sang *America The Beautiful* and *God Bless The USA*. The band also played a medley of military hymns. In the segue between hymns the band's leader asked audience members who were veterans of the military service whose hymn would be played next to stand and be recognized. All branches of the military services – Army, Navy, Coast Guard, Marines, Air Force – were well represented. Goosebumps were breaking out, chills were running wildly up and down spines, lumps were forming in throats, folks were applauding – and cameras were flashing. The band closed its performance with *The Stars & Stripes Forever.* Attendees, with Connie on stage leading, were on their feet, clapping and shouting their praise and gratitude.

When band members, who earlier had accepted our invitation to picnic with us, exited from the theater into The Commons, alumni and teachers again broke into sustained applause. Several alums made a point of shaking hands with all band members. To say that the band's performance was superior – the local newspaper called it "stunning" – would be a vast understatement.

Connie was a whirlwind that weekend. During the opening Friday night assembly in the theater, she shared memories – both poignant and funny – of being in the first class to graduate from the then new building. During the Saturday afternoon assembly in the theater she – wearing a cheerleader uniform – escorted Helen Barkdull Freese, class of 1930 and Shelby's oldest living cheerleader – down the aisle.

A few months earlier I had emailed alumni, explaining that we wanted to make some special recognitions during the all-alumni weekend and asking for ideas. Helen's daughter, Barbara Jane Freese Phipps, class of 1961, replied, suggesting her mom. When subsequently I phoned Helen to describe in detail what I had in mind, her words were, "I'm game." She sure was.

Connie and her cousin DeeDee Milligan, another former cheerleader and also in uniform, had bought a corsage for Helen who also was wearing a cheerleader uniform. All other former cheerleaders in the audience were invited to come forward and 15 or so did. Then Helen – at age 92 – proceeded to lead hundreds of alums in a rousing cheer from 1929. Unforgettable!

But Connie wasn't done. That night at the gala dinner she served as a greeter.

In 2005 she made another major contribution when the alumni association inaugurated the SHS Hall of Distinction. Connie designed the certificate that is handsomely mounted, framed and presented to each inductee. Every year since she has lovingly incorporated personalized text for each new inductee into the certificate's design.

From left: DeeDee Milligan, class of 1963; Helen Barkdull Freese,
class of 1930; Connie Jones Glorioso, class of 1966

Then, too, there's Jodi. Had it not been for the 11-class reunion, I wouldn't have discovered my California cousin. Make that "almost cousin." Jodi Seaton Lowery was only a year ahead of me at SHS, but as with Bill Wilkins and me, she and I were strangers. Then during the 2002 reunion we wound up chatting several times and sitting next to each other during the closing picnic on Sunday.

A week or two later, after Jodi had returned to her San Mateo home, she emailed, saying that I should expect some photos she had taken during the reunion. A few days later a packet of prints arrived. Lynne and I were sitting at our kitchen table, looking at the pictures and commenting that Jodi clearly knew how to skillfully compose photos. Then came an epiphany. I pushed away from the table and said, "I'll be back in a couple minutes." I went upstairs to our bedroom where I opened our family bible. Sure enough, there was the name of my late dad Ralph's first wife – Flossie Olive Seaton.

Back downstairs I went and explained to Lynne what I had just checked on. A day later, October 8, 2002, I sent Jodi an email that read in part: *I must take a moment to pose a question. It's a question that, quite literally, just popped into my mind as I was looking at the photos you sent. If you are standing, better sit down, because this question could knock you off your feet. Ready? Jodi, do you suppose that we might be shirttail relations? Are you still standing or even sitting upright? Or are you out flat? Where in the world, you might be asking, did that question come from? Well, as I was looking at the photos, I thought "Seaton? Seaton? Good Lord, that was the maiden name of my dad's first wife."*

After I sent Jodi the email, I told Lynne how ironic it would be if Jodi were related to Flossie Seaton who had died unexpectedly from a stroke at age 37. And if Jodi and Flossie were related, the irony would be compounded because I had been aware of the Seaton name from my early boyhood. Every Memorial Day my dad and two half-brothers – Dean and Gene, sons of Flossie – would take a wreath to her grave, and sometimes I accompanied them. Which meant that I would see the gravestone with the engraving: Flossie Olive Seaton Johnson, B: 8-6-1900, D: 6-19-1938.

Two days later, October 10, came Jodi's emailed reply: *Oh my gosh!! I'm knocked off my feet and out flat!! I read your email last night and got chills when I read the name Flossie Olive Seaton! You and I are definitely shirttail relatives. Flossie was my dad's aunt – my Grandpa Seaton's little sister!!*

Jodi then went on to say that she had gone searching for stored family photos and historical notes. Among her findings were several references to my dad and two older half-brothers. *This is exciting stuff, Mike. I definitely remember both my dad and mom mentioning – in a very positive way of course – Flossie and Ralph Johnson and sons Dean and Gene. This is blowing my mind!*

By October 2002 Dean had been dead for four years. When I told Gene about this discovery, his memories were equally clear. "Didn't Jodi used to be Georgia?"

"Yes," I replied, "she took to calling herself Jodi during her school years."

Then Gene said, "I knew her very well. I held her when she was a baby. Georgia was certainly the apple of her parents' eyes. She was a very cute girl."

During the last seven years Jodi and I – the almost cousins – have stayed in touch. Lynne and I have visited Jodi and her husband Rob several times in San Mateo, and we have connected a couple more times, including the 2004 all-alumni reunion, here in Ohio. Our most recent visit was in October 2008 when I was at Stanford for a class reunion. The campus is just 15 or so minutes driving from Jodi and Rob's home, and on Saturday afternoon while Rob was meeting with a contractor to discuss a major home remodeling, Jodi motored to Stanford. We spent about two hours sitting on a campus park bench, in the shade of a grove of trees, looking at family pictures and catching up. Which leads to posing one last question: How was it that Jodi, very much aware of the Johnson name, and I, likewise of the Seaton name, could go through the same smallish high school for three years together without so much as thinking even for a fleeting moment about a possible familial connection? The answer, we agree: We were teenagers. Too self-absorbed to be thinking about extended family ties.

If ever there was a testament to the unexpected gems that can be mined from multi-class reunions, the Seaton-Johnson discovery stands as a glittering example.

As a result of attending the 11-class reunion in 2002 you could say that Dave Spangler has become the alumni association's Mr. Everything – and barely been slowed by a health crisis.

Leading up to the 2004 all-alumni reunion Dave recruited two alums who had become ministers to lead the Sunday morning memorial service. He then coordinated all aspects of the service – lovely vocals by an alumna, music and homilies – and served as emcee. Early on the Saturday morning of the reunion weekend Dave joined a gang of alums at a nursery in nearby Mansfield to select and load onto pickup trucks – including Dave's – numerous plants and garden decorations that were to be used to dress the stage in the hall where the Saturday night gala would be held. Then on Sunday afternoon after the closing picnic, Dave led a caravan of vehicles back to the hall to remove and load the plants and decorations, drive them back to the nursery and unload and return them to their proper locations.

Had Janet Page Whitehill's pluck not stood up to massive resistance, well, you get the picture. Caring friends of today would have remained strangers.

And Dave himself has shown plenty of pluck. He has been a standout elementary school teacher for nearly 40 years. He has coached numerous "Odyssey of the Mind" teams. One earned a 1st place ranking in the state competition, thus qualifying for the national competition where it placed 7th. Another of Dave's teams earned a 2nd place finish in the state competition.

In the summer of 2007 Dave's accomplishments were recognized when he was among those voted for induction into the SHS Hall of Distinction. Dave was bowled over.

"I'm really not worthy of this," he said when the voting results were announced. "There are so many nominees who are more deserving." His tone of voice and facial expression underscored his modesty. Clearly, fellow alumni saw his induction as entirely fitting.

At this writing Dave continues his fight with a health crisis. In the summer of 2006 he was diagnosed with cancer – lymphoma. When word reached alums, a deluge of support messages were on their way to Dave. In December, Dave said, "I cannot tell you how heartwarming it has been to receive hundreds of emails and cards from so many SHS alums – many who I have never met. They all sent thoughts and prayers our way, and it has truly touched us all. Many included their stories of battles – and conquests – with cancer either about themselves or a family member. That has made my positive outlook even stronger as I head into this challenge of my life."

By February 2007 Dave had undergone three treatments with five more scheduled. He told his doctors about the hundreds of support messages he had received from members of the "alumni family" – a term coined by Michele Black Abrams, class of '69 – and reported their reaction.

"My oncologist and his staff emphasized how important a strong support system is – and they are amazed by the support we are receiving," Dave said. "They cannot believe – and never have heard of – a high school alumni association having such an impact."

And they never would have had it not been for Janet Page Whitehill.

Late that year tests showed that Dave was free of the lymphoma. Then in autumn of 2008 the dread disease returned. Dave has handled that whipsawing with his customary GUP – grace under pressure.

This second attack required returning to the cancer center in Columbus. While awaiting a bone marrow transplant that took place in February 2009, Dave kept working out – treadmill and lightweights – and continued to communicate in upbeat terms. Oh, and after his immune system recovered from the chemotherapy regimen, he was looking forward to attending alumni association planning team and board meetings in 2009.

Thank you, Ms. Page Whitehill.

CHAPTER 32

DREAMS OF A GODDESS

Bev Highly was hot. A serious student of dance, she also strutted her stuff on football Friday nights as a short-skirted majorette. Pretty? Oh yeah. Creamy complexion, raven-haired, about five feet four inches, trim. Energetic member of the Pep Club as well as student council, choir and yearbook staff.

Question: Would I have considered dating her? Answer: Be serious. She was two years ahead of me and a teen goddess. Her yearbook photo caption conveys precisely why an awkward underclassman would have regarded the goddess as unapproachable: "Exotic dances and personality make Bev mysterious." Amen. Besides, how many awed boys, barely into their teens, consciously think? I'll ask her for a date and set myself up for a disdainful, humiliating rejection. Anyway, as I was to learn later, Bev was in love with a young man two years her senior.

So at last when I did connect with Bev it wasn't so much reuniting as uniting. The engine of connection was that Janet Page Whitehill-inspired 2002 11-class reunion. Leading up to it, as a member of the planning team, I was sending emails to schoolmates, encouraging them to attend. Bev replied, saying that a business-related scheduling conflict might preclude her attendance. In the end, on the Saturday night of the reunion she wrapped up the business obligation in Cleveland and drove straight to the reunion. She arrived just minutes after I'd left to grab some sleep before an early wakeup to be sure everything was set for a Sunday morning memorial service in the Old SHS auditorium. The service's centerpiece was a video that poignantly honored deceased members of those 11 classes. The video slowly and silently scrolled 123 names against a scarlet and gray background accented with the school's crest. When the video ran the only sounds were sniffling, soft weeping and sobbing.

My actual connection with Bev occurred later when we met for coffee in downtown Cleveland after I'd finished a business meeting at my company's advertising agency. We met a second time in Canton where a band Bev managed was performing during the annual Pro Football Hall of Fame Festival. A third meeting occurred at the 2004 all-class reunion. Most recently we reunited over coffee again, this time in a bookstore café. The former teen goddess, I learned, had been ingloriously de-deified – more than once. She had found worry a more frequent companion than worship, and she had learned much about her inner strength and resilience.

Going back to Bev's childhood, her preteen dreams were decidedly ungoddess-like. As early as sixth grade she was envisioning a future that was typical of the time. Recalls Bev, "I asked my dad, 'Is it okay for a woman to be president?' He said, 'Yes, of course.' But I was asking just because I was curious, not because I had any grand aspirations. It was always my passion to have a family. Back then women dreamed of becoming secretaries, teachers, nurses and wives."

That particular dream – becoming a wife – would be realized soon enough. "As I was finishing high school," Bev remembers fondly, "I was thinking mainly about being a wife and mother, and I was very happy with that. I was deeply in love."

Her high school graduation preceded her wedding – barely. "I was married at seventeen – two days after finishing high school. The spring of my senior year I had morning sickness." Motherhood came months later when the first of her two daughters arrived. The second came four years later.

The transition from teenager to parent was jolting. Certain realities of adulthood began surfacing soon and with unexpected force. "There wasn't as much money as I assumed there would be," Bev relates with matter-of-fact candor. "Money to pay for rent and groceries and baby formula. When we were finally able to buy a house, we worried if we could make the mortgage payment, even though it was only ten dollars more a month than the rent."

That reality was painful but instead of consuming Bev with self-pity, it gave birth to her next dream – earning a college degree. She enrolled at nearby North Central Technical College. Balancing studies with spousal and parental responsibilities, she took four years to complete a two-year associate's degree in secretarial science.

Hovering over fulfillment of that dream was a threatening cloud. Her striving was straining marital bonds. Her husband – "a very nice man," Bev smiles – was having difficulty coping with his wife's evolving aspirations and personal development. "The more I went to school the more independent and driven I became – even though I wasn't sure what my ultimate goal was."

The mounting stresses eventually ruptured their marriage and it ended after 14 years. "It wasn't easy. The divorce was hard on us, and it was hard on our daughters."

Four years after the divorce Bev took a fateful airplane flight. Returning from a business trip to New York, she found herself seated next to a pleasant man. They had a brief and seemingly casual conversation. "It wasn't much more than an exchange of names," Bev recalls wistfully. The man was working for Tappan, a Mansfield manufacturer of home appliances. "Later I heard he was asking about me," Bev says. "Shelby's a small town and he was able to find me."

That finding resulted in more than marriage. It led to Bev's departure from her hometown when her new husband left the Mansfield company for one based in Elyria, a city about 25 miles west of downtown Cleveland. The move from Shelby was short in distance but long in how it eventually would affect Bev's horizons, perspective and her dreams.

Initially she was thrilled. Soon after arriving in Elyria, Bev and her husband began building a home in Strongsville, a southwest Cleveland suburb. Soon afterward, though, her new dreams would begin fading, gradually descending into a hellish nightmare that would test her strength and resilience. Her husband, she realized, had a drinking problem that eventually showed itself to be full-blown alcoholism. Employment – his – became chronically problematic. "He went through eighteen jobs in fourteen years," Bev says. "It was up to me to keep us going. I had to make money. I had to pay the mortgage. I had to be sure we had health insurance."

For Bev, among other things, that meant returning to school. She was working as an administrative assistant at a large Cleveland-based company. "I wanted more. A bigger job. More responsibility. I had a talent for design and wanted to do design work, but an associate's degree doesn't count. My boss said, 'You need a degree.' He meant bachelor's degree."

Bev accepted the challenge. She enrolled, with her employer paying for tuition, at Kent State University which has a nationally renowned school that includes both architecture and design – fashion, graphic and interior.   Grittily, Bev began plugging away.   "I took one course at a time, one per semester, for fourteen years."   She smiles wryly, and her next observation manifests self-deprecation that is both remarkable and charming. Advanced math courses, she reveals, were daunting. "I was totally lost. I would sit at our kitchen table on Sunday afternoons, doing homework and crying."

Simultaneously her husband's alcoholism continued worsening and complicating Bev's life. In addition to working her job and commuting from her Strongsville home to Kent, she began attending an Alcoholic's Anonymous program for spouses. "I decided I had to try to learn to deal with it. It wasn't easy," Bev says reflectively, "but looking back I can see it helped me grow and become stronger."

Meanwhile she moved to a different company where she left the ranks of administrative assistants. "I took a marketing and communications position. It included media relations, working as a spokesperson and organizing and managing special events."

She recalls fondly what she terms "a proud moment."   Her employer, under contract with the U.S. Defense Threat Reduction Agency, was responsible for dismantling missile-based weapons systems in the Soviet Union, in particular in Ukraine. It was, to be sure, a politically sensitive mission, and included arranging discussions between some 100 individuals – the company's senior management, U.S. government officials and Soviet high-level military brass. Bev found herself centrally and successfully involved. "Afterward our company president came and commended me for helping engage the Russian generals in meaningful negotiations. For making them feel comfortable and helping accomplish the goals of the meetings."

Her husband's downward spiral was continuing unabated. Spousal abuse was further darkening the bleak picture. A couple separations and reconciliations followed. "I didn't want to be divorced. But the disease kept worsening, and I didn't want to keep taking abuse."

Bev's limits of tolerance were breached when her husband – who would pass away some years later – chased her from one room to another, she fell to the floor and he threatened to beat her.

Her tests hadn't ended. The next one came in 2002. The economic recession, worsened by the after effects of 9/11, proved costly. "I was downsized out of a job."

Quitting on herself wasn't an option. She was single and had no financial safety net. An entrepreneurial spirit began surfacing and flourishing. She forged ahead – "but not without a lot of doubt and fear. Going it alone was new and scary." But Bev was blessed with cheerleaders. "I had great parents who were supportive. I have great daughters and they were supportive too."

Back in Bev's high school years one of her favorite music genres was Latin. She and a classmate once were photographed wearing black tights and dancing seductively to Latin music. In 2001 she connected with Roberto Ocasio. In 1997 he had founded The Roberto Ocasio Latin Jazz Project – a large band that both performed and taught. The group became heavily involved in community enrichment endeavors.

At first Bev worked part-time in an administrative role. But after losing her corporate job she began working with Ocasio full-time. She managed, marketed and merchandised the band and its diverse initiatives. One of those was a distinctive salsa for which Bev worked tirelessly to gain shelf space in food stores.

The next two years were a stimulating and satisfying blur. They ended abruptly with a cruel blow that left Bev stunned and grieving. On January 31, 2004, Ocasio, at age 47, was killed in a car accident. Bev's reaction to the news: "I was just numb."

Quickly, though, her unquenchable resolve and business experience, including training in crisis communications, kicked in. "I was glad for my corporate background." In her grief she took on managing Ocasio's funeral and serving as his family's spokesperson. That was no mean task. "Five thousand people came to his funeral. They included the mayor of Cleveland and city council members, plus federal and state legislators and judges. There was TV and radio coverage. He was so loved by the whole community."

Bev's shock and grief notwithstanding, who would be surprised to learn of her immediate decision to carry on? "After the funeral on the way to the cemetery I told the family, 'We can't let this die.'"

She didn't. Despite initial family doubts and ensuing frequent turnover among band members, Bev kept the Ocasio enterprise going. In addition to scheduling and managing band performances, she is president of The Roberto Ocasio Foundation – www.latinjazzproject.com - that makes the band available for workshops, seminars, camps for music students and lectures which include the history of Latin music from its African roots to the Caribbean to New York City. Moreover she has continued marketing the salsa.

That's Bev the businesswoman. What about Bev the woman? "Being alone is difficult. The hardest part is Friday nights. You come home tired. Exhausted. You want someone there to touch hands with. You want to feel wanted."

Bev falls silent for a few thoughtful moments. Then the former teen goddess brightens. "I still dream. You have to aim high and then match your dreams with realistic possibilities. Don't tell me that something can't be done or that it's never been done before. Unless you dream, unless you reach high, you never know what can be."

CHAPTER 33

"I COULDN'T KEEP HER AT HOME."

I looked hard at him. Really hard. He looked awfully familiar. I squinted, my brow furrowing, struggling to remember. I was standing on the top row of steps, and he was right in front of me. All together there were more than 50 men and women on the Alden Library steps. Then I turned my attention to the photographer. He was positioning us for the obligatory class reunion photo.

After the shoot I again looked at the familiar face. It was black and handsomely bearded, the beard flecked with gray. I tapped his left shoulder and he pivoted toward me.

"Aren't you Chuck Williams?" I asked.

"Yes, I am." His smile was warm and welcoming, and he extended his right hand.

I smiled and said, "I'm Mike Johnson."

"Mike!"

This reunion was not in Shelby which until recent years has had no African-American residents. The town was Athens, site of Ohio University, and the year was 1992. All of the best, most heartwarming reunions aren't limited to high school classes.

Chuck and I had been friends at OU, and we were looking at each other for the first time since 1967. Back then he was best known for two things. As a football player he was a first team all-Mid-American Conference defensive back, and he was half of one of the university's first interracial dating couples. Sue Hudson was his Caucasian girlfriend.

Immediately after graduating in June of 1967, class members scattered to the four winds. Military service. Grad school. Career launches. Weddings and moves to new locales. Most of us quickly lost touch. And unlike high school there was no expectation of reunions. So in 1992 when those of us who chose to accept the university's invitation to a class reunion arrived in Athens, curiosity was intense. Would we know anyone? After all, our graduating class totaled 2,100. Would we bond?

Silly question. Even though each of us knew few of the other attendees, those common OU links pulled us together immediately and tightly for what turned out to be a memorable three days. Highlights included a reception in the on-campus home of university president Charles Ping and his wife Clare and attending a football game as a group. We all stayed in the Ohio University Inn, an inviting hotel on the school's southern edge that featured the same Georgian architecture prevalent on campus. Staying there together meant there was plenty of opportunity for mingling. And blessedly, since that reunion, Chuck and Sue and Lynne and I have remained in touch. We are all members of the Green & White Club, a social and athletics booster organization, and see each other during autumns in Athens.

In 2000 when Chuck learned that our daughter Andrea had moved to Columbus near where Chuck and Sue lived, he pledged to get in touch and did so at her place of work. Chuck's message: if you need help or advice, let me know.

Chuck enjoyed a good career in business, Sue in education, and they have two kids. Retirement brought an unwelcome development – a health crisis. In 2004 Sue found herself in a battle with breast cancer. She underwent surgery and chemotherapy. Although weakened during the ordeal, she continued to accompany Chuck to Athens on football game days. In the end she defeated the cancer.

Now fast forward to March of 2009. I was in Cleveland at a college basketball tournament game pitting OU against Bowling Green. To my pleasant surprise I found myself sitting directly in front of Chuck and Sue.

"How are you doing?" I asked Sue.

"Not so well," she replied with a hint of a catch in her voice.

I reached out, gripping her left shoulder with my right hand.

"Is it back?" I asked.

In the next few moments I learned that in 2007 Chuck and Sue were returning from their son's wedding. Sharp stomach pains began attacking Sue. In short order Chuck drove her to a local hospital for an exam. The verdict: ovarian cancer. "The worst kind," said Chuck.

"I'm going to try some new treatments," Sue said.

"I couldn't keep her at home," Chuck smiled, blinking and eyes misting. He brushed a tear from his cheek, and in another moment he had regained control over his emotions.

Throughout the game Sue cheered for OU, helped "coach" the Bobcats and ragged on the referees.

After the final horn – OU lost – I moved from my seat to the aisle and stepped up to the next row. Chuck stepped out into the aisle to make way for me to step into his row. I bent forward and hugged Sue tightly, murmuring "I wish you the best."

I then backed into the aisle and Chuck and I embraced.

"See you at the football games this fall," he said softly.

"I'll be there."

"Thanks, Mike."

Chuck Williams. Good man. And another reunion treasure.

CHAPTER 34

SPIRITS SEEN SOARING

Some class reunions come as no surprise. You graduate from high school or college, years later receive an invitation to a reunion, and if not expected it hardly comes as a shock. But how about one that has the potential for bringing together classmates from six continents?

My most unexpected reunion brought together members of my Executive Program class of Stanford University's Graduate School of Business. The Executive Program was founded in 1952 and, as we were to learn, none of its classes had ever held a large reunion on campus. That was about to change.

Here's how. On September 4, 2006, Mike Moir, a Scottish classmate who lives in Edinburgh, emailed me with a question: *How do you feel about having a class reunion?*

Sounds good to me, I replied on September 6. *Glad to help. What do you have in mind?*

I'm not sure, Mike answered, *and I don't have much experience planning reunions. I've been involved with only one. Do you?*

Yes.

Why don't you take the lead?

Leading the organization of a reunion for our Executive Program class presented a special challenge: the 140 class members – 19 women and 121 men – had come from 31 nations in North and South America, Africa, Asia, Australia and Europe. That geographic diversity goes a long way toward understanding why such a reunion was unprecedented.

As luck would have it, a week or so later I heard from Bev Smith, longtime director of the Executive Program. She was going to be in northern Ohio in a couple weeks and suggested we connect. We did so – over coffee at a Starbucks in North Canton.

I told her about the email exchange with Mike Moir. Bev's reply was quick and enthusiastic. "If your class decides to have a reunion and holds it at Stanford, we will provide support." Over the years Bev has proven to be an exceptional global emissary for the Graduate School of Business. In addition to directing the Executive Program on Stanford's campus, she has organized Executive Program all-alumni weekend seminars around the world.

"Thanks. The first thing I'll need is an up-to-date roster of email addresses."

"You got it."

True to her word, within a week Bev had assigned one of her staff, Karen Williams, to provide the addresses and serve as my Stanford contact.

Instinct then told me that if this reunion was going to have any chance of becoming reality, certain essentials had to happen. I needed to recruit a planning team whose members would:

- work entirely via email
- be diverse as to geography and gender and
- commit to attending the reunion wherever it was held so that we would be assured of a "critical mass"

On September 21, I learned from Karen, whose support over the next two years would prove exceptional, that at least two of our 140 had died. Another 20 she was unable to locate – no current addresses – business or personal.

I studied the remaining names and emailed 11 classmates, asking how they felt about attending a reunion and if they would be receptive to joining a planning team. Acceptances came from three women – Poh Hong Tan in Singapore, Nancy Shanik in New York City and Laura Olle in Washington, D.C. – and seven men – Kuang-Yi Chiu and Denny Sechrest in the San Francisco Bay Area, Mike Yap in Singapore, Graeme Bethune in Australia, Peter Verveen in The Netherlands, Luis Reis in Portugal and Mike Moir. David Thompson in England regretfully declined because he was changing industry and profession and didn't feel he could devote time to reunion planning. He did, however, say that were we to decide to hold the reunion in England, he would be happy to host the group for an evening at his home outside London. Later, Peter Robinson, another Bay Area classmate, volunteered to join the team.

In January 2007 we queried classmates. We asked for their sentiments with regard to attending a reunion and where and when they might like to see it held.

253

Within days input began arriving in our email in-boxes. About 40 classmates – in addition to planning team members – expressed enthusiasm. In discussing possible venues, there were votes for Europe, the east and west coasts of the U.S. and Asia. The largest bloc of votes was for The Farm, Stanford's enduring nickname, dating from its origins as a stock farm. As classmate Frank Carretta put it, "I think it would be great for all of us to meet at Stanford where it all began."

Said Martin Brydon in Perth, Australia, "I am relaxed as to where the reunion is to be held. The Stanford option probably adds an extra dimension by way of memories – providing it's not compulsory to exercise at 6 a.m." He was good-naturedly recalling that many of us as students had done that very thing, albeit voluntarily.

Scheduling? As I shared the above input with Bev Smith, she told me that if we picked Stanford and chose the right weekend, she likely could arrange to have us housed in the dorm – Schwab Center – we had occupied as students. That was a clincher. Classmates loved the idea.

In consultation with Bev we selected the first weekend in October 2008 – three days when there were no other major happenings scheduled on campus.

Stanford's support? It started strong and got stronger. In addition to Karen, Bev assigned Michaela Cronin to work with us. She said if we decided to have our meals on campus, she would make the arrangements – menus and pricing – with staff of the Vidalakis Dining Room, located in Schwab Center. Done. Then she offered to reserve a dorm lounge – equipped with kitchenette and ping pong table – for our class for the entire weekend. Done. Then Karen offered to provide any sports or outdoor game equipment we might want.

When I mentioned that many of us would have cars and that parking at Stanford, as on most campuses, is at a premium, Michaela pledged to provide parking passes – "A" passes – the best, good for anywhere on campus. She went an extra step and mailed me three passes ahead of time.

"We are really excited about having you guys here," Bev said. Indeed. Soon after that comment, Michaela told us that Stanford would pay for our Saturday dinner.

Meanwhile, planning teammate Poh Hong Tan made a suggestion: learn whether any of our former professors might be willing to meet with us in a classroom setting. Add an academic component to the socializing. Enrich the experience. Our teammates endorsed the idea. So via email I queried faculty members, and four offered to put on mini-seminars. Subjects would include trends in corporate strategy (Professor Robert Burgelman), new techniques for teaching leadership (Professor Charles O'Reilly), the global financial crisis (Professor George Parker) and changes in curriculum (Professor Garth Saloner).

Michaela and Bev then proposed creating a classroom by partitioning off part of the Vidalakis Dining Room. That would simplify logistics. Staff equipped the area with chairs, podium, sound and projection systems, white boards and easels.

Have you ever seen spirits soaring? They were much in evidence in brilliant blue skies over Stanford in early October 2008. The reunion was scheduled for Friday the 3rd through Sunday the 5th. But anticipating that some classmates journeying from afar might want to arrive early, our planning team told classmates we would make the necessary arrangements. Denny Sechrest conducted reconnaissance at area hotels and then negotiated a favorable rate and booked rooms at the Stanford Terrace Inn that adjoins campus.

Peter Verveen, Kuang-Yi Chiu, Ed Yang (another Bay Area alum) and I offered to serve as chauffeurs for arriving classmates who chose not to rent cars. Peter was the first to arrive, on Tuesday, September 30. On the morning of Wednesday the 1st he drove to San Francisco International Airport and picked up Graeme and Sue Bethune. I arrived on Wednesday afternoon, drove to the Stanford Terrace Inn and connected with Peter, Graeme and Sue.

About 6 p.m., I departed for SFO to pick up Poh Hong. Earlier in an email I had told her: *Since we haven't seen each other in 10 years, I'll make it easy for you to recognize me.* Incorporated in the text of that email was a photo showing me wearing a cap with OHIO across the front and a t-shirt with OHIO on the chest. *I'll be waiting for you outside Customs in the arrivals hall, and I'll be wearing this cap and shirt. I doubt if many others at SFO will be wearing OHIO caps and shirts.*

Poh Hong's flight from Singapore via Hong Kong was scheduled to arrive at 8 p.m. Even if on time and she got off the plane quickly, experience told me that if she cleared Passport Control and Customs without delay, it likely would be at least 8:30 before she emerged into the arrivals hall.

I'd arrived early, not knowing how slow rush hour traffic would be between Stanford and SFO. About 7:45 p.m., I was pacing back and forth in the arrivals hall. Then I caught sight of a woman waving vigorously. Poh Hong's flight had landed early. "I saw your OHIO cap right away," she said, smiling widely. We hugged hard.

From left: Tracy Garland, Poh Hong Tan, Carol Fong-Riordan

On Thursday morning Peter Verveen and I, armed with an "A" pass, drove to the center of the sprawling campus, dominated by attractive sandstone buildings with red tile roofs. We parked in a lot smack dab in the center of campus. Our first stop was the Graduate School of Business offices where we met with Bev, Michaela and Karen. Then we walked to the student store to buy Stanford t-shirts and relax in the store's café.

We each ordered coffee and Peter handed the bright-eyed student server five dollars. In making change she handed back four dollars.

"Is this a mistake?" Peter asked, clearly surprised, as was I.

"No," replied the server, smiling, "before eleven coffee is just fifty cents."

Peter and I shrugged, took our coffee to a nearby table and then looked back and up at the menu board. We could see no words communicating such a policy.

"Fifty cents for coffee?" Peter marveled. "At Stanford?"

"Maybe," I joked, "she took note of our gray hair and felt sorry for a couple of obviously senior alums."

"We should tell our classmates," Peter said, eyes twinkling. "There could be a run on the café tomorrow morning."

Meanwhile the reunion was picking up steam as more classmates began arriving. Several of us lunched together, and that evening 16 of us walked from the Stanford Terrace Inn to a nearby restaurant. After dinner we gathered in the inn's lobby. Classmate Martin Brydon approached the reception desk clerk. "Do you have any beer in stock?"

"Yes," she replied.

Martin bought it and within moments the check-in counter more resembled a busy bar. In fact, when a non-reunion guest arrived, he was confused by the loud and large beer-drinking crowd and the array of bottles. "You're in the right place," we assured the poor chap.

At about the same time a lone woman appeared in the lobby entrance. I looked at her, looked away and then did a double take. "Nancy!"

It was Nancy Shanik. She represents the classic immigration success story. Her father had immigrated to the U.S. in 1938 from Poland via France, and Nancy – named after Nancy, the city in eastern France – had risen to a senior position in a large bank. We all moved to greet her. Standing amongst us, Nancy said, "I look different. I let my hair grow." Indeed she had, from a short bob a decade ago to several inches below her shoulders.

I spoke. "We've all been agreeing that we haven't changed much, that we look pretty much the same." I draped my right arm across Nancy's shoulders. "But Nancy's appearance has clearly changed." That comment brought immediate and utter silence. Breaths were being held. What would I say next? everyone was wondering expectantly. I looked at Nancy and then the group. "Ten years ago she was cute. Now she is striking."

Everyone cheered lustily – as much from relief as concurrence.

The next morning, Friday, we all moved to the dorm's lobby where we met more arriving classmates. The gang was increasing from afar and near: Loloy and Ruth Echavez from The Philippines, Chris and Gretel Raats from South Africa, Gerard and Benedicte Roth and Anton and Lianne Hulsink from France, Hanspeter Brunner and Rudi Staempfli from Switzerland, Mike Yap from Singapore, Phillip Vandervoort from Belgium, Klaus and Elfi Stochl from Austria, CK and Chihae Choi from Korea, Tracy Peterson Garland from Washington state, Robert Holleyman from Washington, D.C., Al Perez from Florida, Robin Tauck from Connecticut, Carol Fong-Riordan and John Vitalie from the Bay Area.

After checking in, we walked from the Schwab Center lobby to our rooms. As we pushed open our doors, awaiting each of us was a most pleasant surprise – a bottle of wine and a black Stanford logo'd briefcase filled with "goodies," including a spiral-bound notebook with attached pen, a large notebook, a key ring and a tin of mints – all Stanford logo'd. Cool – and more evidence that, as Bev had said, "We are really excited about having you guys here."

How did it feel to be back in the dorm? Before entering her room, Nancy paused and looked around. Eyes glistening, she said, "It feels like we are home again."

The reunion exceeded expectations. From start to finish, the vibes were genuinely warm. The four professors putting on the mini-seminars were obviously glad to be with us. As was the case when we were their students, they brought to our improvised classroom remarkable physical energy, inspiring knowledge and well-seasoned wit. Two joined us for lunch on Friday and a third for a reception later that afternoon. Another, Jim Lattin, a marketing professor, had accepted our invitation and spent much of Friday and Saturday with us. Bev, Michaela and Karen spent much time with us and were ever attentive to details.

At the Friday lunch Bev announced that Michaela would be succeeding her as Executive Program director in mid-2009 with Bev staying on as business development director. Good news.

Later, in April 2009, Bev, after much deliberation, decided to retire in mid-May. She had worked at Stanford since 1982 and directed the Executive Program since 1995. "I've been the luckiest person in the world to get to do this kind of work," Bev says. "It was a perfect confluence of my experience and my skill set at a time in my life when I could really embrace the role. I don't think that happens too often, and I will always be grateful to Executive Program alumni for their support and affirmation that we really are doing something meaningful."

Should our class have a second reunion and were we to reside again in Schwab Center, we'll be certain to invite Bev to join us as an Honorary Dormmate. A reunion without her just wouldn't be the same. When I told Bev that, her reply was succinct: "I will be there!"

As with other reunions this one led to discoveries. For example, several classmates had made life changes, moving into a giving-back phase. Peter Verveen had retired from the corporate world and now is involved in working to improve health care in areas of South Africa. Carol Fong-Riordan had closeted her corporate suits to become a schoolteacher. After a career in business, Tracy Garland heads up a foundation.

As expected, the lounge's ping pong table proved a hit. Back in our student days Poh Hong ruled the table with quickness and economy of movement. During the reunion she still was blessed with limitless energy and enviable hand-eye coordination. Her eyes still glistened like polished onyx, and she remained lean and lithe – as she showed on Sunday morning while demonstrating Tai Chi – the ancient Chinese slow-motion exercise regimen. Her great-grandmother had immigrated to Singapore from China in the early 1900s. Poh Hong seems to have inherited her sense of adventure; back in 1988, a decade before journeying to Stanford for the Executive Program, she set out for the U.S. east coast where she earned an MBA at New York University. Today she has sons ages 19 and 15 – and at our reunion retained her ping-pong crown.

Another hit. Many attendees had accepted our invitation to bring items that would be given as gifts and used as prizes in two drawings. The result was a cornucopia: wine from California and Australia, jenever (juniper-flavored liquor from which gin evolved) from The Netherlands, port – aged for 20 years – from Portugal, chocolates from Switzerland, large coasters from Singapore featuring historic street and waterfront scenes, books written by classmates and another on Scotland's history, a wood-carved figurine and handcrafted jewelry from The Philippines, lacquered business card cases from Korea, canvas travel bags and so on.

How emotionally satisfying was the reunion? During the Saturday night dinner, Luis Reis was talking haltingly about his departure the next day to his native Portugal. Eyes misting, he said softly, "I am already feeling nostalgic."

Within days after returning to Singapore, Poh Hong emailed classmates. *It was a wonderful reunion. And I am so glad I attended, despite having to fly half way across the world to do so. When I told my friends and family about the reunion, they thought it incredulous that I should fly all that way just for a few days of reunion. I told them that I enjoyed every bit of it, and the journey was more than worthwhile.*

Mike Johnson

Those spirits seen soaring over Stanford during the reunion? They were warm, gentle, embracing and uplifting. During a period of worldwide economic and financial tumult, classmates had shown themselves to be a global treasure.

CHAPTER 35

THE UNSTOPPABLE BOBKITTEN

At this point in my life – ahem, just months away from certifiably being a senior citizen – I find myself mulling a couple questions. To wit:

- Should I be reunioned out?
- Should I throttle back on working to make and sustain friendships?

Broadly speaking, the answer lies in my simple philosophy of life: We get only one walk across the planet and it's nice to take it with friends. Corollary: Go the extra mile; it's seldom crowded.

Speaking more narrowly, the answers lie with the original bobkitten, and she has proved unstoppable.

What's a bobkitten? you ask. No, it's not a feline subspecies found only in Shelby, Ohio. The original bobkitten was born and grew up in a bilingual family – Italian and English – in nearby Mansfield, graduated from St. Peter's High School and, given her story, richly deserves inclusion in this book.

Franscesca Femia Hahn's story is remarkable, especially when you consider the nasty curveballs life has hurled at her. Many women and men would have swung haplessly, missed badly and trudged dejectedly back to the bench to mope or sulk. Fran? She kept coming back to the batter's box, kept swinging and more often than not has smashed homeruns.

Our initial connection had serendipity plastered all over it. It took place in the autumn of 1966 at Ohio University. I was doing an internship for Sports Information Director Frank Morgan. My chief responsibility was compiling and organizing facts and figures for the basketball media guide for the upcoming season. The internship included a few perks. One was hanging out with coaches. Another was a football sideline pass. During games I had much fun roaming the sidelines with a camera.

One early autumn Saturday in Peden Stadium, OU's Bobcats were hosting the University of Dayton Flyers. I was shooting photos of game action, coaches, band members and fans. Then I saw the newly inaugurated bobkitten mascot waving at me. She had been "invented" to serve as a companion for the bobcat mascot that had debuted in 1960 when the men of Lincoln Hall conceived the idea of a comical mascot. They designed the costume but found fabricating its oversized papier-mache head beyond their manufacturing capabilities. After considerable exploration they contracted to have it constructed in France. Total cost: $250, including long-distance phone calls. Lincoln Hall resident Dan Nichols was first to wear the costume that also featured a green jersey with a large block O on the chest.

The new bobkitten's costume also included a comically oversized papier-mache head, a pullover sweater, a short skirt, beige tights – and undies with a large OHIO stitched cross the bottom.

In the first of three black and white photos I took that day, Fran is waving flirtatiously at the camera. In the second the bobcat is pinning a corsage on her. In the third Fran turns her back to the camera, bends over, flips up the skirt and exposes the OHIO. Click. An instantly classic picture.

Over the next few days in the university's photo lab, I carefully enlarged and edited the 2" X 2" negatives and then printed two sets of pictures, one to keep. The other I delivered to Fran at Howard Hall, a red brick, delightfully inviting dorm in the center of campus. When she entered the lobby, what did I see? Well of course there were the same shapely legs that so nicely occupied her costume's tights. But what did I see now that wasn't hidden under that papier-mache head? Peering up at me from her five feet two and a half inches was a pair of the warmest, most penetrating eyes ever to meet mine. They were hazel or, as Fran laughingly says, "not quote brown and not quite green."

How did Fran Femia Hahn become the original bobkitten? The girl she was at St. Peter's High School gave her an edge in the competition to become OU's first female mascot. As was common in the early to mid-1960s, St. Pete's offered no varsity sports for girls. But Fran was an athlete and a versatile one. She roller-skated, ice-skated, biked and played tennis and softball. Had girls varsity sports been available, says Fran, "I would have run track and played tennis." St. Pete's had outstanding – as in state championship – boys basketball teams, and Fran was a member of the cheering section.

In addition she was a member of the school's choir and a thespian. She played supporting roles in stage productions all four years and in her senior year played the lead of Sharon in *Finian's Rainbow*, singing *Look, look, look to the rainbow, follow it over the hill and stream, look, look, look to the rainbow, follow the fellow who follows a dream.*

Not surprisingly, Fran was popular. The entire St. Pete's student body elected her secretary of student government.

Fran's dream for post-high school had her headed east – to Manhattan where she envisioned attending New York University and studying theater. "But I got a scholarship to OU," she says, "and they had a great theater program. And I could only afford a state school."

In September of 1965 Fran the freshman arrived at Howard Hall. Quickly she became a dorm leader. "I was social chairperson and did a lot of skits and performed for all kinds of dorm events."

The dorm's social group spawned the idea of creating a bobkitten to pair with the bobcat who, tradition held, was perennially a Lincoln Hall man. "We auditioned and I was selected. My theater background probably helped." How did she react? "I was elated and nervous, but just thrilled!"

Soon the bobkitten became a campus celebrity. Or at least her shapely legs did. Otherwise her identity remained closely guarded among the Howard Hall women and a select few others.

One afternoon Fran and a girlfriend were strolling from classes back to Howard Hall. Behind them were walking two male students.

"Do you think that's her?" said one of the men.

"I think so," said the other. "Look at those legs."

"They're talking about you," said Fran's girlfriend.

"Oh, no, they are talking about you." Fran's girlfriend was particularly pretty.

"No," the girlfriend smiled, "it's your legs. That's what they recognize."

Fran heard the first man say, "You're right. That's got to be her."

"Hey," said the second man, "let's get a look at her face."

Hearing that, Fran, without looking back, began running toward Howard Hall. "I wanted to preserve the mystique of the bobkitten."

The men began chasing but athletic Fran held the lead and escaped into the sanctum of Howard.

Another of her favorite memories centers on then university President Vernon Alden and his lovely wife Marion. (Doctor Alden, now in his mid-80s and a Boston resident, remains an active supporter of OU, but Marion passed away on August 26, 1999.) "It was at a football game," Fran recalls, "and we were winning. He and his wife were sitting in their box, and he waved me up. His wife had borrowed my bobkitten outfit for Halloween for two years. I sat down on his lap and gave him a big hug and kiss! It was great! I was so excited, and he just laughed and laughed."

In March of 2009 Doctor Alden laughed again when I saw him in Cleveland and told him that that incident would be included in this book. He immediately reached inside his jacket pocket, extracted a business card and said, "Please be sure to send me a copy."

Fran remained the bobkitten through her senior year. She had helped design the bobkitten costume, and it underwent an unexpected alteration after her sophomore year. Sports Information Director Frank Morgan, admiring Fran's mascot work, gave her a green varsity letter sweater with a large block O on the front. "Wow! It was so cool!"

By the time Fran graduated in 1969 with a bachelor's degree in communications with a double major in English and theater arts, I was in the Army in Korea. We had lost touch. Years went by. Two decades, actually. Then in 1988 OU published its first alumni directory. It was indexed three ways and had the heft of the Manhattan white pages. The day it arrived, Lynne and I took it to bed. We laid the volume between us and began paging through it, remembering names and reminiscing. Among others I spotted Carl Vandy, my freshman roommate and a friend to this day; Pam McCabe, a girl a year younger whom I'd met at a mixer and who became a judge; John Edwards, one of my closest buddies, a former OU footballer and today a Methodist minister; Jane Bond, a girl I'd dated and who also became a judge and whom I saw again in the late 1990s at an alumni event Lynne and I had organized; Bruce Cryder, another close buddy and now a lawyer.

I had a brainstorm. The next morning I went to my desk where I knew I'd find a dozen postcards. I addressed them to 12 of the names I'd seen in the alumni directory. In the limited space available on each card, I wrote simply that I'd seen his/her name in the new directory, hoped he/she was doing well and invited a response.

Most responded, some with postcards, others with letters. Fran wrote a letter. During the ensuing 21 years she and I have remained connected via letters, phone chats and emails.

Life has made a nasty habit of clawing at the original bobkitten. It attacked Fran the first time in 1966 when her dad died unexpectedly. In 1977 she was stricken with a blood disease. "It started the roller coaster ride," Fran says. In 1983 her body began to betray her in mysterious ways. That was her worst time. "For the next two years I didn't know what I had. It's better to know the beast, so you can work to defeat it."

Fran's beast? "I had what looked like bug bites on my legs, and it was the weekend of the *Live AIDS* concert. But the bites did not go away." In 1985 the beast was diagnosed. Lupus. One of the autoimmune diseases. No known cause. No cure.

"I was devastated," she says. "And sad. I thought my life would change drastically. It did at first." Her strength waned. "I couldn't even lift a teacup. I was out of work for six months."

By chance I learned about Fran's lupus in 1993 during Lynne's 25-year OU class reunion. Nancy Petty Klimo, a friend of Fran's, was among the attendees. When talk turned to Fran, she told us about the disease.

But the original bobkitten's spirit was unquenchable. "I refused to quit work and decided to fight."

Which she has. Fran went on to build a stellar career. For 15 years she taught high school – two years at Tri-Way Regional High School near Wooster, Ohio and then 13 at Morristown High School in New Jersey. Her specialties were English and theater arts, and she made the move to Morristown High because she was given an opportunity to build her own arts program. She directed two shows each year. During summers she directed and choreographed plays for adult groups. In addition she pursued and earned a master's degree. Then in 1985 she began working as a fiscal analyst for the state of New Jersey and served in a variety of administrative positions. In 1997 she again launched a new career, taking a position in government relations for a major pharmaceuticals company and later joining another leading company in that industry.

Life, though, hasn't stopped clawing at Fran. In 1990 lupus attacked again. "It was a serious bout," she says and again was forced out of work for six months. Because lupus will continue lurking within her, she works to try to keep the disease from worsening and symptoms from resuming their assaults. "I've been taking prednisone every day since 1985. Five mg's a day." The drug has kept her alive and going but can produce a plethora of side effects that range from irksome to dreadful. "I have good coping skills," Fran says, "but I ask myself how long I can keep this up." She has lost strength and endurance and can no longer move as fast as the original bobkitten would like.

Life's claws have mauled her in other ways too. Fran's older sister has been diagnosed with Alzheimer's Disease. For Fran that has meant making sad, frequent trips from New Jersey to Ohio to see her sister and help her brother-in-law and his sons make the necessary adjustments.

Francesca Femia Hahn

Clawing scars notwithstanding, Fran could conduct seminars on *Look, look, look to the rainbow.* "Life – every day – is a joy," she says with bobkitten spirit undimmed. "It is not the years you have but how you live the years. My greatest joy is the arts. So I hope to start my fourth career soon. I just started piano lessons, and I write lyrics. I want to leave a legacy before – hopefully – my time ends upon this earth. I want to give back through my words and through love. I loved teaching and directing shows. I loved my government days and met so many wonderful people. I've loved my pharmaceutical lobbying days and met so many interesting political figures and traveled to some great places. But my joy is in the arts. So some day I want to leave my words in music for all the world to hear and enjoy. It will fulfill my spirit and what lies deep within my soul. I have a saying that I hope someday will be on my final resting place: *Life is to be enjoyed, not endured.* It's a 'Frannieism,' one of my many little quotes. It says it all."

Indeed, it does, and does anyone doubt the original bobkitten's tenacity? Her resolve? As Fran adds, "No isn't in my vocabulary."

One thing does remain undone. As I've said, we have written to and talked with each other and we have exchanged emailed pictures. But we haven't reunited. It's been 43 years since we last saw each other in the flesh – and outside her papier-mache head. It's another reunion to look forward to.

CHAPTER 36

A SINGULAR MAN OF THE CLOTH

Strapping on shoulder pads. Taking fierce hits on the football field. Leading a prayer circle and gladly accepting requests to include strangers. Enduring poverty. Demonstrating perseverance. Dealing with heartache. Helping the elderly. Hanging onto a playful sense of humor. Package it all and to me you have a working definition of a man.

Add to the mix phoning unexpectedly from an ocean beach, a New England town or Great Britain while visiting his Air Force son just because he's thinking of you, and remembering to consistently ask about your wife whose health he knows to be fragile, and what do you have? A friend worthy of that word.

"Hello?" said the richly resonant voice on the other end of the line.

"Might this be John Edwards?"

"Yes, it is."

"Are you standing or sitting?"

"Standing."

"You'd better sit down. Before your knees buckle."

"Mike! Mike Johnson!"

"Bingo! I'm surprised you recognized my voice. After all, it's been more than twenty years since you last heard it."

"Doesn't matter. I'd know that voice anytime."

Like Francesca Femia Hahn, John Edwards had received one of those dozen postcards I'd sent after receiving the Ohio University alumni directory in 1988. John had replied with a four-page letter. But what I don't remember as vividly as my first encounter with Fran on that football sideline is when I first crossed paths with John. More than likely it happened in

268

Gamertsfelder Hall where we both wound up living for four years or across the street in Shively Hall's cafeteria.

By the time we graduated, we felt as much like brothers as dorm mates. A strong tendril of our friendship's roots was football. In high school while I was playing guard for Shelby's Whippets, John was winning first-team All-Ohio recognition as a quarterback for Lancaster's Golden Gales.

After his senior season John had two football scholarship offers – from OU and Miami. In choosing OU he pretty much stripped emotion from his thinking.

"At Lancaster," John recalls, "I was a left-handed quarterback and we ran an option offense. Miami already had a left-handed quarterback (Ernie Kellerman who went on to play defensive back for the Cleveland Browns) and ran a pro-style offense. The OU system seemed a better fit for me."

Then John laughs. "Of course, after I signed my letter of intent, OU changed offenses and went to a pro-style. I could run well which was a strength for an option quarterback, but I didn't really have the arm for a pro-style offense." As you can see, John was suffering few football illusions.

He played all four years at OU but saw little action at quarterback. Through his junior season most of his playing time was at wide receiver. His senior season he played defensive back. John stood about six feet, had a square jaw and close-cropped blonde hair. His wit was as quick as a striking mongoose and as sharp as a Samurai sword. But I never heard him use it to injure or cut deeply. Often his wit was directed at himself, and when he did poke fun at a friend, it was done gently and with a smile.

If in one regard John wasn't unique, he certainly qualified as unusual. Teasingly, I once asked him, "How many guys arrive at college as all-state quarterbacks on a full-ride scholarship – with the intention of becoming a minister?"

John's answer was a grin and a shrug. Pastoring was his aim and he didn't miss the target.

While at OU one of our frequent diversions was playing catch with a football on a grassy strip across the street from the rear of Gam Hall. We did it mostly for fun and relaxation. And we both loved the feel of throwing and catching the spiraling leather. While John was toiling for the Bobcats, I was player-coaching Gam Hall's intramural team and serving as the dorm's athletics director. We figured we were unique among other

OU guys who also might have been playing catch. Reason: we both threw left- handed. We both were sure-handed, but John could put a bit more zip on the ball than I.

Mike Johnson and John Edwards

John was a stickler for obeying football team rules. Once while we were playing catch, he was feeling pretty down. His first two years at OU, the Bobcats had done well, winning a conference crown in our freshman year. But our third autumn was descending into a gridiron abyss. Injuries ravaged the Bobcats and losses were piling up.

"Hey, John," I said, trying to buoy his spirits, "how about we go uptown tonight and share a pitcher of beer?"

"I don't think so," he replied dejectedly.

"My treat."

"Thanks, but it's against team rules, drinking during the season."

"You sure? Odds of anyone spotting you at the Union Bar on a week night are pretty slim."

"Yeah, I'm sure."

And he was. His left arm might not have been quite strong enough to quarterback a pro-style offense, but his moral fiber was all-pro.

During our years together in Gam we shared plenty of laughs. Many had to do with a photography course I was taking in the autumn of 1966. Or more accurately, they had to do with the course's unexpected and not unpleasant consequences. One of them was meeting and dating Jane Bond, the lovely dark-haired girl mentioned in the preceding chapter who became Judge Bond.

"I think you bumped into her – on purpose – in the dark room," John teased.

Another such consequence – and attendant laughter – resulted from John's daring me. Here's the backdrop. He and I were living in single rooms down the front hall from each other on Gam's third floor. Our rooms overlooked tree-shaded East Green Drive which – except for move-in and move-out days – was closed to vehicles. Across the street was Shively Hall with its cafeteria where we ate. Both Gam and Shively featured the Georgian red brick with white trim architecture that makes the campus so gloriously and warmly picturesque.

It was early on an autumn Sunday afternoon that was sunny and brisk. John and I were lounging in his room, chitchatting. I was puffing a pipe filled either with Cherry Blend or Mixture Number 76. Was John puffing too? "Never got into smoking. I quit when I was about 10," he recalls, tongue in cheek. "Chewing tobacco did me in. Thought I would die. Even the smell of it made me dizzy."

Across the street a girl emerged from Shively and began walking past Gam toward the far side of the green. She was striking – and strikingly attired. Her blonde hair was straight and hanging several inches below her shoulders. She was wearing black stretch pants, black boots and a fake-fur white jacket with large black spots. In the crisp late autumn air she was striding purposefully.

"Beautiful girl, isn't she?" I said.

"She's really sharp," John replied. "Do you know her name?"

"Tanis Galik. She was a member of the homecoming court. Lives in Jeff." (Jeff was short for Jefferson Hall, a handsome Georgian-style block-long girls dorm with its own cafeteria and branch library where I had a job checking out books. Tough duty.)

"Do you know her?" asked John.

"Not really. She works the serving line at Shively and I've said hi."

"I'm surprised you haven't said more than hi."

"Yeah…Hey, I just had an idea."

"What?"

My lips pursed and eyes closed in concentration as my idea took shape. "For my photography course my next assignment is a series of action photos. Doesn't matter what kind of action. That's up to us. I'm thinking I'll call Tanis and ask her to be my model."

"Oh, come on, Mike. You just said you don't know her."

"So? I'm thinking of giving her a call."

"When?"

"Right now. Well, in a couple minutes after she gets back to Jeff."

"You wouldn't dare."

Without another word I put down my pipe, stood, exited John's room and went walking to one of the two hallway phones that served our section of Gam's third floor. In-room phones were still years away. John came striding behind me. I paused briefly and then lifted the heavy black receiver from its cradle.

"You're really going to do this," John said, his incredulity slowly giving way to imminent reality.

I smiled and dialed Jeff.

"Jefferson Hall," the student operator said cheerily.

"May I please speak with Tanis Galik?"

"Just a moment please. I'll see if she's in." When a dorm operator rang a hallway phone, getting an answer depended on a student hearing the rings and leaving her or his room to pick up the receiver. You learned to be patient. If there was no answer, the operator slipped a message into the student's lobby mail box.

"I still don't believe you're actually doing this," John said, grinning and shaking his head.

"You dared me."

John rolled his eyes upward. Long moments of silence finally ended.

"Hello?" Her voice was soft and curious.

"Tanis?"

"Yes."

"My name is Mike Johnson. You don't know me. I live in Gam and have said hi to you in Shively."

"Hi, Mike." Her greeting was friendly and encouraging.

"Tanis, you're probably wondering why I've called. Let me tell you. I'm taking a photography course, and I have to take a series of action photos. I have some ideas and I'd like you to be my model. What do you think?"

Bam! How was that for getting right to the point?

I glanced at John and his eyebrows were raised, his head shaking again in disbelief.

"Okay. That sounds like fun." Just like that. No hesitation. Tanis was game.

"Great." I winked at John.

"When do you want to do this?" Tanis asked.

"How about now? This afternoon. It's sunny."

"Okay. Give me a few minutes."

"Okay. See you in a few minutes in Jeff's lobby."

I hung up. John was staring at me. "You old son of a gun. You actually did it."

Yes, and that afternoon turned out to be the first of two afternoons Tanis spent modeling for me. She was a really good sport. For the second shoot I asked her to wear the same black and white outfit she was wearing the afternoon when I first phoned her. We walked to a nearby elementary school playground which included an overhead horizontal ladder. I had Tanis stand beneath it, then reach up and grasp a rung. She was smiling before I asked her to. Next I moved in close, the lens capturing her from chest to just above hands. I asked her to keep smiling, and she complied, eyes glittering happily. More than 40 years later I wonder if Tanis still has the prints I gave her?

June 4, 1967, saw the last OU commencement ceremony held outdoors on historic College Green. Ohio Governor James Rhodes was the speaker. OU, founded in 1804, is the oldest university in what had been the Northwest

Territories. Stately Cutler Hall on College Green was built in 1816 and still serves as the university's central administration building. In the university's early years, College Green also served as a community cow pasture. Beginning in 1968, commencements would be held in the soon-to-be completed Convocation Center – seating 13,000 on upholstered comfy chair-type seats and air-conditioned for those sweltering graduation days.

Commencement Sunday was sunny and steamy and sweat was running freely beneath our heavy black gowns. The day and the ceremony also were bitter sweet. There was the elation that attended being handed a diploma with my family present. There was the pleasure of meeting my girlfriend Lynne's parents who had journeyed north from Marietta, Georgia for the graduation of Lynne's older sister Dianne. There also were throats thickened from saying goodbye to friends we might never see again. One was my close friend Andy Blank to whom my second book, *Fate of the Warriors*, is co-dedicated. Just nine months later, March 1968, Andy would fall to cancer that was detected during his graduate school physical. And there was saying goodbye to John. We shook hands warmly.

The next morning, June 5, I volunteered Army. Less than a month later, on July 2, John would marry Pat. Ironically, only a day earlier, I had arrived in Marietta, Georgia to visit Lynne who, a Spanish major, would be spending her senior year in Madrid.

In the autumn when I flew off to basic training at Fort Gordon, Georgia, John began his divinity school studies in Columbus at Evangelical Lutheran Theological Seminary (Trinity Lutheran Seminary following a merger). After earning his master's in divinity and his ordination in 1971, the years flew by. And not without their tests.

John's first assignment was in his hometown where he served as associate minister at Lancaster United Brethren in Christ Church. Not long after he moved to Fort Wayne, Indiana where he pastored for 10 years. Then it was on to Florida and the Daytona Beach area where he served for four and a half years. "We didn't have much money," John recalls in his understated way, "barely enough to live on. We wanted kids but I'm not sure we could have afforded them. Things were pretty tight." The former footballer clearly wasn't chasing glitter and glory.

His next assignment brought him back to Ohio – Zanesville and Coburn United Methodist Church where he served as associate pastor.

John and Pat still wanted a family and chose to act boldly. They decided to adopt – two kids born in 1978 – a boy, Dan, and a girl, Dina, not siblings by birth. Dan's birth father was Panamanian Mestizo, his birth mother a Mennonite. Dina's birth mother was 8th grade educated and very young when Dina was born. And then as happens not infrequently to adoptive parents, a bio child was not long in coming – in 1983. As John put it drolly in that 1989 four-page letter, "Darci just happened after 16 years."

In June of 1991 John and his family moved from Zanesville to Baltimore, a village in southeast Ohio. Heartache struck in January 1992 when his mom died. Just afterward he and I decided it was time to see each other. On March 20, 1992, Lynne and I parked in front of 301 West Market in Baltimore and ascended the steps to the front porch of John's parsonage.

Twenty-five years of separation dissolved in a hug worthy of the power of a sheet metal stamping press. During the course of a long afternoon we caught up and met Dan, Dina and Darci – good-looking kids all. Pat, who had done some modeling, retained her youthful beauty.

One thing hadn't changed for John. Pastoring seldom brings riches, especially when serving small, rural congregations. John not only was handling ministerial demands with energy and aplomb, you could see he still was genuinely savoring certain components of his work. "I enjoy singing with the choir and working with youth groups," he told us.

1992 brought more change for John. With his kids growing older and expenses increasing, the Golden Gale quarterback called another set of signals. John took the steps necessary to become – as he puts it – "bi-vocational." Translation: he became qualified to serve as administrator for two nursing homes. "Man, I just had to bring in some more money."

In January 1994 John and family moved to a new home just outside Somerset, another small southeastern Ohio community, and we visited again soon afterward. At first he continued leading the congregation in Baltimore. Next he began pastoring a congregation closer to Somerset.

In 1995 he shifted from administering the two nursing homes to taking a position with the Helen Purcell Home for women in Zanesville where he remains today. John tested himself further in 1997 when he took on ministerial duties for two congregations near Newark. He kept up that draining regimen – which also meant piling up the miles on his car – until the end of 1999 when he began leading a congregation closer to home in Hopewell where he continues as minister.

Heartache struck again on August 14, 2002. On August 20 John emailed me. *Yesterday we had my father's funeral in Lancaster, Ohio. He died last Wednesday, about noon to 1 p.m., at the park where he often walked. A jogger found him slumped over, sitting at a picnic table. She called EMS, but I believe he was already gone. He could not have scripted it much better except that he may have preferred simply not waking up or walking in his front door and just dropping over, but had he had it that way, then I would have most likely found him that evening, after about eight hours, when I planned to stop in and check on him. The Lord does know best and for this we are all thankful. I will talk with you later, but for now he is surely where he wants to be, and though sad we are all blessed that much he feared (hospital, nursing home, etc) was graciously avoided. Blessings, John*

Reading that email caused an image to emerge from my bank of memories. On Dad's Day during the 1966 football season, while prowling the sideline with my camera, I snapped a photo of a handsome father. He was wearing a fedora and a long topcoat and was standing proudly shoulder-to-shoulder with his equally proud son.

During his long ministerial career John has counseled hundreds of troubled congregants – men and women, husbands and wives, teenagers. But he'll tell you as he has told me that the stiffest counseling challenge arrives when the trouble resides within your own family. For John that most difficult of ministerial missions confronted him when one of his kids made some distressing choices. Working through the situation has taken a painful toll on John and his family but progress has been made.

That, however, doesn't mean that life's propensity to complicate has ceased sparing John. To try to augment the family coffers, John bought some Alpacas, the docile creatures that are cousins of Llamas. Breeding them, he had learned, could prove lucrative. They quickly won his affection. One morning John went walking to the Alpacas' enclosure – to find torn and bloody carcasses. Wolves or coyotes or feral dogs had attacked during the night.

John felt shock – both emotional and financial – and acute pain. "I had really grown fond of those animals." Give up? There was a survivor and John has been working to rebuild the herd, now numbering six.

Through it all John remains a tower of outward-looking strength. Just one example: he runs an active prayer circle. When I first asked him if he would consider including a stranger – colon cancer-stricken Pat Papenbrock – John's reply was fast in coming: "Any friend of Mike Johnson is a friend of mine. We'll certainly make room on our list for an ex-Whippet." Later his reaction was the same when I asked if he would add lymphoma-stricken Dave Spangler. As you might have concluded, I expected nothing less from the ex-Golden Gale and fellow former Bobcat.

CHAPTER 37

TWICE A SOLDIER

There is much to admire about Jim Williams. Valor, for example.

Serving as a soldier, especially in a combat zone, is seldom a Sunday stroll in the park. Doing so a second time – at age 56 – brings a special set of challenges. Jim proved up to the mission.

After graduating from SHS, Jim moved on to Ohio Northern University where he earned a bachelor's degree in 1968. A scant 18 days after the commencement ceremony, Jim found himself stepping forward to pledge to defend the constitution of the United States as he began Army service. After training, Jim was ordered to Vietnam where he saw combat, served with distinction and paid a price that didn't stop him from getting on with civilian life.

After completing military service in 1970, Jim began a career in computer programming with the state of Ohio in Columbus. He also became a regular attendee at class reunions.

In 1984, 14 years after returning from Vietnam, Jim joined an Air National Guard unit. "I really did it as kind of a lark," Jim says. "A friend thought it would be a good thing to do," he adds modestly, "and I signed up."

Signing up meant participating in obligatory annual summer camps and doing monthly weekend duty. One summer he spent two weeks at an air base in Massachusetts. While there he squeezed in a visit to Cape Cod and took in a baseball game at Boston's legendary Fenway Park.

As the years rolled by, in addition to building a successful working career, Jim developed other interests. They included running (he ran a marathon in Cleveland and finished in four hours and thirty-three minutes) and cycling (of the two-wheeled pedal pumping variety, and he often rode the 24-mile roundtrip to work and back home). Jim also competed in biathlons (once finishing third in his age group, 45-49), and he trained for and competed in triathlons (the demanding events that incorporate long-distance running, cycling and swimming). When not engaged in those pursuits, he enjoyed boating and carpentry.

Life was good. Then came September 11, 2001 – 9/11. Shortly thereafter the United States launched its assault on al-Qaida in Afghanistan. The U.S. military needed to build local infrastructure – fast. Base camps, bridges, helicopter landing sites and so on. In other words, the military needed civil engineering expertise. Right, a specialty of Jim's Air National Guard unit was civil engineering.

The call-up from the Pentagon wasn't long in coming. Training commenced. In a subsequent email, Jim wrote: *Of course, no one can see into the future, and I did not anticipate the forthcoming adventure.*

He and his fellow unit members had very little time to prepare for departure and to say goodbye to their families. *I have stated numerous times in the last two days, 'I am too old for this shit.' Pardon my profanity, but it is how I feel at the moment.* That was a sentiment that many of his contemporaries could no doubt understand and sympathize with. *I have a year and a half left to accumulate my 20 years of service and receive a pension. The next few months will be difficult for me and my wife.*

By December 2001 Jim was halfway around the world in Afghanistan and Pakistan, working hard and long hours. In harsh mountainous terrain and biting winter weather, Jim was living in a tent, eating two meals a day in a mess tent and one from ration tins. Latrines were, shall we say, inconvenient. Each week Jim had a couple hours of access to email and sent this message: *It makes for a long walk in the middle of the night when nature calls.*

What helped Jim endure the demanding regimen and perform in a tough environment at age 56 was his exceptional physical conditioning. Training for triathlons was providing him with unexpected dividends. And remembered lessons from his first overseas duty a quarter century earlier likely added to his ability to cope.

On December 12 Jim sent another email: *We are much closer to the actual fighting than I would prefer. On our base you see lots of weapons. I initially asked myself, 'What is a Guard unit from Columbus, Ohio doing in the middle of this?' Of course, the answer is duty.*

Mike Johnson

After his return from Afghanistan, Jim and I met for lunch on a Saturday in Columbus in an east side restaurant. Taking a break from weekend Guard duty, he was wearing his fatigue uniform. He was looking fit and trim. Soft spoken and easy smiling, Jim has been content to stay out of the spotlights. I for one am proud to be his classmate and friend. Whatever the duty, he has done the job – and our nation is better for it.

CHAPTER 38

THE FINAL REUNION

July 19, 2008.

After just a few minutes, Jim began weeping. He sniffled, wiped his eyes with a tissue and apologized. "I get so emotional. I'm sorry."

"Don't worry about it," I replied, shrugging.

We were in Jim's bedroom. He was wearing a t-shirt and shorts and sitting at the edge of his bed. I was beside the bed, sitting on a low stool.

Twice more during the next 30 minutes tears welled in Jim's eyes. Each time he dabbed them with his soaked tissue.

This was the Jim Henkel who had cajoled me back in 1983, who had urged me to attend my first class reunion. Now Jim was just weeks from dying. It was clear he was too weak to even consider attending our 45-year reunion only three weeks away.

Jim's end began in September 2007. Shelby had become a subject of national news coverage a month earlier in August when heavy, unrelenting rains pushed the Blackfork over its banks, cresting at the height of the goal post crossbars at adjoining Skiles Stadium.

The flooding inflicted heavy damage on the middle school (Old SHS) and adjacent Central Elementary School. Damage to Main Street businesses was so severe that the owners of two decades-long enterprises – Britt's (formerly Ben Franklin) and Shelby Furniture – chose not to continue. In one residential neighborhood surging waters collapsed foundations, forcing the razing of those homes.

As Shelby's conscientious mayor, Jim was in the vortex of the flood crisis and its aftermath. He worked frantically and tirelessly to ensure the safety of the town's people. He attended endless meetings with state and federal disaster relief officials. He gave numerous interviews to news media – local, area and national. There was precious little time for rest. Few Shelbians have been more supportive of the community than Jim. Twice he served as mayor and in between as a city councilman.

He also chaired and served on the boards of numerous civic groups as well as the SHS Alumni Association.

Jim Henkel – 1945-2008

After the waters receded, fatigue was weighing heavily on Jim. His wife Susie could see how rundown he was. She urged him to see a doctor, just in case. No need to run undue risks to his health, she told him. Amidst meetings with insurers, health officials, citizens, news media and others, Jim acquiesced and made time for a checkup.

That precautionary visit to a doctor led to tests and a stunning diagnosis: Jim had been stricken with an aggressive strain of leukemia.

"You can't imagine what a jolt it is to get that kind of news," Jim told me 10 months later during the July 19 visit to his home. "But everyone has been so supportive. There has been so much support." He choked up and added haltingly, "I'm still hoping for a miracle."

Treatment had begun almost immediately and in late 2007 a doctor told Jim he could detect no sign of leukemia. "You are cancer-free," the physician told him. "It's a medical miracle."

Jim's spirits soared – only to be crushed soon thereafter when the same doctor told him the cancer had returned.

To me the sudden and all too brief remission did in fact qualify as a "medical miracle," or the physician somehow had committed a colossal blunder.

From that juncture onward Jim's regimen consisted largely of repeated rides from Shelby to a cancer treatment center in Columbus. During my July 19th visit Jim told me, "They put me through ten different kinds of chemo. They even found a donor for a bone marrow transplant." But the treatments had so depleted his immune system that he had been rendered too weak to withstand the procedure. And he had decided against more chemo; he was tired of being sick to his stomach.

Did the flood-fueled stress trigger Jim's leukemia? Or hasten its development? No one can be certain, but some in the medical community theorize that most if not all humans carry potentially lethal viruses and that stress can be the activator. That theory often is linked to the onset of autoimmune diseases, including MS, lupus and dermatomyositis.

During our last conversation – I had also visited him in 2007, just weeks after the diagnosis – I told Jim that one of my goals was to avoid saying something stupid. He smiled. On greeting him in his bedroom, I managed to avoid asking, "How are you?" After about 30 minutes as I stood to say goodbye, I told myself, "Don't say see you soon or take it easy or hang in there or something equally witless."

Jim began to stand and I said, "There's no need to get up." And then I bent over and we hugged. A lump was forming in my throat.

"Thanks for coming, Mike. I really appreciate it."

I backed away and nodded. "That's all right."

In Jim's living room his wife, a son, older sister and friends were gathered, and I paused to chat with them. Then Jim surprised me by entering the room. He sat and some light conversation – punctuated by frequent laughter – ensued. Jim's doctor had told him he had perhaps six weeks to live. "The way I feel right now," Jim said, eyes brightening, "I could last a lot longer."

After another 10 or so minutes, I said my goodbyes, and Jim and I shook hands.

Two weeks later, vote tallying for 2008's SHS Hall of Distinction induction took place on Saturday, August 2. Jim was the leading vote-getter, by a wide margin. Anticipating the outcome, I had asked Connie Jones Glorioso to design Jim's induction certificate and another schoolmate, Marlene Steele Adkins, to get it matted and framed. Normally the certificates aren't presented to new inductees until the October induction ceremony. Clearly this wasn't a normal situation. So after the voting results were announced, I asked if someone would like to volunteer to deliver the framed certificate to Jim's house right after the meeting adjourned. Two schoolmates, Dave and Sue Robertson Winans, immediately took on that mission.

The text on Jim's certificate reads: *In recognition of your outstanding accomplishments that demonstrated clearly the educational foundation received at Shelby High School and in particular for your distinguished service to Shelby citizens as both mayor – twice – and councilman and to Shelby students as a teacher's aide, the SHS Alumni Association proudly inducts you into its Hall of Distinction.*

That certificate inscription managed only to touch on Jim's accomplishments. He had also shown a strong zest for business. In late 1988 while still working for a mortgage company, Jim had bought a flower shop in Ashland. Then in early1989 he had acquired a laundromat in Shelby.

Achievements and recognition notwithstanding, modesty came naturally to Jim. "My Jim never was good at tooting his own horn," says Susie. "He'd always say, 'Working from the outside in is always the best way.' That was his belief for handling union contracts and other issues."

There would be no miracle. Jim died at 8:55 a.m., in his home, on August 19.

The classmate who had all but lassoed and dragged me to my first reunion had attended his final one. He was a caring man, a good man.

CHAPTER 39

THE LAST ORDER OF BUSINESS

Whether a school class is large or small, you can't have a successful reunion without effective leadership. So, how does a class go about lining up a planning team leader or committee chairperson? Stay tuned.

At the 1988 25-year reunion, Ralph Thauvette had just wrapped up his portion of the emcee duties. He went to sit with his wife. At the same time, reunion committee chairman Bob Blankenhorn was making his way to the front of the hall.

"Thank you, Ralph," Bob said, smiling benignly. "Great job, as always. Now, we have to take care of one more order of business. We need to select a chairman for our 30-year reunion. Now, in the past, we've tended to use a freight train to select the next chairman." That remark caused laughter to erupt. "That's how I got the job for this reunion. For the next one, though, I think it would be a good idea if we were a little bit more democratic. There shouldn't be any need to railroad anyone. In fact, what I would like to see is a spontaneous outpouring of support for a uniquely qualified individual. You know, someone we all can be confident will carry the ball all the way." As those words carried through the hall, I'm pretty sure there were some nervous ex-ballplayers. "In fact, it would be nice if this were like a political convention," Bob continued. "You know what I mean. Everyone gets all excited and comes together to support one candidate. A groundswell, that's what we need." By this time, I think most of us were concluding that Bob had something up his sleeve besides his beefy arm. "We need some convention excitement. You know, where everyone parades around the hall." Bob paused. "I said we need a *parade*...Hey! Is anybody listening? We need a *parade*! Uh, how about a parade?"

At that moment, among growing giggles and hoots, six of our classmates began parading from the back of the hall toward the front. Each held aloft a large placard which read "Ralph for Chairman" and "We Want Ralph" and "Class of '63 for Ralph" and so on.

They reached the front of the hall, waving and pumping their arms up and down, and then began parading around the perimeter of the hall as the rest of us began clapping and chanting for Ralph. (Courtesy of classmate Marilyn French, I have videotape of this; what a hoot!)

Ralph? He was looking poleaxed. Meanwhile, Bob was struggling to get his own laughter under control and then he said, "It sure seems like a spontaneous demonstration, and it definitely seems unanimous. But I need to ask, 'Are there any other nominations?' Is there a second for Ralph? Is their *anyone* who doesn't want Ralph to chair our 30-year reunion?" Silence, relatively speaking. "Then all who want Ralph Thauvette to chair our next reunion say Aye!"

"Aye!" we roared. Probably roaring loudest were some class members who had begun to worry that they were about to become the subject of this "spontaneous" outburst of support.

Ralph stood slowly and began shuffling toward the front of the hall. Sort of a condemned man's walk. Bob moved to greet him. "Congratulations, Ralph," Bob said, vigorously pumping Ralph's hand. "I'm so glad you've agreed to do this."

Ralph still was looking more than a little stunned but was too gracious – and maybe too shocked – not to accept.

I couldn't have been more pleased by the outcome of this democratic process. We knew Ralph would do a fine job. And he would have help. Within minutes, Mary Ellen May Hall and Gail McMeeken Adams approached Ralph and offered to help. And I knew that he could count on others as well.

Five years later in 1993, the 30-year reunion went splendidly, as we had expected. And guess what? At the conclusion of that three-day reunion – our class's first multiday gathering – Ralph volunteered – *really* volunteered – to chair the 1998 gathering. Naturally, his offer was immediately and resoundingly endorsed by all.

THE LAST WORD

At this juncture, what are you thinking about reunions? How much do you think you would enjoy going to your next class reunion? Or a multi-class reunion if one were organized? How much do you think you would value it? What old wounds might it heal? What old bonds might it reinforce? What new bonds might it create?

Here's the way I've come to see them. It's not particularly profound so I won't be particularly wordy. We've got only one opportunity to walk this planet and limited time to do it. It's nice to take that walk with friends – old, familiar, trusted friends. Want that validated? When you receive an invitation to your next reunion, buckle up and get going.

What about qualms? What about risks? Well, of course, we all know it's easier to decide not to do something.

There's an aphorism that I like and it goes like this: *Friends are like stars. You can't always see them, but you know they are there.*

If we've made a friend, we can lose touch and still call a friend a friend for life. Ah, but actually seeing and being with those friends from time to time can provide nourishment for the spirit. Chris, David, John, Jim, Pat, Joel, Mary Ann, DeeDee, Ralph, Suzon, Jane Bell, Jeff, Malcolm, June, Anne, Bill, Diane, John, Randy, Larry, Tom, Dave, Connie, Jodi, Fred, Elaine, Margie, Rich, Kathy, Dick, Bob, Janet, Mary Ellen, Chuck, Fran, Poh Hong, Peter, Luis, Nancy, Denny, Graeme, Chris, Robin, Robert, Loloy, Carol, Phillip, Tracy, Mike, CK, Martin, Klaus, Rudi, Ed, Al, Hanspeter, Anton, Gerard, John, Bev. Reunions as nourishment, a healthy way to think about them.

Oh, and invite your teachers or professors. You'll be glad. So will they.

ACKNOWLEDGEMENTS

Pretty darned lucky. That's me.

Let me explain. In recent years readers frequently have asked me, "Don't you wish you'd begun writing books sooner? When you were younger?"

The question is understandable. After all, I was 60 when my first book debuted. But my answer is simple enough: "If I'd begun writing earlier, I couldn't have written the books I've done."

Over the decades numerous sturdy building blocks have strengthened the foundation of my life – or my continuing education. They included: my parents Ralph and Bea, my brothers Dean and Gene, my sisters Linda McBride and Laurie Parrish. Lynne Haley – my wife, friend, mother of our kids and chief critiquer and preparer of my manuscripts. My alma maters – St. Mary's, Shelby High School, Ohio University, Marshall Law at Cleveland State University, Stanford University's Graduate School of Business – and their alumni, faculty and staff – my friends. The United States Army and my fellow soldiers in Korea, including Mike Hood, Emmett Zimmerman, Mike Schwartz, Don Schauer. My friends in disparate and far flung lands – Alexandra Dinita and Raluca Topliceanu in Romania; Andre van der Merwe, Lea Rassler, Laura Ramaschi, Joachim Kramer and Marc and Carmen Rohfritsch (who own Maison des Tetes, my favorite hotel in the world, built in 1609 in Colmar) in France; Peter Bohnenblust in Switzerland; Peter Bloomfield, Celia Turner and Tony Sharpe in England; Marzena Witek in Poland; Xiaoli Yuan in China; Shuri Fukunaga in Japan, Won Chong Hee and CK Choi in Korea, and so many others. They all have contributed to my education and enriched my life.

More such building blocks came in the form of places I've been blessed to visit and that travelers seldom see: the Diaoyutai State Guesthouse in Beijing; the Members Tea Rooms in Britain's Houses of Parliament; the early books vault – with its ebullient curator Francis Gueth – in the Colmar, France Library; England's Royal Military Academy; Poland's University of Warsaw; the ruins of the one remaining gas chamber at Auschwitz; the vast wine cellars beneath the streets of French villages Ribeauville and Riquewhir; and others.

Only with all of those building blocks – and the foundation they have provided – could I have even imagined writing my books.

Lastly, I owe so much to readers who have taken time to send me emails and handwritten letters and others who have managed to track down my phone number – not an easy trick when you are searching for one of the many thousands of Mike Johnsons – to thank me for my research and writing. I am equally grateful to war veterans who have sent me their memoirs, thinking – correctly – that they might prove useful in my research. Reader feedback – all of it – has provided nourishment for the soul.

Postscript:

The Original Bobkitten and this author reunited in person. Forty-three years after last seeing each other at Ohio University and more than two decades after reconnecting via letters and then staying in touch through more letters, emails and phone conversations, we met face-to-face on April 23, 2009 in Columbus, Ohio, on the front steps of the state capitol. It was her 62nd birthday, and it was a happy reunion.

The author and his family – Lynne, Ben, Andrea, Zach – in 1983 when he attended his first reunion and Lynne suggested he write notes recording what he had experienced and learned.

SOURCES

- The Daily Globe. May 15, 1962. Whippets Top Tygers 10-4; Kidwell Gets 3rd
- The Daily Globe. April 19, 1963. Whippets Nip Mansfield 7-6
- *Scarlet S* yearbooks from 1930 onward
- The Daily Globe. November 1970. Baldridge Is Coach At Harrodsburg
- The Daily Globe. January 9, 1971. Internship Year Completed, MA Degree Awarded
- The Daily Globe. July 1973. Former Shelbian Dies In Plano, Texas
- The Daily Globe. July 1973. Baldridge Named Line Coach
- The Daily Globe. January 1984. Baldridge Named Morehead Mentor
- Mansfield News Journal. October 1985. Shelby's football craze sure to go down in history
- *The History of Shelby Football – 1894-1985.* Fred Eichinger
- The Daily Globe. January 29, 1987. John Crum's career is on a roll – finally
- The Plain Dealer. September 27, 1988
- The Plain Dealer. September 29, 1988
- The Daily Globe. October 26, 1989. Baldridge resigns Morehead post
- Alumni News, Views & Memories. April 29, 2003. Lillian Rae Bowman
- Alumni News, Views & Memories. May 3, 2003
- Ohio University – The Spirit of a Singular Place – 1804-2004.
- Whippet Echoes. December 2005. Harryet Snyder Memorial Edition
- Whippet Echoes. September 5, 2006
- *Just As Though You Were Here.* CD. 2007

Printed in the United States
149981LV00005B/2/P